PRAISE FOR *VISUALIZING GENERATIVE AI*

"An engaging, cartoon-illustrated guide that makes complex AI concepts accessible to everyone. This book demystifies how GenAI works, blending clarity (and fun!), perfect for beginners and a refreshing perspective for practitioners too."

—*Dr. Marily Nika, author of* Building AI-Powered Products

"As someone who has been standing on the sidelines, I've finally found a way to catch up on the fundamentals behind GenAI without dedicating all my free time."

—*Kelsey Hightower, distinguished engineer and author of* Kubernetes: Up and Running

"More than just a technical guide, this book is a blueprint for building responsible Generative AI applications at scale. It provides the architectural patterns needed to balance creativity with the risk, cost, and latency that every platform leader obsesses over."

—*Gabe Monroy, SVP/GM, Workday Platform*

"AI doesn't have to be intimidating. This beautifully visual approach transforms GenAI from a mysterious black box into understandable technology that anyone can learn and leverage effectively."

—*Vanessa Lyon, managing director and senior partner, BCG*

"The most approachable introduction to GenAI available. Cuts through the AI hype with clear visual explanations of how GenAI actually works under the hood. Perfect for developers and leaders building AI applications."

—*Mona Mona, GenAI Specialist, AWS*

VISUALIZING GENERATIVE AI

How AI Paints, Writes, and Assists

PRIYANKA VERGADIA AND VALLIAPPA LAKSHMANAN

VISUALIZING GENERATIVE AI
How AI Paints, Writes, and Assists

by Priyanka Vergadia and Valliappa Lakshmanan

Published by O'Reilly Media, Inc., 1005 Gravenstein Highway North, Sebastopol, CA 95472.

O'Reilly Media books may be purchased for educational, business, or sales promotional use. Online editions are also available for most titles (*oreilly.com*). For more information, contact our corporate/institutional sales department: 800-998-9938 or *corporate@oreilly.com*.

ACQUISITIONS EDITOR: Megan Laddusaw
DEVELOPMENT EDITOR: Sarah Grey
PRODUCTION EDITOR: Ashley Stussy
COPYEDITOR: Liz Wheeler
PROOFREADER: Krsta Technology Solutions
INDEXER: BIM Creatives, LLC
COVER DESIGNER: Susan Thompson
INTERIOR DESIGNER: Ron Bilodeau
COVER AND INTERIOR ILLUSTRATOR: Tanvi Agarwal (SillyStrokes)

October 2025:   First edition

REVISION HISTORY OF THE FIRST EDITION

2025-10-14: First edition

978-1-098-17230-5

[LSI]

CONTENTS

PREFACE

Generative AI has captured the world's imagination like no other technology. Within months of ChatGPT's release in November 2022, everyone, from CEOs to college students, was experimenting with AI-powered tools that could write, code, create images, and solve complex problems. The enthusiasm is infectious—and justified. But as the initial excitement settles, a sobering reality emerges: building production-ready applications with generative AI is fundamentally different from using ChatGPT for quick tasks.

We wrote this book because we've seen countless teams struggle to bridge the gap between the promise of generative AI and the reality of deploying reliable, responsible applications at scale. The technology is powerful, but it's also nondeterministic and prone to hallucination, and it requires careful architectural decisions to balance creativity, risk, cost, and latency. Traditional software engineering practices need to evolve to accommodate these unique challenges.

WHAT MAKES GENAI APPLICATIONS DIFFERENT

Generative AI applications aren't just traditional software with an AI component bolted on. They require a fundamentally different approach to development, testing, and deployment. Unlike deterministic software, GenAI applications produce different outputs for the same inputs. Unlike traditional AI models trained for specific tasks, foundation models are general-purpose tools that can be applied to countless problems—but also carry new risks around bias, toxicity, and misinformation.

The result is that teams often start with impressive prototypes but struggle to move to production. The demo that works perfectly in the conference room fails when exposed to real user inputs. The chatbot that provides helpful answers during testing starts hallucinating facts when deployed. The content-generation tool that saves hours of work suddenly becomes a compliance nightmare.

WHY WE WROTE THIS BOOK

Both authors have spent years helping organizations navigate these challenges. At Google, Microsoft, and at a number of other companies, Priyanka and Lak have helped countless developers and organizations adopt cloud technologies and have witnessed firsthand the architectural decisions that make or break AI implementations.

We've written this book to be an approachable guide to what we believe will remain core ideas in building GenAI applications for real-world use. It's not about the latest model architectures or research breakthroughs—it's about the practical engineering decisions, architectural patterns, and responsible AI practices that separate successful deployments from expensive experiments.

WHAT YOU'LL LEARN

This book takes you on a journey from understanding how generative AI works to deploying responsible applications at scale. We start with the fundamentals: how these models generate text and images, why they behave the way they do, and what makes them both powerful and unpredictable. From there, we show you how to build applications that harness this power while mitigating the risks.

You'll learn to architect GenAI applications that balance creativity with reliability, implement agentic systems that can reason and act autonomously, and deploy monitoring and evaluation frameworks that ensure your applications remain safe and effective over time. Most importantly, you'll understand how to make responsible choices about when and how to use this technology.

Throughout the book, we use real-world examples and provide code you can run and adapt. Every prompt, every architectural pattern, and every code sample is available in our GitHub repository (*https://github.com/lakshmanok/visualizing-generative-ai*) , allowing you to experiment and build upon our examples.

WHO SHOULD READ THIS BOOK

This book is written for several overlapping audiences:

- *Software engineers and architects* who need to integrate generative AI into existing applications or build new AI-powered systems. You'll learn the architectural patterns, engineering practices, and infrastructure considerations needed to deploy GenAI at scale.

- *Data scientists and ML engineers* transitioning from traditional machine learning to generative AI. While many concepts carry over, GenAI requires new approaches to evaluation, monitoring, and model management, which we cover in detail.

- *Product managers and technical leaders* who need to make informed decisions about when and how to adopt generative AI. Understanding the technology's capabilities and limitations is crucial for setting realistic expectations and making sound investment decisions.

- *Anyone building with AI* who wants to understand responsible development practices. As generative AI becomes more powerful and pervasive, building safely and ethically isn't just good practice—it's essential for sustainable innovation.

WHAT YOU NEED TO KNOW

We assume you have some familiarity with APIs and web services. If you've worked with machine learning before, that's helpful but not required—we explain the concepts you need as we go.

More importantly, we assume you're curious about building applications that work reliably in the real world. This book is hands-on and practical. We'll show you how to implement every pattern we discuss, and we encourage you to experiment with the examples.

HOW THIS BOOK IS ORGANIZED

The book is structured to take you from understanding to implementation:

- Chapters 1 and 2 establish the foundation: what generative AI is, how it works, and how to use it effectively through better prompting and API integration.

- Chapter 3 explores real-world use cases across industries, showing how organizations are successfully deploying GenAI applications today.

- Chapters 4 and 5 dive deep into building applications: implementing agentic systems, choosing the right architectures, and balancing the competing demands of creativity, risk, cost, and latency.

- Chapter 6 addresses the critical topic of responsible AI, covering everything from value alignment and human-AI interaction to environmental impact and governance frameworks.

Each chapter builds on the previous ones while remaining modular enough that you can focus on specific topics based on your needs.

A LIVING TECHNOLOGY

Generative AI is evolving rapidly. By the time you read this book, new models will have been released, new capabilities will have emerged, and new challenges will have surfaced. Rather than trying to keep up with every development, we've focused on principles and patterns that transcend specific models or providers.

The architectural decisions you make today will determine how easily you can adapt to tomorrow's innovations. The responsible AI practices you implement now will shape how your applications scale and evolve. The engineering practices you adopt will determine whether your GenAI applications become reliable, valuable parts of your technology stack or expensive technical debt.

Our goal is to help you build applications that not only work today but continue to deliver value as the technology evolves. Welcome to the future of software development.

Priyanka Vergadia and Valliappa Lakshmanan

June 2025

## Chapter 1

GENERATIVE AI EVERYWHERE ALL AT ONCE

Generative AI (or GenAI) is the ability of machines to create new content. It is a branch of artificial intelligence (AI), which is the field of computer science that tries to make machines autonomously carry out tasks that we associate with human cognition or creativity. Today, GenAI is capable of creating images, essays, poems, music, and even videos at a human level.

While research on GenAI has been going on for over a decade, it burst onto the public consciousness with the release of ChatGPT (*https://oreil.ly/hg_Ii*) by OpenAI in November 2022. ChatGPT provided an ability for users to ask for open-ended text (such as "Write a limerick about an office party" or "How do you reverse an array in Python?") and get answers. ChatGPT became the fastest-growing application ever (*https://oreil.ly/ONnn3*) , reaching 100 million users in just two months. For comparison, it took TikTok (which was based on an already viable Chinese product called Douyin) nine months and Instagram 2.5 years to reach the 100 million mark.

In this chapter (see Figure 1-1), we will discuss what GenAI is, how it works, why it has gotten so much better recently, and the challenges that remain. Generative AI has taken off because the technology has recently become powerful, and people are discovering that it can greatly improve existing products and ways of working. Discussing the growth curve of GenAI will allow us to provide context for both the technology underpinning generative AI and the products that take advantage of it.

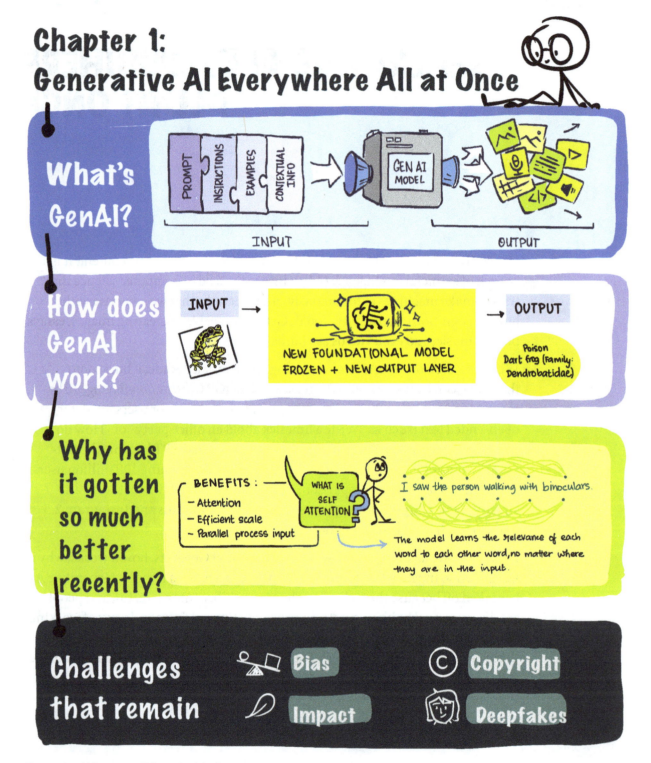

Figure 1-1. What you will learn in this chapter.

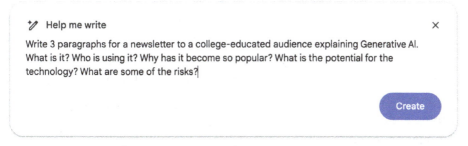

Figure 1-2. Screenshot of Google Docs "Help me write" tool.

WHAT IS GENERATIVE AI?

The best way to start a book or talk about GenAI is with a demonstration of its capabilities. This will help us understand both the promise and the shortcomings of the technology. Can we get a GenAI tool to generate this book's introduction for us?

Mandatory Parlor Trick

We are writing this book in Google Docs, which includes a *Help me write* capability to which we supplied the textual input "Write 3 paragraphs for a newsletter…" that is shown in Figure 1-2.

Textual input, typically consisting of instruction, examples, and contextual information (see Figure 1-3 top panel), that is provided to the GenAI model is called a *prompt*. Google Docs uses GenAI, specifically a GenAI model called Gemini, to handle the previous prompt. The following sidebar contains the output.*

It's amazing that an AI is able to create such fluent text. GenAI has gotten so popular (see Figure 1-3, middle panel) because it is so easy to use, and is embedded in popular products like Google Docs. Also, the output text is created in seconds, compared to the minutes to hours it would take to write those paragraphs on your own. Plus, GenAI technology keeps getting better all the time.

It's also eminently clear that our jobs as writers are safe for now—the generated text has no personality and is quite forgettable (compare it with our introduction to GenAI in the pages that follow if you are unconvinced!). The only real details in the generated text were already in our prompt.

Note that if you try out our previous prompt, the results you get will be different. This is not just because the model has changed in the meantime (from Gemini 1.0 to Gemini 3.0 perhaps), but also because GenAI models inherently use randomness when generating new content. This randomness, as we will discuss later in this chapter, is what keeps the generated text from becoming monotonous and repetitive.

---

* Generated using Google Workspace with Gemini. May 2024.

Generative AI: A New Frontier in Artificial Intelligence

Generative AI, a subset of artificial intelligence, has taken the world by storm. Unlike traditional AI, which analyzes and interprets data, generative AI creates something completely new, such as text, images, or music. Its rapid adoption, impressive capabilities, and potential for revolutionizing industries have made it a hot topic of discussion.

One of the key reasons for generative AI's popularity is its user-friendliness. Anyone can generate text, images, or music with just a few clicks, making it accessible to a wide range of people, both tech-savvy and non-tech-savvy alike. Another reason for its popularity is its speed. Generative AI can generate high-quality content in a matter of seconds, which saves users a significant amount of time. Finally, generative AI is constantly improving. With each passing day, it becomes more sophisticated, capable of producing more realistic and creative content.

The potential for generative AI is enormous. It has the potential to revolutionize industries such as customer support, marketing, and entertainment. For example, generative AI can be used to create personalized customer support experiences, generate high-quality marketing content, and create realistic visual effects for movies and TV shows. However, as with any technology, generative AI also brings unique risks. For instance, it can be used to create fake news, deep fakes, and other forms of misinformation, which could lead to serious consequences. Additionally, the widespread adoption of generative AI could lead to job displacement, as more and more tasks become automated.

Generated text can function as a great starting point for structural outlines and talking points that human writers can elaborate upon. It is rare, however, that you can surface generated content directly to users in any situation where there is a high expectation of quality.

Even though GenAI does not (yet) reach the level of the world's best at any specific task, the outputs are good enough that we see it being rapidly adopted in certain types of use cases (see Figure 1-3, bottom panel). It's used for personalization at a scale that would be impossible to do using human labor. It's used to augment humans such as doctors to perform tasks that detract from their "real job" and to reduce errors. You see it used in situations like customer support to increase business efficiency and in cases like fraud detection to increase the number of checks that can be performed.

GenAI Can Help Humans

GenAI is not a replacement for humans, especially humans who are experts at the particular type of content being produced. However, it can function as an excellent assistant to humans.

A 2023 study from Harvard Business School (*https://oreil.ly/PNtex*) showed that, on tasks that lie "within the frontier" of what AI can do well,

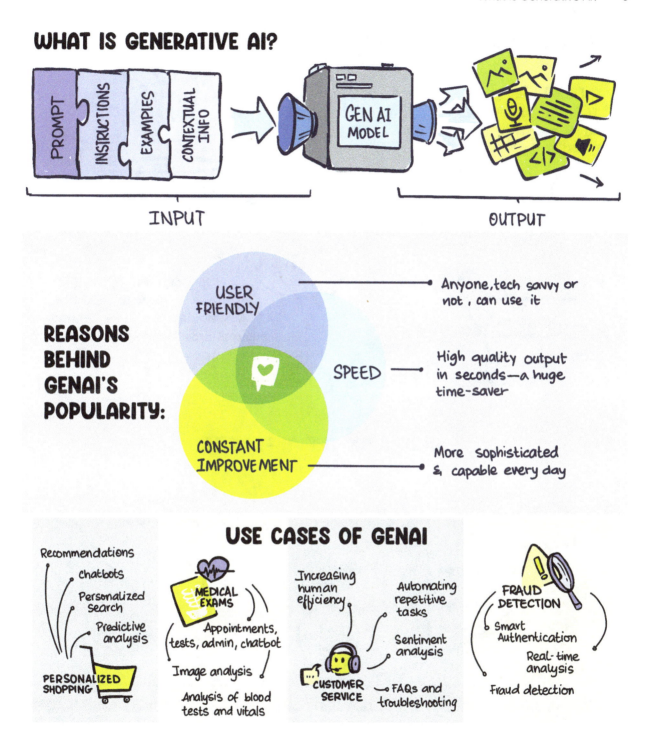

Figure 1-3. GenAI is being rapidly adopted for all kinds of use cases. Think about how these use cases reduce friction and improve accuracy, scale, and efficiency.

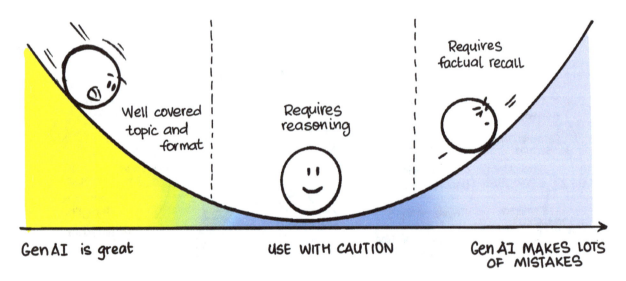

Figure 1-4. Understanding the AI frontier.

content created by humans with the assistance of GenAI is better than what humans or AI alone could produce.

Think of yourself on a sailboat (see Figure 1-4, top panel) with the wind blowing away from the shore and toward the sea. In this analogy, the task ("heading to sea") is what you want to do. The sail can either help (if you want to move in the direction of the wind) or it can make things harder (if you want to move against the wind). In this way, the sail is analogous to AI—sometimes AI can help, and other times, AI can make things harder.

A *frontier task* is a task that AI is capable of doing—if you want to head out to sea, you'll get some movement using just the sail. Sailing in the direction of the wind is a frontier task, and on such a task, the sail (AI) will be assistive. Of course, just as you have to know how to manipulate the sail to catch the wind, you need to know how to use AI effectively.

A cautionary tale from the same study was that for tasks "outside the frontier" of what AI can do well, subpar AI suggestions can detract humans from doing their best work! In our sailboat analogy, sailing back to land when the wind is blowing you out to sea would be a task that is outside the frontier. The sail is a hindrance to such a task, and you are better off not using the sail.

Over time, as AI has been employed in a variety of industries, the community has developed an understanding of the kinds of use cases that are within the frontier of the technology. Thus, we see GenAI being used to generate recommendations, implement chatbots, and personalize the search function in shopping sites.

We followed our own advice when writing this book, using GenAI as an assistant only on tasks that it is known to be good at. Specifically, we used GenAI tools as a way to brainstorm, to rephrase sentences, and to skim research papers. Unless clearly marked (as with the paragraphs quoted in this section), the text and illustrations in this book were all created by humans. AI assisted, but it did not create.

What's on the Frontier?

It is important to develop an intuitive understanding of what tasks AI can do well, and use it only for those tasks. Let's look at a few example tasks, one within the frontier, two on the fence, and the fourth beyond the frontier of GenAI. We'll ask ChatGPT from OpenAI (*https://chat.openai.com*) to perform these tasks.

> **NOTE** Throughout this book, we encourage you to follow along with us whenever possible. You can repeat our actions in this chapter by trying out our prompts on *chatgpt.com*. Note that the responses will vary because the models may have improved between the time we did it and when you are reading this book, and because model responses are nondeterministic.

Generating text on a topic that is well covered by the training dataset is within the frontier of GenAI—this is a task at which it excels. For example, we asked the GenAI model to

```
Write a 1-sentence explanation of
Fermat's last theorem
```

and received this response:

```
Fermat's Last Theorem states that there
are no three positive integers
x,y, and z that satisfy the equation
x^n+y^n=z^n for any integer value of
n>2.
```

This is perfectly correct because Fermat's last theorem is well covered by the internet data on which ChatGPT was trained—there is a Wikipedia page on Fermat's last theorem, and thousands more web pages on the topic. You can use this explanation as is, and it's unclear that a human could improve on it significantly.

What if we ask the AI to *explain* the theorem, not merely parrot it? For example, we asked ChatGPT:

```
Why does Fermat's last theorem specify
n > 2?
```

We received a response that included the following text:

```
When n=2, the equation becomes
the famous Pythagorean theorem:
x^2+y^2=z^2. There are many integer
solutions to this, known as Pythagorean
triples.

...

The difficulty for n>2 comes from
the rapid growth of the powers x^n,
y^n,z^n. For these higher powers, the
relationships between x, y, and z
become much more constrained and do not
allow for solutions in integers, a fact
that was only proven conclusively by
Andrew Wiles in 1994.
```

The previous explanation sounds *plausible*, but is it true? The fact about the Pythagorean theorem is true, and Pythagorean triples are, indeed, solutions for n = 2. However, the part about relationships being constrained is a logical fallacy commonly referred to as "circular reasoning" or "begging the question"—it assumes as true what it is trying to prove. GenAI is not good at logical *reasoning*. Always double-check the logic behind explanations and rationales generated by GenAI, since plausible isn't necessarily correct.

What if we ask, not for a one-sentence explanation, but for a limerick on the topic? Presumably, there is no limerick on this math theorem in ChatGPT's training data (that might change once this book is published!*). When we asked the GenAI model to

```
Write a limerick about Fermat's last
theorem
```

we received this response:

```
There once was a theorem, quite grand,
Fermat left it unproved by hand.
He said "no cubes or squares,
Can sum in such pairs,
For n greater than two, take a stand!
```

It's a limerick (has the AABBA rhyme scheme) and is on the topic we requested. On close examination, though, the limerick falls apart—the crux of Fermat's theorem is that there are triples for n = 2, but not for n > 2. So, the third line ("no cubes or squares") is wrong—there are squares, but there are no cubes. The last line makes no sense (who's supposed to take a stand?) and is obviously shoehorned into fitting the rhyme

---

* Large language model providers often monitor forums where people report problems and fix their models to handle the reported issue, if not the underlying problem. So a limerick on Fermat's theorem may start working once this book is in early access, but a limerick on Euler's primes or some other mathematical theorem may not.

scheme. Generating a limerick on Fermat's theorem requires being able to understand the theorem and its history and use this understanding to plan out text that fits a limerick's rhyme scheme. Such *reasoning and planning* is not something that GenAI is not yet good at, although researchers have been making progress in special cases.

Even though GenAI is a technology built on mimicry of large datasets, GenAI tools struggle to correctly reproduce factual information. For example, asking ChatGPT the following:

```
Who did Andrew Wiles' student who
helped him prove Fermat's last theorem
collaborate with afterwards? Cite the
paper
```

yielded the following response (in November 2024):

```
After their groundbreaking work on
Fermat's Last Theorem, Richard Taylor
continued his own research, including
further contributions to the study of
Galois representations and modular
forms. He has written influential
papers in these areas. One significant
later collaboration was with Laurent
Clozel and others on the Langlands
program, which is a broad and deep set
of conjectures in number theory and
algebraic geometry.
A notable paper from this later work
is:
Laurent Clozel, Richard Taylor,
"Automorphic forms and Galois
representations,"
Publications Mathématiques de l'IHÉS,
99 (2004), 1-218.
DOI: 10.1007/s10240-004-0010-5.
```

While Richard Taylor did work on the topic of Galois representations with Laurent Clozel, the citation is wholly made up—volume 99 of the IHÉS journal in 2004 (*https://oreil.ly/VHp_B*) has four articles, none of which match the previous citation. The generated text is plausible, but it is not correct. This sort of plausible, but incorrect, information is called a *hallucination*. Never use information generated by GenAI without double-checking its factuality!

> **NOTE**
> Doubtless, by the time you read this book, GenAI will have advanced past some of the shortcomings we are pointing out in this section. However, for a long time to come, there will continue to be a frontier beyond which GenAI will not be reliable. As you read about new GenAI capabilities and encounter new products and tools that use GenAI, update your understanding of where the frontier currently is.

The inability of GenAI to reproduce factual information can be very surprising when you encounter it for the first time. Which do you think GenAI is better at? Making an exact copy of a painting, or making an artistic impression of one? In **Figure 1-5**, we show the results from the Imagen GenAI model (built into Gemini; try it by going to *gemini.google.com*) when we asked it to

```
generate an image of the famous
painting "The Scream". Match the style
and colors of the original painting
closely.
```

 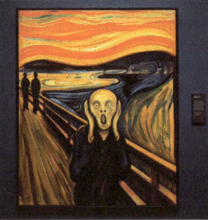 

Figure 1-5. The Scream. (a) Actual painting by Edvard Munch, 1893, from the Google Art Project. (b) Painting as reproduced by GenAI. (c) Painting reimagined using GenAI.

versus when we asked it to

```
create an image that looks like the
famous painting "The Scream", but set
the picture in a cornfield. Replace
the people in the background with
scarecrows.
```

It's clear that the reproduction in the middle is recognizable but not faithful to the original, whereas the image on the right is obviously created in the style of Munch's painting, but following our instructions.

We tend to assume that computers are good at exact reproduction but bad at making artistic modifications. GenAI is the opposite! It struggles with exact recall, but excels at mimicry. This is because GenAI does not involve extracting text or images from a database of everything that it has encountered in its training data. Instead, GenAI is generating pixels and text based on what is probabilistically likely (we'll discuss the exact mechanism later in this chapter). It is important to keep this probabilistic nature of GenAI firmly in mind as you use it. Otherwise, you will end up being surprised by the results.

In the rest of this chapter, we'll build up to an intuitive understanding of the probabilistic nature of GenAI. We'll start with a quick introduction to AI.

AI GIVES MACHINES HUMAN CAPABILITIES

Artificial intelligence is the field of computer science that imbues machines with human-like capabilities. When Facebook tags people in photographs or when you deposit a check into your bank account by taking a picture of it, you are relying on machines' ability to "see" and recognize faces, text, and numbers. When authors of Apple Books use AI to create an audiobook from their written content, the machine has become able to "speak." When an iRobot vacuum makes

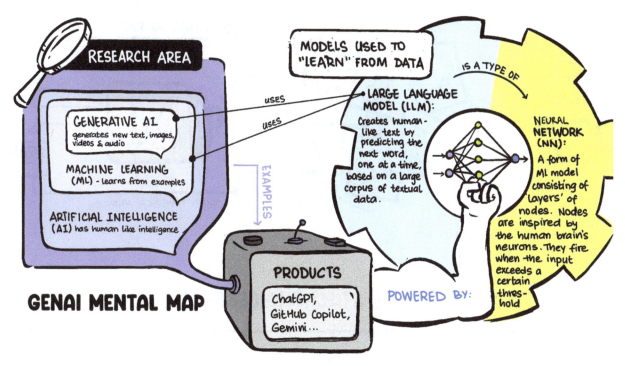

Figure 1-6. The GenAI ecosystem consists of products that incorporate GenAI, models that employ the technology, research that advances it, and software stacks that are needed to operationalize it.

its way around furniture, it is relying on a sense of "touch." Smart speakers such as Alexa and assistants such as Siri can "hear" and react to spoken commands. AI doesn't taste yet, but there are AI models that can predict how wine will taste based on the growing conditions of the grape.

All of the previous examples involve AI built into products (such as Facebook, banking apps, or Apple Books). AI is a powerful way for the companies that make these products to reduce friction, improve accuracy, increase scale, and reduce cost. Technology that *doesn't* make its way into products is just a curiosity and will have limited impact on the world.

As an example of AI technology and products, let's consider how AI analyzes retinal scans.

GenAI Ecosystem

The term *generative AI*, or *GenAI*, is used to refer to models, products, research areas, and software frameworks (see **Figure 1-6**). GenAI models like GPT-4, built by OpenAI, provide the ability to generate images and text. GenAI products like ChatGPT incorporate these models and provide a nice user interface. Research in the field of GenAI advances the capability of the models. GenAI software stacks are needed to operationalize these models and products. Together, these form the GenAI ecosystem.

Figure 1-7. How machine learning works.

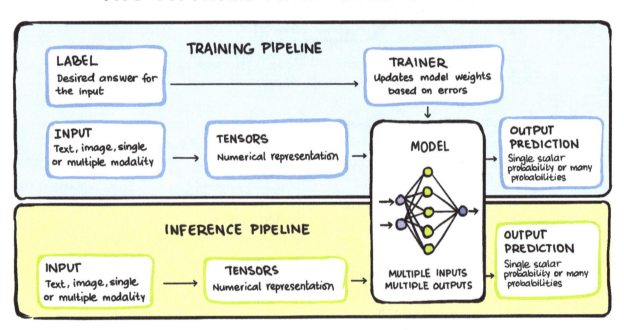

Figure 1-8. For machine learning, you need a software stack for the training pipeline and another one for the inference pipeline.

From a research area perspective, retinal scans involve *machine learning* (ML), a type of AI where the machine learns by looking at hundreds of thousands of images (see Figure 1-7). These images are *labeled*, meaning each image is marked with its classification (such as healthy, diabetic, or glaucoma).

A *neural network*, so called because it is inspired by the neurons that are part of biological nervous systems, is a common model that is used to learn from data. The neural network (NN) is a mathematical function that is usually represented (both in code and visually) as layers of connected nodes. In the example of classifying retinal images, the input to the NN is an image and the output is a word from a very limited vocabulary (such as diabetic or healthy).

Generative AI is a form of machine learning, because the AI is taught using large amounts of data, but its output tends to be much more open-ended than that of most ML applications. The output of GenAI models can be videos, audios, etc. Large language models (LLMs) are GenAI models that are trained on textual inputs to generate natural language text. ChatGPT is an example of a GenAI product that is powered by an LLM.

There are two software stacks necessary for machine learning. The first is a training pipeline that is used to tune the model weights based on large amounts of data (See Figure 1-8). Because these models can operate only on numbers, the input data will have to be represented as multidimensional numbers, termed *tensors*. Once a model has been trained, it can be used to perform predictions on new inputs. The software stack to do this is called the inference stack. The inference pipeline is similar to the training pipeline except that labels are not necessary.

An AI-infused Product

What is the advantage of doing retinal scanning using AI? Retinal scanning was possible before AI, but it involved considerable friction and was not scalable.

I remember going to an eye doctor who would drop medicine into my eyes to dilate them. The doctor would then look into my eyes with an instrument, to see the state of my retina. Like many people of Indian descent, my pupils are larger than average, and the doctor would usually be worried that it was glaucoma. This would involve further tests, and then I'd get to go home, driving home, dangerously, with still-dilated eyes.

Now, there are machines that can scan retinas noninvasively. Because the doctor has the retinal scan from previous years, they can easily compare the images from past years to see that each pupil remains the same size.

Less friction. More accuracy.

What's true of my eyes is true for millions. In India, 60% of people live in villages without access to eye doctors—but medical technicians can mount the machine onto a vehicle, drive it to villages, and provide eye scans with the help of an optometrist working remotely (*https://oreil.ly/zjbLQ*). In many cases, the AI can quickly determine that there is no problem, and this makes the whole process more efficient, with increased scale.

A 2023 blog post by Verily (*https://oreil.ly/dYZ6p*) notes that bringing such an AI-infused product to market requires high-quality data, the early involvement of cross-functional experts, validation in real-world environments where the AI is designed around humans, and continuing to proactively monitor the performance of the AI system.

If you are a developer or product manager who hopes to use GenAI, it's worth focusing your work around this question: how will using GenAI in your product improve accuracy, scale, and/or efficiency? This, then, is the lens with which we will look at generative AI in this book. We will discuss how the technology works, but we will also discuss how you can use it to reduce friction, improve accuracy, increase scale, or reduce costs associated with the ways you do things today.

Is This AI?

A good way to start a debate among technologists is to ask if some AI-infused product is truly AI. Are the featured snippets in Google Search AI? How about Google Maps figuring out which subway exit you should take? Facebook suggesting the people to tag in a photo? Microsoft Copilot summarizing a document? Amazon recommending what other people buy when they look at this product? Are these AI?

John McCarthy is credited with the statement "as soon as it works, no one calls it AI any more." Once we become familiar with an application of AI, the AI contribution to the feasibility of the application vanishes into the background, and the use case becomes just another feature of a widely used product.

Betram Raphael made the point that AI is a collective name for problems that are not effectively solved by computers. However, the nature of scientific and engineering progress means that the goalposts of what constitutes AI, and what is merely software, keep moving.

Indeed, with the 2024 Nobel Prize in Physics going to Hopfield and Hinton, who were among the pioneers of neural networks (a form of machine learning, which is a form of AI), we could complete John McCarthy's statement by positing that "once it works, we call it physics"!

Our recommendation is to stop worrying about whether or not you are using AI. Focus on whether what you are doing reduces friction or improves accuracy, scale, or efficiency.

HOW GENERATIVE AI WORKS

Generative AI is a form of machine learning where the output of the NN is open-ended images, text, audio, or video. This goes beyond the simple AI models that can only recognize images or do one-to-one mapping of words to speech. Instead, a generative AI model "paints" entire images, "writes" entire paragraphs, "speaks" for minutes, and synthesizes long videos. How does it do this?

In this section, we'll discuss how generative AI creates images, text, music, and video. But before that, you have to understand how machine learning works, because GenAI is a form of machine learning.

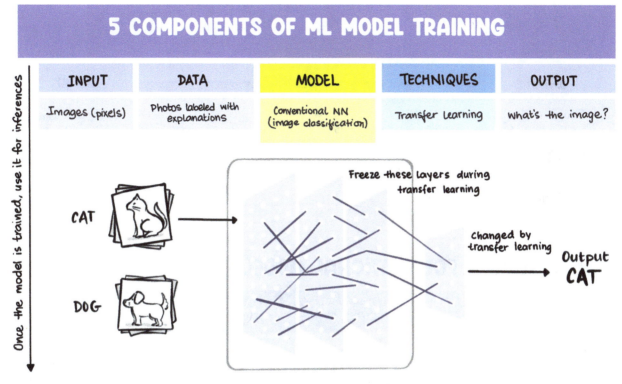

Figure 1-9. The five key components of training machine learning models, and which characteristics are still applicable during inference.

How Machine Learning Works

Typical computer programs consist of a bunch of rules: *If the user clicks "like," then increment the like button count by one. If the user clicks "dislike," hide the post.* But what if the action involves judgment? *If the user clicks "like" on a cute cat photo, show them more photos of cute cats.*

How can the machine determine that an image is of a cat, let alone that the cat is not feral? We could try to write rules such *look for a cuddly animal with whiskers*, but this begs the question of how to program the meaning of *cuddly* or identify whether a thin line in the image is a whisker.

Machine learning provides a data-driven approach to this problem. In our example, we'd show the neural network a bunch of labeled photographs of cats, dogs, and anything else we want it to be able to recognize (See **Figure 1-9**).

ML models have parameters called *weights* that are adjusted in a process called *training*. We'd train the model by evaluating the output and adjusting the weights until the NN outputs the correct label for each of the labeled photographs. This is called *backpropagation*. We still may not get 100% accuracy because models are not perfect and because some images may be mislabeled or ambiguous, and that's often okay—we can stop adjusting the weights when the accuracy stops improving.

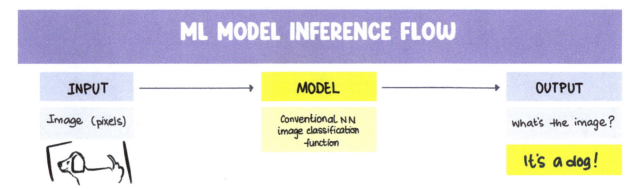

Figure 1-10. The ML model inference flow.

FINE TUNING A FOUNDATIONAL MODEL

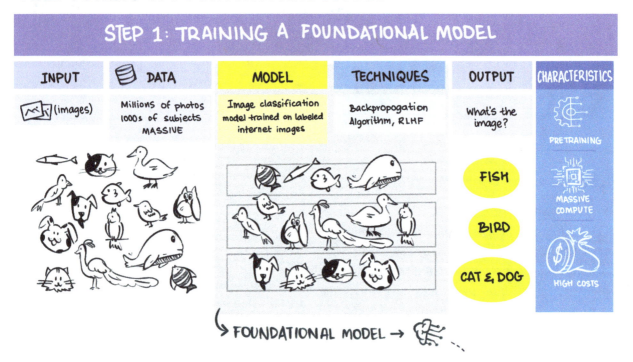

Figure 1-11. Step 1 of transfer learning involves training a foundational model.

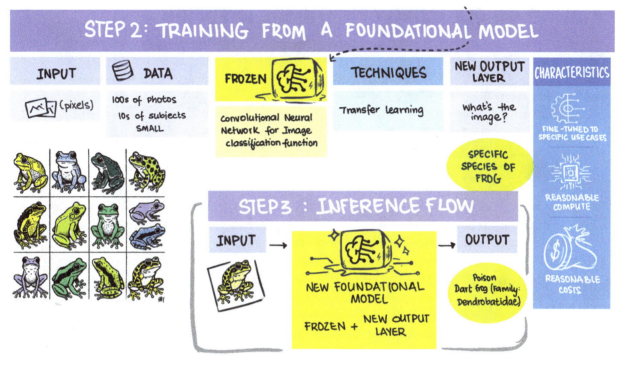

Figure 1-12. Step 2 of transfer learning involves fine-tuning. Fine-tuning lets us start from a foundational model and train a bespoke model for our task based on a much smaller dataset.

After the model has been trained, we deploy the model and let our application's users upload photos to it (see Figure 1-10). The model takes each unknown image, runs it through the NN, and sends back the output (which is *cat, dog,* etc.). Based on this output, the application can decide whether or not to show a specific image to users who want to see cute cats. Using a trained machine learning model to do what we trained it to do (to classify what's depicted in photos, for example) is called *inference*.

In many cases, humans can provide feedback, either implicit (they look at relevant pictures longer) or explicit (they click the "Like" button). This sort of human feedback is used to further train the model using a technique called reinforcement learning. Reinforcement learning

from human feedback (RLHF) is a key reason that AI models have become so much better, and why many technologies focus on building a large user base that can provide such feedback.

Training a machine learning model from scratch typically requires a lot of data. A model capable of photograph classification will have millions or billions of weights, and training it (as a rule of thumb) would require roughly that number of examples. Fortunately, we don't need millions of labeled cat photos. *Transfer learning* lets us start with a model trained on other image datasets (called a *foundational model;* see Figure 1-11) and adjust the weights of a small part of the NN (this is called *fine-tuning;* see Figure 1-12). The resulting model consists of the

CREATING IMAGES USING CONDITIONAL DIFFUSION

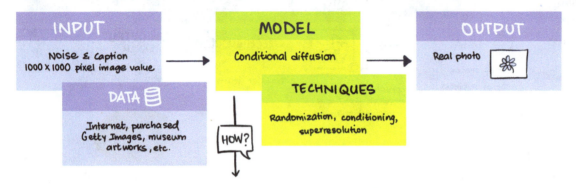

Figure 1-13. Conditional diffusion is a technique that can generate images using self-supervised denoising, progressive generation, text conditioning, and superresolution.

foundational model with a newly trained output layer that is focused on our problem.

Let's identify some of the key characteristics of this machine learning model:

Input

The input to the model is an image (really, the pixels of an image).

Data

The data needed to train the model is a set of photographs and labels that say what is in the image.

Model

The model is a mathematical function that works really well at image classification, such as a convolutional neural network.

Technique

Because the model has millions of parameters and we are unlikely to have millions of labeled images specific to our application,

we'll need to fine-tune a foundational model using transfer learning.

Output

The output of the image is one word (cat, dog, tiger, etc.) of a limited vocabulary.

Whenever you look at a machine learning use case, it's important to identify these five characteristics. In this chapter, we'll do this as we discuss how GenAI can create different forms of output—images, text, audio, and video.

Creating Images

The first form of GenAI that we will discuss is image generation. How can you create a machine learning model that can generate new images? In image generation, the input and output are both images (see **Figure 1-13**).

Modern image generation models use a method called conditional diffusion. There are four key ideas underlying this technique (see **Figure 1-14**): self-supervised denoising, progressive generation, text conditioning, and superresolution.

4 TECHNIQUES OF CONDITIONAL DIFFUSION

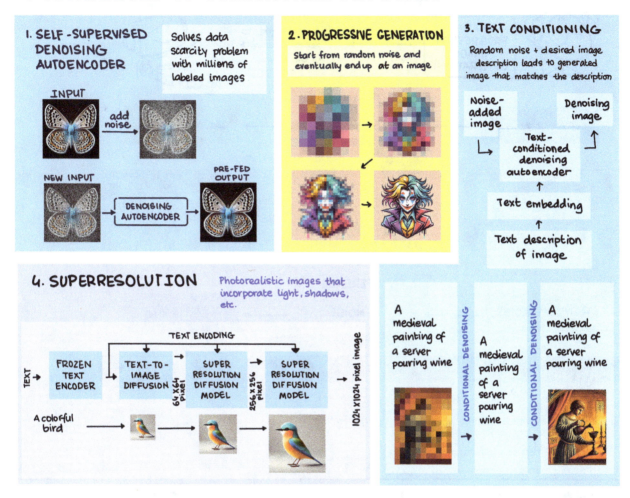

Figure 1-14. Four techniques for conditional diffusion.

This contrasts with image classification (shown in Figure 1-11), where the output is a word, such as "dog," from a limited vocabulary.

Self-supervised denoising autoencoder

Remember that in supervised machine learning, such as the image classification example to teach a model to identify cats, you need a large dataset of labeled images with one label per image.

For image generation, you'll need 1000 × 1000 output pixel values for each image. The size of the training dataset you need scales with the number of weights you need to train, and when you have one million outputs per image, you will need one million times as many weights to train, and therefore, one million times the size of the dataset that we would need for image classification! How are we going to create a labeled dataset of sufficient size?

PROGRESSIVE IMAGE GENERATION & CONDITIONING

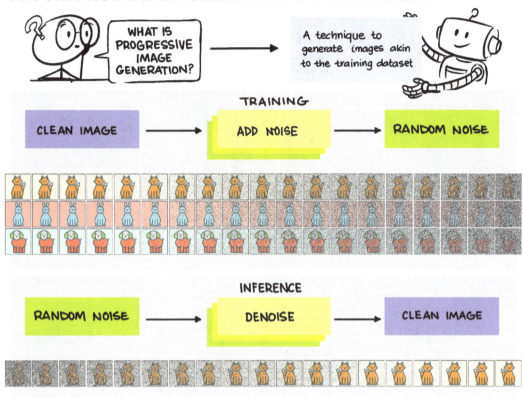

Figure 1-15. How diffusion models use progressive generation.

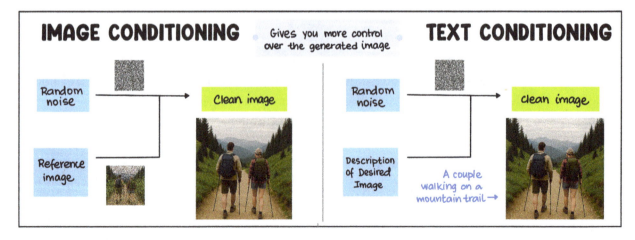

Figure 1-16. Image and text conditioning give you more control over the images that are generated by the model.

Diffusion solves this data scarcity problem using a brilliant idea: take an image, add small random variations to the image (this is called *noise*), then use the noisier image as input and the clean image as output (see Figure 1-14). This sort of technique where the ML model can synthetically create training data without needing humans to label the inputs is called *self-supervision*.

Because the input of the ML model is a noisy image and its output is a clean image, the ML model learns how to *denoise* an image. Any model that essentially returns its input is called an *autoencoder*. Here, because the output image has less noise, it is called a *denoising autoencoder*.

To create a good denoising autoencoder, you need millions of images—but you don't have to spend time labeling them. Once you train the model on these millions of images, it will be capable of denoising images with a small amount of noise.

Progressive generation

Instead of doing the denoising only once, you can do it multiple times. In *progressive generation*, the idea is to start with a clean image and add noise in steps (Figure 1-15). If each step consists of adding only a small amount of noise, the denoising autoencoder will be capable of reversing each individual step. At some point, you can start with pure noise, and the model will be able to reconstruct an image by doing the denoising operation one step at a time (Figure 1-16).

What kind of images can such progressive generation create? If you start from random noise, you will end up with an image that's akin to the images in the training dataset. This is great if

you train the model on a dataset of faces and are happy to end up with a face, any face.

What if, though, you want to control the image in some manner? Then, you need a technique called *conditioning*—instead of starting with purely random noise, you would start with a mix of random noise and a desirable image that you want to match (see left panel of Figure 1-16). If you want to generate an image that is like something in your training dataset, you can start with that desirable image, suitably degraded, and ask the generative model to denoise that image progressively so that you end up with a similar image.

This is rather hit-and-miss, though—two images could be alike because they both depict outdoor scenes, or because they both depict mountainous areas. What level of detail should the similarity capture? What if you'd like to be able to generate images that are completely unlike anything in your training dataset, and so you don't have a desired likeness to start from?

Text conditioning

It would be ideal if we could condition based on text—perhaps we can provide a sentence that describes the image we want ("two hikers walking up a mountain"). To do that, you have to first train the generative model on text-to-image pairs. If you are training on images in books, you could use the image caption or the sentence that references the image as the text that is used to train the model.

Rather than train a denoising model purely on the noisy image, we also tell it what's in the image, so that the denoiser in each step has two inputs: the noisy image and a caption or description. The output remains the clean image. This is how the model is conditioned to operate on text.

Once such a text-conditioned model has been trained, you can use progressive generation—start from random noise and a caption that describes the image you want, and end up with a generated image that matches the description (see right panel of Figure 1-16).

Superresolution

The approach we just described is sufficient to create a simple illustration, but it can't create photorealistic images or fine paintings. For that, you need a model that can learn how to handle light, shadow, and other aspects of style. So, modern diffusion models employ yet another machine learning model to go from low-resolution images to superresolution, photorealistic images. Such a model can also be trained in a self-supervised way by starting from high-resolution photographs and paintings, progressively coarsening them, and then repeating the process in reverse during inference (see Figure 1-14).

Creating Text

As shown in Figure 1-17, the input to a GenAI model that generates text can be purely text or it can be multimodal (consisting of interleaved images and text). While many popular foundational models such as Gemini and Claude are multimodal, we'll simplify the discussion in this section by focusing on text inputs only.

There are a few key concepts that underlie text generation models: next-word prediction, transformer architecture, prefix tuning, human feedback, conversation state, and instruction tuning. Let's look at these one by one. These ideas are roughly in chronological order, with each idea building on previous inventions.

Next-word prediction

Text generation models are set up to predict the next word given a context. For example, given the following context (see Figure 1-18):

"We were climbing the"

The text generation model identifies the next most likely words:

```
We were climbing the [hill, mountain,
tree, …]
```

It chooses one of them based on the candidates' likelihood, adds it to the context, and then proceeds to identify the word most likely to follow:

```
We were climbing the mountain [when,
at, on, …]
```

This method of iteratively predicting one word at a time is what powers many phones' predictive text models (Google Search's autocomplete predicts multiple words at once, but is similar). You may have seen the memes where you plug in a prompt and see what your phone gives you: "I like talking to…." Using this method of iteratively predicting one word at a time, a text generation model can generate paragraphs, pages, and even entire books.

How does the model know which words are likely in a given context? It is shown billions of sentences where the training data consists of N words, and the model needs to learn to predict the N +1th word. The size of the training corpus (billions of words) is such a

CREATING TEXT USING GENAI

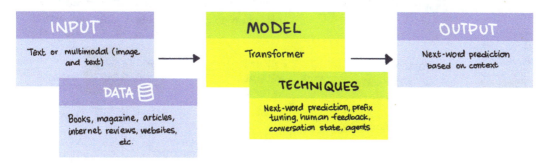

Figure 1-17. Basic workflow for GenAI models to produce text.

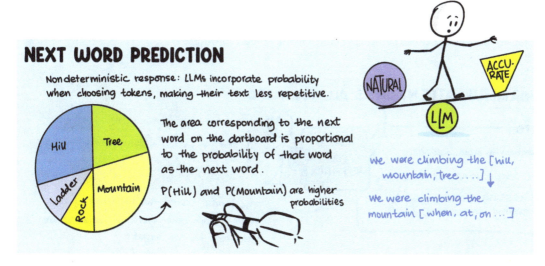

Figure 1-18. LLMs predict the next word in a sequence.

defining characteristic of this approach that it gives text generation models their name: *large language models*.

An LLM that always chooses the most likely word would result in repetitive and robotic text. In practice, therefore, an LLM chooses among the most likely set of words in proportion to their relative probabilities. Think of the LLM as throwing a dart at a dartboard where the area corresponding to each candidate word is proportional to the probability of that word being

found in the training data. This is one of the reasons why when you ask a chatbot the exact same question, you are not guaranteed to get the same answer. Text generation is not *deterministic*.

The term "next-*word* prediction" is not strictly accurate. Modern text generation models do not operate on words. Instead, they operate on *tokens*. This is because there are many things in text that are hard to represent as just words.

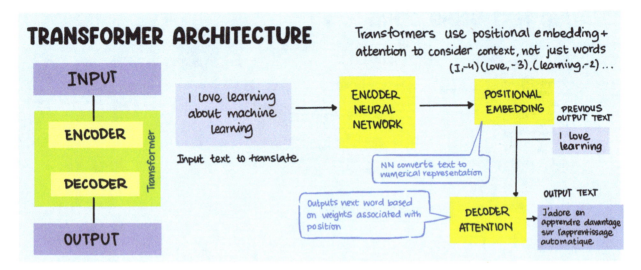

Figure 1-19. How transformers are structured to include context in their predictions.

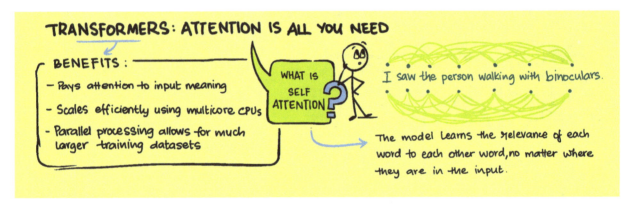

Figure 1-20. The "Attention Is All You Need" paper introduced the idea of self-attention.

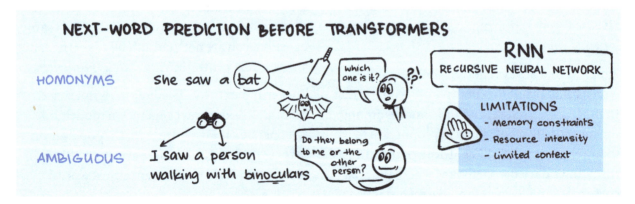

Figure 1-21. How next-word prediction worked before transformers.

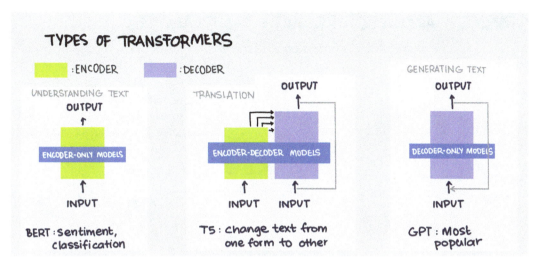

Figure 1-22. Different types of transformers are used for different tasks.

Imagine a sentence like the following:

```
I bought the GenAI book by Vergadia and
Lakshmanan for $45 on amazon.com.
```

It would be almost impossible to represent the words here using a finite vocabulary—after all, there will always be unique and rare names, and the set of possible numbers is itself infinite. Instead, what models do is to break the sentence up, and split any word that is not a common word into one- or two-character sequences called *tokens*. A *tokenized* version of the sentence might look something like this:

```
I bought the Ge n AI book by V erg ad
ia and La k sh ma nan for $ 4 5 on
amazon . com.
```

The list of these tokens is now finite, and it is possible to represent anything in a corpus of text using them. However, one potential drawback of such tokenization is that text generation models have to work harder to understand the likelihoods of citations (such as lists of people's names) and numbers.

Transformer architecture

Modern generative AI is based on a technology called transformers (**Figure 1-19**), which was introduced in a famous 2017 paper called *Attention Is All You Need (https://oreil.ly/cgw-WN)*, originally for translation problems (see **Figure 1-20**). It solved several problems associated with previous attempts at language problems like translation, homonyms, and word order (see **Figure 1-21**).

In a transformer architecture, the input text is converted into a numerical representation called an embedding, using an NN called an encoder. This embedding, along with preceding words of translated text, is provided as input to a second NN, called a decoder, which outputs the next word of the translation. While translation requires both an encoder and a decoder, other language problems like sentiment analysis and next-word prediction can be addressed with only an encoder or only a decoder (see **Figure 1-22**).

TRANSFORMER ARCHITECTURE WITH AN EXAMPLE

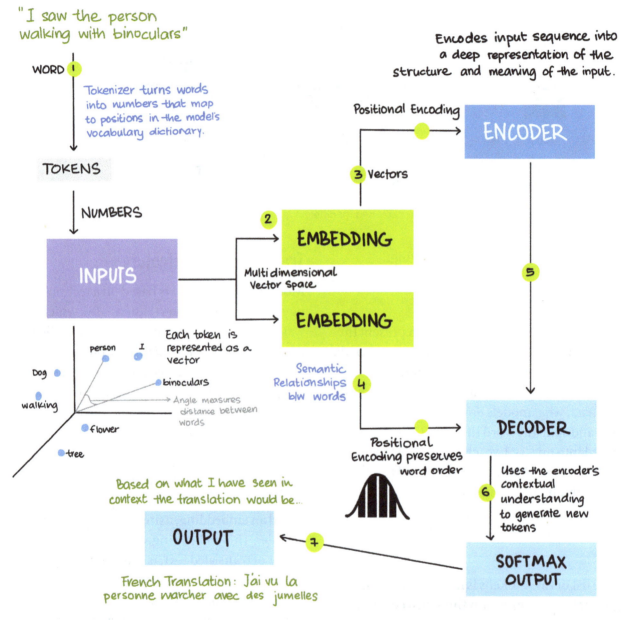

Figure 1-23. The transformer architecture involves two concepts, attention and positional embeddings, that together solve the problem of word order in translations.

There is one wrinkle: translating between two languages is almost never word-for-word. The word order within sentences varies. One language may have gendered pronouns where the other doesn't; some words may have different translations depending on the subject. The standard way to handle this in early machine learning models was to imbue them with memory so that they could remember the words that came before, and to feed in words in sequence. Such recurrent neural networks didn't work very well.

The authors of the transformer paper introduced two concepts—positional embeddings and attention—that provided a brilliant solution to this problem (see **Figure 1-23**). Positional embeddings are exactly what the term sounds like: instead of just creating tokens for each word encountered in the input text, models using this technique also append a relative position. So, if we are "on" the word *person* in the sentence *I saw the person walking*…, the representation of the previous words would be (I, -4), (saw, -3), and (the, -2).

The output of the decoder depends in part on the weights associated with these positions, so that the translation of any word depends in different ways on the words that came before—for example, the weights of the words "I" and "saw" would be high when determining the first word of the translated phrase into French ("j'ai") because this depends on tense—"I see" would be "je vois". We say the model is paying attention to the words "I" and "saw" when decoding the word "j'ai".

Similarly, the third word of the translation ("la") would require heavy weights on "*the*" and "*person*" because French is gendered—had I seen a waiter, it would have been "le garçon." In this way, the decoder learns to pay attention to different words, even to the point of "reasoning" that the person was walking *holding* the binoculars ("marcher *avec* des jumelles"). Hence, the title of the famous paper: "Attention Is All You Need" (it's also a homage to the famous Beatles song "All You Need Is Love").

While encoder-decoder models continue to be used for translation and summarization, many modern language models tend to specialize—they either have only an encoder or only a decoder! Models with only an encoder are limited to producing embeddings, but embeddings are all you need for a variety of language tasks, including text classification, topic modeling, and search. Models with only a decoder are used to generate open-ended text. GPT-4, Gemini, and Claude are all encoder-only models.

The data used to train an LLM tends to come from many publicly available sources such as Common Crawl, Wikipedia, US patents, and corpora of books. Recently, foundational model providers have been striking agreements with content owners such as Reddit and Stack Overflow for the right to train their LLMs on copyrighted data.

Prefix tuning

A decoder-only LLM is capable of generating text, but we usually want to control the form and content of the text, not just generate what is statistically most likely given the starting point. One way to do this is by fine-tuning the model to follow instructions. Some example prompts are shown in the following:

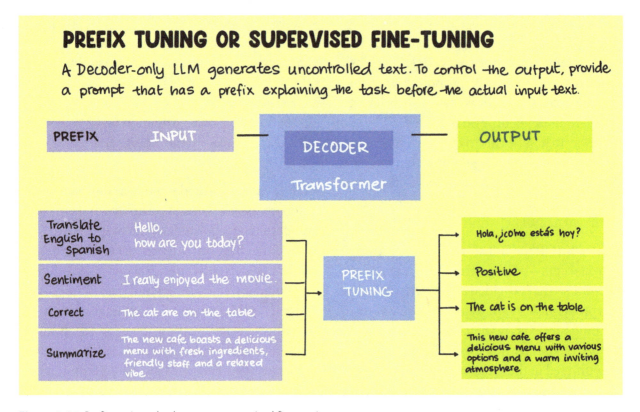

Figure 1-24. Prefix tuning, also known as supervised fine-tuning.

- Create an outline of a book on GenAI

- Write a poem to celebrate an athlete's 30th birthday

- Summarize the following paragraph in two sentences (followed by a paragraph of text)

- Translate the following text into German (followed by some text)

The way that foundational model providers imbue their next-word prediction models with these capabilities is called *supervised fine-tuning* (SFT) or prefix tuning (see **Figure 1-24**).

The model trainer adds a description of the task to be done and prefixes it to the input text they provide to the model. The trainer appends this

example to the labeled training data for each of the tasks—the result is one massive dataset covering a wide variety of prefixes (each of which is an instruction to the model). The model is thus trained to produce the desired output text given a wide variety of prompts. This way, the LLM learns to follow a wide variety of instructions, instead of being able to do only one specific task.

While the T5 model from Google *(https://oreil. ly/YYpTJ)*, which introduced prefix tuning in 2020, supported only a limited number of tasks, OpenAI's GPT-3, introduced in 2022, was described as being *task-agnostic*. It appears that, as the number of tasks a model supports increases and as the size of the model increases, the model starts to be able *(https://oreil.ly/yrWlK)*

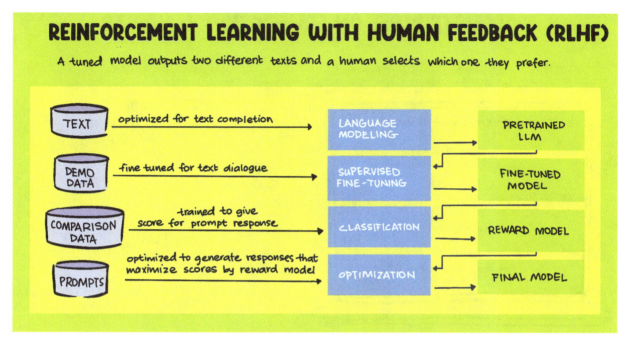

Figure 1-25. Reinforcement learning with human feedback (RLHF).

to do tasks that it was not explicitly trained to do, as long as there was some similar task in the training dataset. This is only a hypothesis, however. Between 2020 and 2022, the leading foundational model providers ceased being open about their methods, so it's unclear what other changes (like meta-prompting; *https:// oreil.ly/noTPQ*) OpenAI employed to make their models task-agnostic.

Human feedback

The basic transformer approach worked fine for generating short snippets of text or highly conditioned text (such as translations). For more open-ended tasks, the text got less coherent the longer it got.

To address this, OpenAI introduced the idea of *reinforcement learning with human feedback*

(RLHF) with its GPT-2 model. Incorporating human feedback (*https://oreil.ly/Ewqox*) remains an important part of modern LLMs, although an elegant mathematical result called *direct preference optimization* (DPO) has enabled LLMs trained after 2024 to incorporate human feedback while avoiding reinforcement learning.

The basic idea is to have the tuned model output two different texts, then have a human select which text they prefer (see **Figure 1-25**). Once you have enough pairs (in practice, 100,000 to 1,000,000 examples), it's possible to train a *reward model* to predict which text a human would select. The LLM is then fine-tuned to assign higher probabilities to word continuations that would be more pleasing to humans.

Pretrained foundational models such as GPT-4, Gemini, and Claude are LLMs that have been

PRODUCTS BUILT ON FOUNDATIONAL MODELS

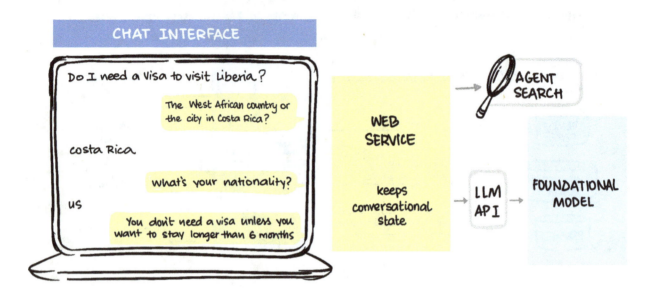

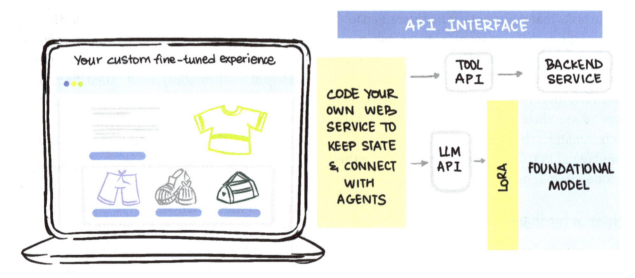

Figure 1-26. Products built around foundational models.

CREATING AUDIO & VIDEO USING GENAI

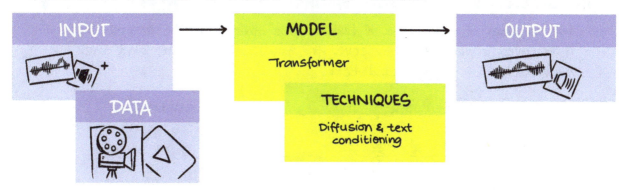

Figure 1-27. Basic audio and video workflow for GenAI models.

prefix-trained to support multiple tasks or to be task-agnostic, then fine-tuned on human feedback. If you use Gemini through Google Cloud Vertex AI or Claude 3 through Amazon Web Services (AWS), you are using a pretrained model. This is important because it's possible to further fine-tune such a model on your own data, using a parameter-efficient fine-tuning (PEFT) method such as low-rank adaptation (LoRA), both of which we'll discuss later in this book.

Productionizing the foundational model

When you use OpenAI's GPT-4 (*http://chat. openai.com*), Google's Gemini (*http://gemini. google.com*), or Anthropic's Claude 3 (*http:// claude.ai*) through their web services, you are not getting the foundational model. Instead, you are getting a product that is architected around the foundational model.

A service such as ChatGPT is an API endpoint to a web service that is *powered* by the foundational model but also includes a host of additional capabilities (see Figure 1-26). The web service keeps *conversational state*—in other words, it asks the

LLM to summarize the previous conversation and automatically adds the summary as additional context to the prompt of the next question you ask. The web service might also maintain long-term *memory* from past sessions—for example, it might use your past queries and follow-up instructions to provide answers that are better aligned to your personal preferences.

Many web services often let users invoke external tools, such as the ability to search the web and incorporate the search results directly into the context of the query. The foundational model, on the other hand, can only generate text based on the training dataset. If you're a developer using a foundational model and you want to fine-tune it to your dataset, include previous conversation state, or call out to some web capability, you'll have to code that up yourself.

Creating Audio and Video

Compared to creating images and generating text, the enterprise use cases for creating music and videos are narrower and more specialized (see Figure 1-27). There is also the additional

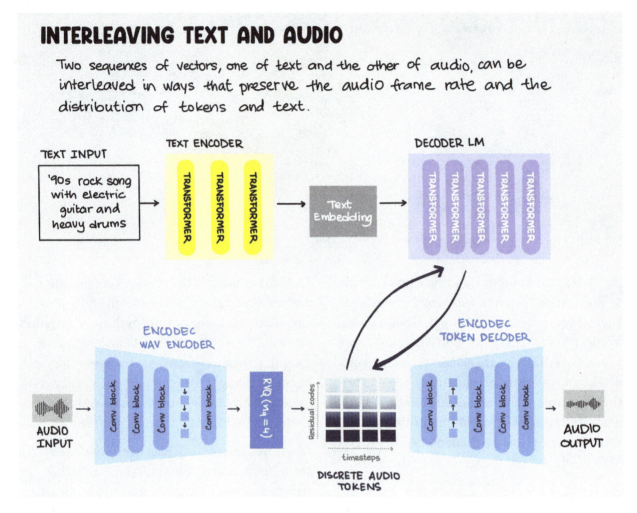

Figure 1-28. Interleaving audio and video models involves specialized architectures.

complication that audio and video have an element of time. So, we'll provide only a very high-level overview of how music and video generation work.

Audio

In 2023, Meta introduced an open source family of models called AudioCraft (*https://oreil.ly/1T4eg*) to generate music and sound effects in response to a text prompt. Rather than training these models starting from music

representations such as MIDI files or sheet music, Meta started from raw audio signals (see **Figure 1-28**).

Two important concepts here are encoding and interleaving:

Encoding audio

Dealing with raw audio signals directly would require processing millions of time-steps per minute of audio. So, the first step is to train an autoencoder that functions on raw audio, but also quantize the intermediate embedding to make it small enough for the remaining steps to handle.

For example, if you want the audio output at a quality of 48 kHz (the quality of CD recordings), it is possible to reduce the size of raw audio signals by over 10 times.

Interleaving text and audio

Text input is converted into a vector representation using standard text-embedding models. Because the raw audio has been converted into audio tokens, we now have two sequences of vectors, one of text and the other of audio. These need to be combined to create the input to the GenAI model. But there is a complication: the audio tokens are spread over timesteps, whereas the text input is static.

The Meta researchers solve this complication by interleaving the two sequences in various ways that preserve the frame rate of the audio and have the same distribution of tokens and text. The interleaving algorithm picks subsets of the audio token sequences or introduces delays within which the text can be interleaved. The specific subsets and delays are determined beforehand (these predetermined patterns are called *codebooks*) and applied to all the audio and text pairs in the training dataset.

As with image and text generation models, the interleaved sequence up until a timestep forms the input to the transformer model, and the model is trained to predict the audio tokens of the next timestep. These audio tokens are then decoded with the original decoder to create the audio output.

Video

In 2024, Google published a paper (*https://oreil. ly/Be0fQ*) explaining how to generate video conditioned on text prompts or on an initial image. Called Lumiere (*https://oreil.ly/lNH89*), the approach is new in that it processes all the frames of a short video simultaneously, instead of working on time samples (as the Meta audio model, discussed in the previous section, did). With this approach, video generation is exactly like image generation using diffusion (see Figure 1-29), except that video generation operates on one more dimension than image generation! The exact same concepts apply.

Model architecture

The encoder part of the model architecture consists of progressively downsampling the 4D input sequence (one temporal dimension, two spatial dimensions of height and width, one dimension of RGB values) using a specific kind of neural network layers called convolutional layers. Convolutional networks find structure in images by operating, not on individual pixels, but on all the pixels within a pixel's neighborhood. At the coarsest resolution, the resulting stacks are stacked across time and input into an attention layer, as shown in Figure 1-30. This way, the model can learn to pay attention to different timesteps and parts of the frame. The layers are then reconstructed by upsampling back to the original dimension. This allows the model to learn how to form videos.

VIDEO: MODEL ARCHITECTURE AND CONDITIONING

Video generation model architecture that utilizes a Space-Time U-Net to process the entire video sequence at once, capturing complex motions.

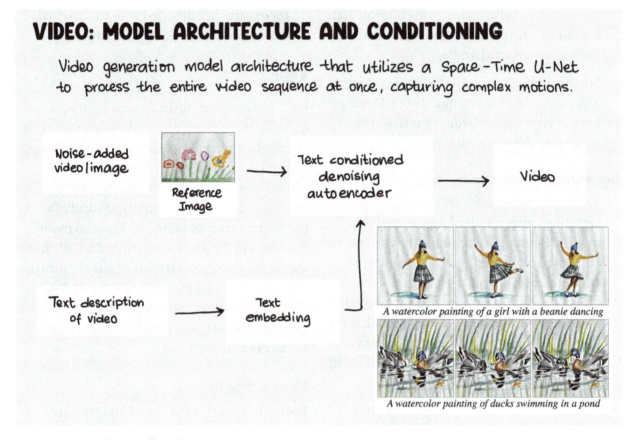

Figure 1-29. Conditioning for video generation.

VIDEO GENERATION: MODEL ARCHITECTURE

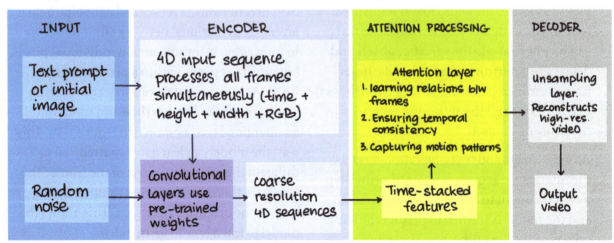

Figure 1-30. Model architecture for video generation.

As with image generation, this video autoencoder architecture can be used to denoise an input video to which random noise has been added. Thus, we can train a diffusion model to generate a video starting from random noise. The Lumiere paper showed that it was possible to freeze the weights of a pretrained image diffusion model and to train only the newly added time parameters.

Conditioning

As with image generation, we don't want to generate some arbitrary video; we would like to control the content and style of the video. Video generation too can be conditioned off a text prompt. It can also be conditioned off an image that provides the style of the desired video. By 2025, video generation models such as Sora, Runway, and Veo had greatly improved on the Lumiere approach and are now capable of creating long, quite realistic videos.

We hope that this tour through the technologies underpinning GenAI has helped demystify the models. Just understanding the technology doesn't really do it justice, though. You need to understand what you can do with these capabilities. For that, you have to look at these technologies through the product capabilities lens. What can we do now that we couldn't do just a few years ago?

FROM TRANSFORMERS TO CHATGPT IN SIX YEARS

The 2017 paper that introduced transformers, "Attention Is All You Need," was hugely influential in machine learning research, but the technology was not yet ready to get into the hands of the general public.

Writing Poetry

In 2018, one of the authors of this book (Lak) collaborated with one of the "famous eight" engineers who wrote the transformers paper (Lukasz) to use the ideas in that paper to generate poetry (*https://oreil.ly/REIcH*). The idea was to feed in one line of a real poem, and have the model generate a possible next line.

We created a training dataset by downloading 22,000 lines of poetry from Project Gutenberg (*https://gutenberg.org*) and extracting pairs of lines, so that the input was a line of poetry and the target output was the next line from the same poem. For example, Shakespeare's 14-line sonnet on absence would contribute 13 training examples, as shown in Table 1-1.

We trained the transformer on these input-output pairs, deployed the model, and asked people to try it out. As a demonstration of the technology, it was powerful. For example, we prompted it with a line from a poem by the Persian poet Rumi:

```
where did the handsome beloved go
```

The model output:

```
where art thou worse to me than dead
```

In 2018, the fact that we could get a *fluent* line of poetic text, rather than just gibberish, from just

Table 1-1. Training examples for the poetry model

INPUT	TARGET OUTPUT
Being your slave what should I do but tend	Upon the hours and times of your desire?
Upon the hours and times of your desire?	I have no precious time at all to spend,
I have no precious time at all to spend,	Nor services to do, till you require:
Nor services to do, till you require:	Nor dare I chide the world-without-end hour
Nor dare I chide the world-without-end hour	Whilst I, my sovereign, watch the clock for you,
Whilst I, my sovereign, watch the clock for you,	Nor think the bitterness of absence sour
Nor think the bitterness of absence sour	When you have bid your servant once adieu:
When you have bid your servant once adieu:	Nor dare I question with my jealous thought
Nor dare I question with my jealous thought	Where you may be, or your affairs suppose,
Where you may be, or your affairs suppose,	But like a sad slave, stay and think of nought
But like a sad slave, stay and think of nought	Save where you are, how happy you make those;—
Save where you are, how happy you make those;—	So true a fool is love, that in your will,
So true a fool is love, that in your will,	Though you do any thing, he thinks no ill.

22,000 examples was amazing. However, the resulting poetry was not *coherent*—the first line is about absence, whereas the model's completion is about disappointment.

What happens if we try that same line with some modern GenAI models in 2024? Because we have not trained these models on our task, we'll prepend an instruction to the input:

```
You are a poet. I will give you the
first line of a couplet. Please suggest
a potential second line.
First line: where did the handsome
beloved go
Second line:
```

In Table 1-2, we show you our results and provide a URL where you can try it yourself. Note, however, that the results you obtain won't match ours because the models use randomness in their generation.

All these models exhibit both fluency and coherence, although the smallest model is somewhat prosaic.

What changed between 2017 and 2024?

One Small Step by OpenAI

In 2022, OpenAI released ChatGPT as a research preview (*https://oreil.ly/3rD1K*), introducing it as "a sibling model to InstructGPT, which is trained to follow an instruction in a prompt and provide a detailed response." It was an incremental improvement, just one step in a long set of improvements to transformers (see Figure 1-31), but it turned out to be the step that moved the technology from being a research curiosity to something laypeople could use.

Priyanka vividly remembers encountering ChatGPT amidst the whirlwind of her MBA program, where every day seemed to be a race

Table 1-2. Poetry completion by a few selected GenAI models in April 2024

Model and URL to try it out	Parameter count	Suggested completion(s)
ChatGPT 3.5 (OpenAI) *https://chat.openai.com*	175 billion	Leaving behind traces of his whispered echo
Gemini 1.0 Pro (Google) *https://gemini.google.com*	Not published	Option 1: Focused on longing and mystery Where did the handsome beloved go? His absence leaves my spirit low. Option 2: A more whimsical, nature-inspired approach Where did the handsome beloved go? Perhaps the wind his secret does know.
DBRX (Databricks)	132 billion	Beneath the moon's soft glow, his heart still beats in rhythm with your own.
Claude 3 Sonnet (Anthropic) *https://claude.ai*	70 billion	leaving my heart to ache and soul to woe
Mistral-7B (Mistral AI) *https://hugging-face.co/mistralai/ Mistral-7B-Instruct-v0.2*	7 billion	perhaps in the twilight, he sailed across the sea. or perhaps he hid within the forest's secret heart. or perhaps he left to chase the setting sun.

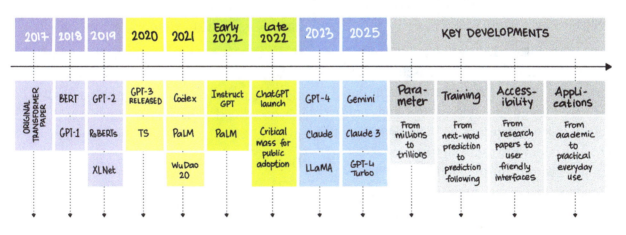

Figure 1-31. A long set of improvements to the original transformer model.

against time. With a stack of company case studies towering over her desk, she often found herself drowning in the details. It was during one of these overwhelming moments that she explored ChatGPT, which was all the buzz at the time. With a simple prompt, it effortlessly condensed the intricate narratives of each case study into concise yet insightful summaries. This newfound efficiency transformed her study sessions, allowing her to grasp the essence of each case study without getting lost in the minutiae.

As her MBA journey progressed, ChatGPT became an indispensable tool in her arsenal. Whenever she hit a roadblock while brainstorming paper topics, she turned to it for inspiration. Its ability to generate diverse ideas sparked her creativity and helped her uncover fresh perspectives to explore. For Priyanka, the most valuable aspect of ChatGPT was its talent for brevity: with word limits on every assignment, it helped her trim down her papers without sacrificing substance. ChatGPT, she felt, effortlessly sculpted her verbose drafts into sleek, polished compositions that fit snugly within the confines of her professors' expectations.

Your other author, Lak, wasn't as easily convinced that ChatGPT could be useful. He still remembered the incoherent text that came out of his poetry language model in 2018, and couldn't believe that a simple next-word predictor would produce fluent and coherent text. There is a famous theorem (*https://oreil.ly/fWt7E*) by Claude Shannon that, in simple terms, says that to create an LLM capable of learning the entire corpus of text available on the internet, the LLM would need as many parameters as it would take to store the internet in compressed form.

Knowing that no practical LLM could ever be large enough to capture all human-generated text, he even wrote an article in 2022 titled "*Why Large Language Models Like ChatGPT Are Bullshit Artists*" (although he did cover his bases somewhat by adding the subtitle "and how to use them effectively anyway"; *https://oreil.ly/hYd3A*).

What did Lak miss?

Advances Between 2017 and 2024

Lak missed that (a) billions of parameters are enough to capture the gist, if not the entirety, of the most commonly needed information, and (b) the culmination of many technology improvements is that GenAI models have vastly improved. In this section, we'll quickly run through these improvements.

Generative AI's widespread adoption stems from three key factors: its user-friendliness, enabling anyone to utilize it regardless of technical expertise; its speed, delivering high-quality results rapidly and saving considerable time; and its continuous advancement, leading to increasing sophistication and capabilities.

If you are skeptical about the capabilities of LLMs, as Lak used to be, perhaps this will help bring you over to a more optimistic outlook. If you have a colleague or boss who is skeptical about LLMs, share this chapter with them.

The improvements have happened in four broad areas: model architecture, data quality, algorithmic improvements, and customizability.

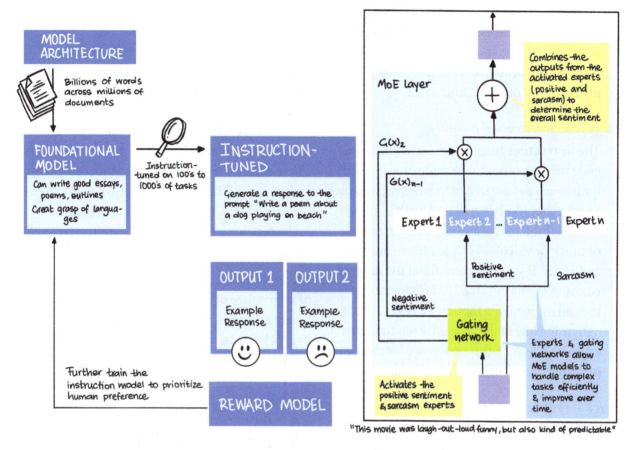

Figure 1-32. Four stages of training in newer models.

Model architecture

The transformer model that Lak used in 2018 was tiny—he had to train it on eight 2018-era graphics processing units (GPUs) in a day or so. The number of parameters in that model was in the millions. The number of parameters in modern LLMs is in the hundreds of billions to trillions.

Lucasz and Lak trained the poetry model from scratch: it had to learn how English works, how poetry works, and how to maintain context across consecutive lines. That is not the case with newer models.

As depicted in **Figure 1-32**, newer models are trained in four stages:

Stage 1: Foundational model training

The LLM learns to understand language by looking at billions of words across millions of documents, so it starts out with a much better grasp of English.

Stage 2: Instruction tuning

The language model is instruction-tuned on hundreds or thousands of tasks. Humans generate good answers for these tasks and these answers are used to train the model to perform those tasks. Because of this second stage of training, modern GenAI models start out being able to write good essays, good poems, good outlines, and so on.

Stage 3: Reward model training

The instruction-tuned model is made to generate two responses to the same prompt, and both responses are shown to humans, who pick the one they like better. Based on this, a reward model is built that prioritizes text (or images or music or video) that is pleasing to human audiences. If you look carefully at the suggested completions in Table 2, you'll notice that they all rhyme, even though we never asked for a rhyming line in the prompt. Even though not all poetry rhymes, this preference for rhyme is probably a result of human feedback.

Stage 4: Preference optimization using reward model

The reward model is used to further train the model to prioritize human preferences, even for instructions or tasks that were not explicitly shown to users. While humans may have written 100 limericks (Stage 2), and selected which version of a limerick they preferred 1000 times (Stage 3), Stages 2 and 3 are limited by the cost of human labor. It is Stage 4 that allows the model training to scale. For example, the model trainer can ask the model to generate 100,000 pairs of limericks and have the reward model choose between them.

The interplay between these four stages is a key reason that modern LLMs are so much better than the model Lak trained in 2018.

The model architecture at each stage of this multistage process can be quite a bit simpler than if you had a single model that needed to do all the steps. Thus, the foundational model (Stage 1) that learns language can look ahead and use only the encoder part of the transformer architecture. Meanwhile, the model in Stage 4 needs to focus only on next-word prediction and can use only the decoder part of the transformer architecture. These more streamlined architectures and training tasks enable the models in each stage to be trained in a more effective way.

Modern architectures are also much more efficient than the basic transformer. They consist of a "mixture of experts" (MoE in Figure 1-32), where an *expert* is a path through the NN. Each expert is sparse and uses only a subset of the weights in the model, and different experts are activated in different situations. The use of experts allows for more efficient use of the parameters of the model—for a given model size, having more experts leads to performance akin to that of a much larger model. Researchers have found (*https://oreil.ly/pryxR*) that encoder experts tend to focus on specific aspects of the input, such as punctuation, proper nouns, verbs, and so on, while decoder experts are less specialized.

In summary, modern architectures are larger, more specialized, more streamlined, and more efficient than the early transformer architectures from 2018.

Data quality

Machine learning is driven primarily by data. Larger models are better primarily because they can better capture the insights from larger datasets. However, it is intuitively obvious that size

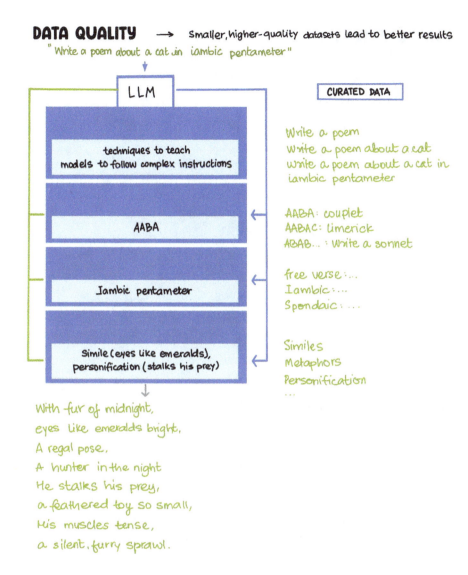

Figure 1-33. Smaller, higher-quality datasets lead to better results.

cannot be everything—more data is not going to lead to better models if that data is garbage.

Can a smaller dataset of higher quality lead to better results than a larger, lower-quality dataset? A number of Microsoft researchers in 2023 proved that, yes, "Textbooks Are All You Need" (*https://oreil.ly/d8A_K*). They did this for a coding model named phi-1 by intentionally selecting clear, self-contained, instructive code ("textbook-quality" data). They supplemented this with synthetically created tutorials and coding exercises that were generated by a language model. The coding model they trained using this dataset performed better than one trained on a much larger corpus of code that happened to be in publicly available repositories.

The organizations creating foundational GenAI models have taken this lesson to heart: they employ humans whose job is to create demonstration data (see **Figure 1-33**). The demonstration

ALGORITHMIC IMPROVEMENTS

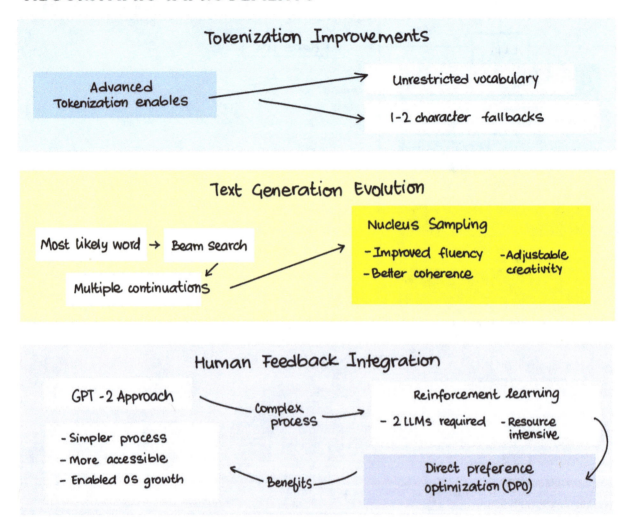

Figure 1-34. Improvements to algorithms lead to better results.

datasets keep growing because once the models are released, users ask these models to do more and more tasks and often provide increasingly complex instructions in their prompts.

Tutorials usually involve simple instructions. How can we teach GenAI models to follow complex instructions? For example, the prompt to Midjourney that won the Colorado State Fair's annual art competition (*https://oreil.ly/xgaH6*) would have been something along the lines of "concept painting of epic space opera scene, epic golden portal, red nebula in background, Victorian spacesuits, planets and stars visible beyond huge golden portal, reflections and orna (sic)" (*https://oreil.ly/IQHvf*). You can be sure that would not have been in any training dataset.

How does the model learn to respond to such complex instructions?

One technique to teach models to follow complex instructions is called *Evol-Instruct (https://oreil.ly/HQS7O)*. It works by taking a simple instruction and then evolving it in some specific ways, often by taking the results of other instructions.

The Microsoft researchers who created phi-1 not only trained it on textbook-quality data, but also added synthetically created tutorials in the form of Python notebooks, coding exercises, and solutions to those coding exercises. To create these tutorials, they used GPT-3.5, a much larger model. In spite of the *Inception*-like connotations of using LLM-generated data to train an LLM, the idea of creating pristine synthetic data to supplement a training dataset has proven quite valuable (*https://oreil.ly/wkfuQ*)in a lot of settings.

The final piece of the puzzle in increasing data quality has been commercial agreements to take advantage of proprietary, copyrighted, and/or up-to-date information. We'll discuss these agreements in more detail shortly. For now, let's just note that using timely, high-quality data that has been vetted by human experts contributes to the overall quality of GenAI models.

How does all this play into the poetry problem? In 2018, Lak's poetry model was trained on 22,000 lines culled from three anthologies of out-of-copyright poetry. Today's LLMs have access to textbooks (poetry-writing guides, rhyming dictionaries, and critical analysis), poems in increasing order of complexity (ranging from nursery rhymes to iambic pentameter),

demonstration guides (limericks, haikus, sonnets, etc.), and commercial agreements to use more recent poetry. The quality and size of the data available to modern LLMs far exceeds that minuscule dataset used to train a model from scratch in 2018. This larger data is also organized in such a way that models can be successively refined on more complex data, as shown in **Figure 1-33**.

Algorithmic improvements

Model architectures are greatly improved, and the data quality is higher. The techniques used within the models have also gotten better (see **Figure 1-34**).

Here we'll take a quick look at three examples—tokenization, nucleus sampling, and human feedback:

Tokenization

Recall from earlier in this chapter that instead of restricting training data to a small vocabulary of words, tokenization—using one-character and two-character tokens as fallbacks—allows us to use any and all text in the input to the model.

Engineers make choices in the model tokenization scheme to prioritize the use cases the model is being trained for. For example, OpenAI's GPT-3 and GPT-4 models explicitly represent common Python reserved keywords and variable names with a single token each. Not only does this make representing code more efficient, but it also makes it easier for the LLM to understand the relationships between different coding symbols. By contrast, Google's Gemini uses a common tokenizing scheme across hundreds of languages. This allows it to understand multilingual content much better (such as when text messages use a mix of Hindi and English words).

Nucleus sampling

When generating text, choosing the most likely next word results in text that is degenerate and not at all fluent. In 2018, the way this was solved was *beam search*, where continuations were maintained for a certain length, and then the most likely series of words was chosen. Modern LLMs use *nucleus sampling,* where they consider the relative probabilities of potential continuations along with the user's desired creativity level. We'll explain nucleus sampling and the parameters associated with it in Chapter 2. For now, suffice it to say that fluency and coherence are greatly improved by this method of choosing the next word.

Human feedback

OpenAI was the first to use human feedback in the LLM training process. In GPT-2, they used human feedback on pairs of generated text to train a reward model that would make choices similar to a human's. Then, they fine-tuned it using *reinforcement learning*—the unmodified LLM would create some text, the reward model would choose the text that was better, and this was used to create a fine-tuned version that would assign a higher likelihood to this text. The problem with this approach is that it needed two LLMs and was so expensive that only well-funded companies could afford to do it.

Stanford researchers changed this dynamic in 2023 when they published an elegant mathematical proof, "*Direct Preference Optimization: Your Language Model Is Secretly a Reward Model*" (*https://oreil.ly/gIqAO*). They showed that it was possible to avoid reinforcement learning and directly optimize the first LLM based on human feedback, known as direct preference optimization. The availability of DPO changed the economics of LLMs and made it possible for open source models to catch up in quality to proprietary models.

Customizability

So far, we have looked at why large models such as OpenAI's GPT-4, Google's Gemini, or Anthropic's Claude are better than the models available in 2018. However, it is not enough that these large proprietary models have gotten better. Large models getting better is insufficient for enterprise use cases because it may not be possible to use large models in enterprises, for a few reasons:

Cost

Large models are costly to train and very costly to deploy—every call to the LLM involves utilizing very expensive hardware.

Confidentiality

Enterprises may be reluctant to send confidential data to an API that is outside their organization's boundary. Foundational models may, therefore, not have access to confidential and transactional information that is business- or domain-specific.

CUSTOMIZATION FOR ENTERPRISES

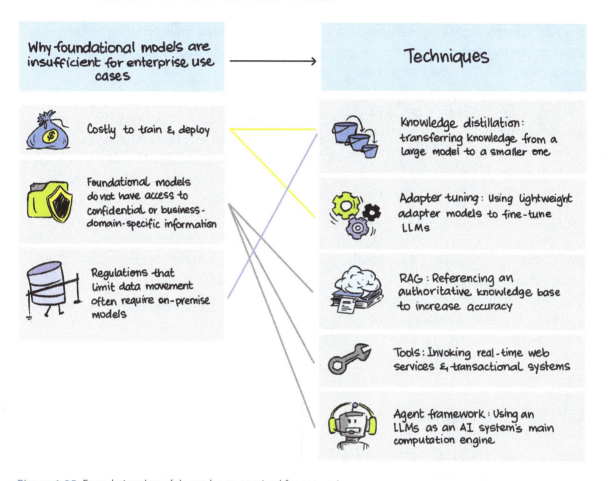

Figure 1-35. Foundational models can be customized for enterprise use cases.

Compliance

There may be regulatory and legal limitations on the storage and movement of data in regulated environments.

Because of these reasons, enterprises need to be able to train, host, and run their own models.

Enterprises have been able to adapt foundational models to their needs using techniques such as knowledge distillation, adapter-tuning, retrieval-augmented generation, tools, and agent frameworks (see Figure 1-35). We will cover these customization techniques in Chapter 4. For now, it's enough to be aware that you can use GenAI without having to call out to foundational models via proprietary, pretrained APIs. The ability to customize foundational models to (1) meet different cost versus quality tradeoffs, (2) train/tune them on confidential data, and (3) run them on-premises has made LLMs suitable for a wide variety of enterprise use cases.

CHALLENGES WITH GENERATIVE AI

As early as 2021, researchers were warning of the dangerous consequences of using LLMs. In a famous paper titled *"On the Dangers of Stochastic Parrots: Can Language Models Be Too Big?"* (*https://oreil.ly/gAeiK*), Emily Bender, Timnit Gebru, Angelina McMillan-Major, and Shmargaret Shmitchell pointed out the risks associated with unanalyzed datasets, bias, and toxicity, as well as the environmental costs.

These are all valid concerns, and the rapid adoption of GenAI has made this pushback more pervasive. Concerns have arisen on economic, legal, environment, technical, and ethical fronts (see Figure 1-36). In this section, we'll discuss these concerns in the approximate order in which they were discovered or raised.

Bias

The capabilities of an LLM are largely limited by its training data. Because they are trained on so much internet data, LLMs are much better in areas that are well represented as digital text (computer code, politics, science) and languages (English, German) than in areas (deep-sea ecology) and languages (Bhutanese) that are not.

Note that the training data here is text, not actual ground truth. For example, LLMs exhibit gender bias and stereotypes (*https://oreil.ly/NmJcS*) that are prevalent in articles and books about a profession, even if the actual labor statistics are less biased. For example, even though women make up a slim majority of first-year students in US medical schools, a lot of training texts refer to doctors as men, and so the LLMs will exhibit a bias toward using male pronouns when generating text about doctors. In this way, LLMs amplify bias.

Many of the capabilities of an LLM to perform tasks without further training, called *zero-shot* capabilities, emanate from human feedback. However, the human raters employed by LLM providers are not experts in the topics of the content they are rating, so they tend to choose text that looks convincing. This makes LLM-generated text extremely good at *sounding* right and confident, even if the information being presented is wrong or wholly made up.

Because the choice of words captures tone and reveals biases, LLMs will tend to reproduce the tone and bias of the articles in their input corpus. Overconfident, sexist, or racist, it will reproduce all the shortcomings of the internet datasets that are its primary sources.

Reasoning, Planning, and Math

Critics argue that LLMs are capable only of remixing their training data, not of independent thought. For example, Yann LeCun, inventor of convolutional neural networks and head of AI at Meta, says (*https://oreil.ly/zTr3m*) that LLMs have no idea of the underlying reality described by the language they generate. Subbarao Kambhampati, professor at Arizona State University, dismisses (*https://oreil.ly/9hT8S*) many supposed LLM reasoning capabilities, ascribing them to the "clever Hans" effect. These critics point out the implications of this lack of underlying reality—even though LLMs can

CHALLENGES WITH GENAI

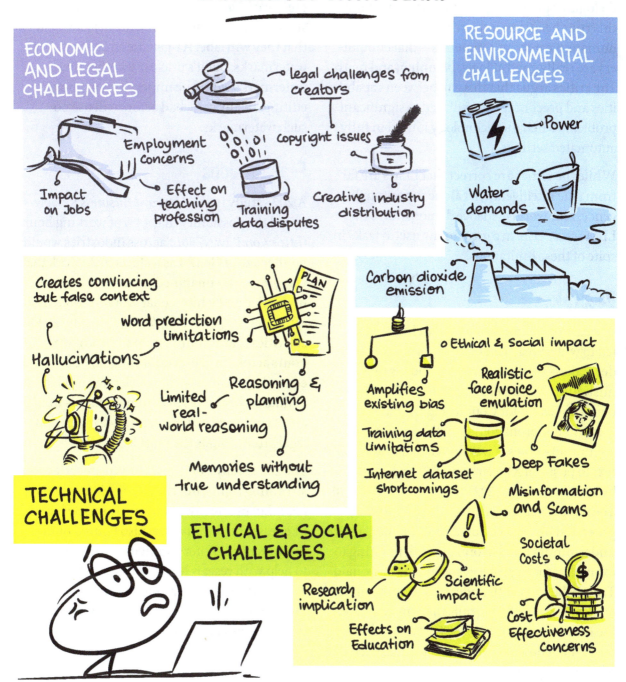

ECONOMIC AND LEGAL CHALLENGES

- legal challenges from creators
- copyright issues
- Employment concerns
- Impact on Jobs
- Effect on teaching profession
- Training data disputes
- Creative industry distribution

RESOURCE AND ENVIRONMENTAL CHALLENGES

- Power
- Water demands
- Carbon dioxide emission

TECHNICAL CHALLENGES

- Creates convincing but false context
- Word prediction limitations
- Hallucinations
- PLAN
- Reasoning & planning
- Limited real-world reasoning
- Memories without true understanding

ETHICAL & SOCIAL CHALLENGES

- Ethical & Social impact
- Amplifies existing bias
- Realistic face/voice emulation
- Training data limitations
- Internet dataset shortcomings
- Deep Fakes
- Misinformation and Scams
- Societal Costs
- Research implication
- Scientific impact
- Cost Effectiveness concerns
- Effects on Education

Figure 1-36. Some of the challenges with GenAI.

mimic thought, they cannot think, so they can't do logic or planning or math. Unfortunately, this runs headlong into preconceptions that humans have about computers—that computers are really good at logic, planning, and math. The critics argue that this gap between capabilities and preconception will lead to significant problems when the technology is used in fully automated settings.

While the critics are correct that LLMs are far from true intelligence, let alone super-intelligence, real-world evidence demonstrates that LLMs can perform a great many useful tasks in spite of these limitations.

Deepfakes

The ease of creating content with LLMs has led to widespread fear of misinformation from deepfakes—realistic images or videos that misleadingly depict an event that did not happen. The Center for Countering Digital Hate, a British nonprofit, found that the number of community notes (a way for readers to add context to posts on X) referencing AI had gone up by 130% a month in 2023 (*https://oreil.ly/feE_q*). The nonprofit claimed that misleading AI-generated images, videos, and audio media were undermining the electoral process, pointing to examples, such as a fabricated image of Donald Trump dancing with underage children (*https://oreil.ly/T-Zty*) and robocalls that impersonated Joe Biden (*https://oreil.ly/jN5ZV*) to say things he never did. Foreign governments are suspected of using deepfakes to spread misinformation on social media (*https://oreil.ly/QKBAc*).

GenAI providers such as OpenAI (*https://oreil.ly/qfZ0t*) and social media companies such as Meta (*https://oreil.ly/jRiVd*) have said that they will label AI-generated content with watermarks, but it's unclear whether these watermarks would be impervious to photo editing. In any case, bad actors will use no such watermarks.

Fear for Jobs

A 2023 study in the *Harvard Business Review* raised the possibility that 44% of working hours (*https://oreil.ly/N73bL*) across industries would be affected by GenAI as it starts to do work that was previously imagined to be the sole province of creative and white-collar workers. McKinsey estimates (*https://oreil.ly/m5xLL*) that by 2030, activities that account for up to 30% of work hours across the US economy could be automated, with this trend being accelerated by GenAI. Unlike earlier waves of automation, this would affect engineers, teachers, creative types, and legal professionals the most (see **Figure 1-37**).

The 2023 Hollywood strike was primarily about streaming rights, but the use of AI (*https://oreil.ly/0IuLo*) in screenwriting and the use of actors' likenesses in new material also figured quite prominently. Writers wanted AI to be used only to help with research and not as a tool to write entire scripts. Actors wanted limitations on studios' ability to create new content by training AI to mimic the actors' voice and face patterns.

Web 2023
future-of-work
Exhibit 3 and 13 of 21

With generative AI added to the picture, 30 percent of hours worked today could be automated by 2030.

Midpoint automation adoption[1] by 2030 as a share of time spent on work activities, US, %

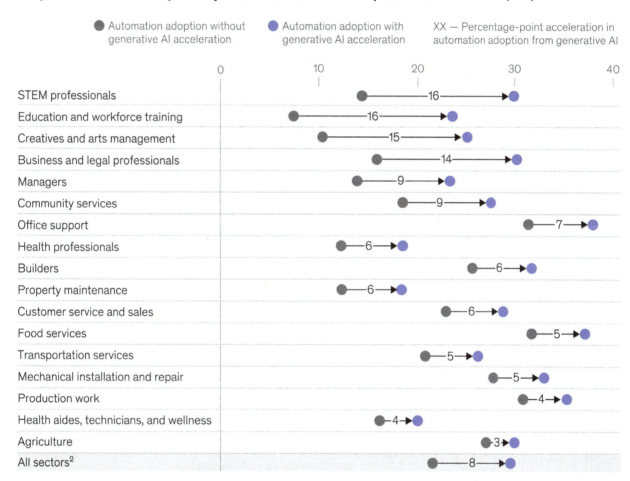

[1]Midpoint automation adoption is the average of early and late automation adoption scenarios as referenced in *The economic potential of generative AI: The next productivity frontier*, McKinsey & Company, June 2023.
[2]Totals are weighted by 2022 employment in each occupation.
Source: O*NET; US Bureau of Labor Statistics; McKinsey Global Institute analysis

McKinsey & Company

Figure 1-37. GenAI has the potential to automate parts of many jobs. Source: McKinsey. *https://oreil.ly/EfDP-*.

Copyright

In late 2023, *The New York Times* sued OpenAI (*https://oreil.ly/LXIEc*) over its use of the newspaper's copyrighted material in LLM training. The *Times* claimed that OpenAI used millions of its articles and reproduced product reviews from its technology vertical *Wirecutter* verbatim, while stripping the affiliate links out. The lawsuit claims that GenAI is not fair use, is creating a competitive product, and leads to trademark dilution. Also in 2023, Getty Images sued Stability AI (*https://oreil.ly/Lv3Yz*), a GenAI image model provider, on very similar grounds. Perhaps the content deals GenAI model creators have started to strike are a response to these lawsuits. Google signed up Reddit and Stack Overflow. OpenAI signed up Alex Springer, which owns *Politico*, *Business Insider*, and many other publications.

Hallucination

At heart, GenAI models are next-token predictors. Image models predict a value for every pixel in an image and text models predict a next word to follow an existing text, whether or not the subject of that text is an area they know anything about. If the training source is not nonexistent, the prediction could be quite arbitrary. If training sources conflict, the prediction could be a nonsensical muddle.

GenAI models' tendency to hallucinate can cause significant issues, especially when they sound confident and use the right jargon. A Stanford study found that LLMs hallucinated in 70% of legal tasks (*https://oreil.ly/XlA24*), struggling the most with local laws and practices that

were presumably not in their training datasets. This issue isn't just abstract. For instance, one New York lawyer filed a brief using text created by ChatGPT and it turned out that none of the law articles it cited actually existed (*https://oreil.ly/6Vnyb*). And a chatbot at Air Canada made up a nonexistent refund policy (*https://oreil.ly/Ub2p7*), which the courts then forced it to honor. As long as such hallucinations are possible, enterprise use of GenAI is fraught with danger.

There is also the fear (*https://oreil.ly/LJ0SD*) that the increasing amount of generated content is polluting future datasets, creating a negative feedback loop of low-quality AI content that will lead the quality of AI content to decline further in the future.

Societal and Environmental Costs

A final concern is about the societal and environmental costs of the technology. A 2024 study in *Nature* (*https://oreil.ly/69RRm*) estimates that GenAI's carbon footprint will lead to a 0.12% increase in global carbon dioxide emissions, and that the technology will consume as much water as 328 million adults. In 2024, a Sequoia report (*https://oreil.ly/a06sL*) estimated that $200 billion had been spent on training GenAI models, but the economic value of what had been created was only $3 billion.

There is also widespread concern (*https://oreil.ly/qq2xT*) about the use of GenAI in education. Will it lead to students learning less? Or can GenAI lead to more personalized education? Finally, evidence is mounting (*https://oreil.ly/P-fdf*) that many scientists are using GenAI to write research papers. The quality of peer review might be decreasing as well, with a 2024 study estimating that as many as 16.9% of peer reviews *(https://oreil.ly/soVjo)* may have been substantially modified by LLMs. It's unclear how much this affects the quality of the science itself.

ORGANIZATION OF THE REST OF THIS BOOK

In this chapter, we have discussed what GenAI is, how it works, and the techniques used to generate text, images, and video. You learned about the advances in GenAI over the past few years and the challenges that remain.

In Chapter 2, we will look at tools that enable consumers to use GenAI and products that have GenAI built in. You'll learn how to prompt GenAI models, employ APIs to call GenAI models, and adapt the models' responses.

In Chapter 3, we'll examine real-world case studies and practical implementations to shed light on the tangible benefits and transformative potential of GenAI across diverse fields. You will learn how organizations are leveraging GenAI to achieve operational excellence, enhance customer experiences, streamline workflows, and drive innovation.

In Chapter 4, we'll discuss approaches to designing AI applications around the current limitations of LLMs. You will learn how to use agentic architectures to go beyond reasoning and planning limitations, a RAG architecture to provide the LLM with fresh and confidential data it didn't have access to during training, and SQL agents to reduce hallucinations of factual data.

In Chapter 5, we'll explore different architectures of individual agents that give you the ability to balance considerations such as creativity, risk, latency, cost, and engineering complexity. You will also learn how to fine-tune an LLM to perform a specific task and to distill a small language model from an LLM.

Finally, in Chapter 6, you'll learn about some of the ethical, societal, and environmental considerations that you may need to keep in mind as you build GenAI applications.

SUMMARY

GenAI is a branch of AI where machines create new content like text, images, music, and videos. It gained widespread attention with the release of ChatGPT in 2022. While not a replacement for human experts, GenAI can be a valuable assistant for "frontier tasks"—those within its capabilities. However, it struggles with reasoning, factual accuracy, and planning, necessitating careful review of its output.

We discussed how different types of GenAI models work. Image generation uses conditional diffusion, involving denoising autoencoders, progressive generation, text conditioning, and superresolution. Text generation employs next-word prediction (based on tokens), transformer architecture (using positional embeddings and attention), prefix tuning, and human feedback (via RLHF or DPO). Audio generation uses specialized techniques like interleaving text and audio. Video generation is similar to image generation but operates on an additional time dimension.

We also discussed the evolution of GenAI, highlighting improvements in model architecture (including multistage training and "mixture of experts"), data quality (using textbook-quality data and synthetic tutorials), algorithmic refinements (like tokenization, nucleus sampling, and DPO), and customizability.

Despite these advances, GenAI faces challenges like bias amplification, limitations in reasoning and planning, the potential for deepfakes and misinformation, concerns about job displacement, copyright issues, hallucination, and societal and environmental costs.

The remainder of the book explores GenAI use cases, application design, agent architectures, fine-tuning techniques, and ethical considerations.

## Chapter 2

USING GENERATIVE AI

In the previous chapter, we discussed what Generative AI is and how it works. Users, however, consider a technology as being transformational only if it significantly makes their lives easier. Therefore, what matters is how useful and how good the products that incorporate the technology are. On this front, GenAI has been compelling.

In this chapter, we will look at tools that enable consumers to use GenAI and products that have GenAI built in. We'll also show you how to prompt GenAI models, employ APIs to call GenAI models, and adapt the models' responses (see Figure 2-1). We'll look at enterprise use cases of GenAI in the next chapter.

To make it convenient for you to follow along with us, we've posted all the prompts and code in this book's GitHub repository (*https://github.com/lakshmanok/visualizing-generative-ai*).

GREAT FIRST DRAFTS

The general public has rapidly adopted tools that enable consumer uses of GenAI. The public uses GenAI as a *general-purpose technology*—it is used by multiple age groups, multiple nationalities, and for multiple tasks. ChatGPT gained 100 million users in two months—the fastest product adoption rate in history to date (see Figure 2-2). Just about everyone is using GenAI tools such as ChatGPT, Gemini, and Midjourney for quick brainstorming and illustrating slides and reports. Professionals now use them to create art, write headlines for corporate blogs, and create background music for films.

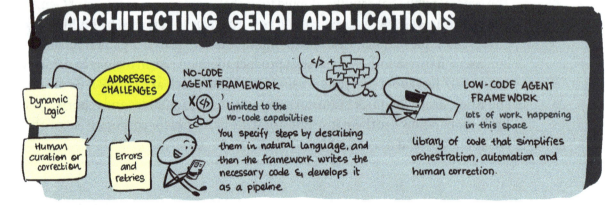

Figure 2-1. What you'll learn in Chapter 2.

GENAI DEMOCRATIZATION & USE CASES

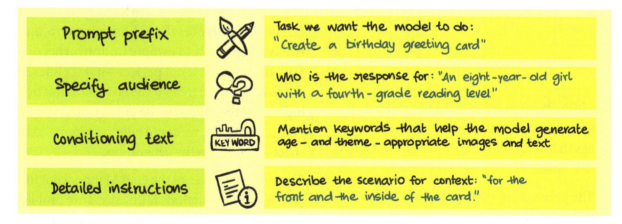

Figure 2-2. (Top) GenAI is a general-purpose technology that nontechnical users can use for everyday tasks. (Bottom) Depending on your use case, you'll structure your prompt differently.

In this section, we'll look at three examples of ways in which lay consumers might use GenAI (pictured in Figures 2-3 to 2-7): creating a greeting card, writing a complaint letter, and creating a packing list. We will also encounter common failure modes of these models—instruction-following, hallucination, completeness—and discuss ways to address them.

Creating a Greeting Card

Let's use a GenAI model to create a greeting card for our eight-year-old niece's birthday. We'll turn to Gemini, which is a *multimodal* model (meaning it can generate both images and text), and ask it to create a card:

```
create a birthday greeting card for
an eight year old girl named Laura
who lives in Boston, loves Dora the
Explorer, trains, and has a Golden
Retriever named Flux.  For the front of
the card, create an image showing her
dog wearing a Chilean hat and riding
a train through the Torres del Paine.
For the inside of the card, write a
funny limerick about everything she can
look forward to when she is nine years
old. The poem should be at a fourth
grade reading level. Make sure to
include Boston, Laura, and Flux in the
limerick.
```

While the prompt seems to be natural language instructions, it takes advantage of a few things that we already know about how GenAI models work:

- The prefix of the prompt includes the task we want it to do: "create a birthday greeting card."

- It specifies the audience: an eight-year-old girl with a fourth-grade reading level.

- It uses text to condition the model, mentioning Boston, Dora, trains, and the golden retriever. All of these will help the model generate age- and theme-appropriate images and text.

- It provides detailed instructions for both the front of the card and for the inside.

The results Gemini returned for us are shown in Figure 2-3. As you learned in Chapter 1, your results will vary, because the models are nondeterministic and use randomness in generating text. At first glance, all four images depict what was requested, but the model's *instruction-following* is not perfect. For example, in the second image, the dog is not wearing a hat. Note also that the poem refers to Flux as a toy, not a dog!

The images also have different styles: the third image is photorealistic, while the fourth is a children's book-style illustration that is not to scale. If the style matters to us, we could edit the prompt and rerun the generation.

The limerick generation also looks great on first glance—it references the T, Boston's metro, and is about being able to explore Boston on her own. Still, the limerick is not perfect—it is six lines, not five, and if we treated the last line as not being part of the limerick, the poem would end on a comma. Again, we could edit the prompt to be stricter and rerun the generation.

These are examples of the GenAI model not following our instructions faithfully. This problem is not unique to Gemini—all GenAI models occasionally fail at instruction-following. If that's important for your specific use case, you should

CREATING A GREETING CARD WITH GEMINI

PREFIX (TASK)

PROMPT : Natural-language instructions to the model

AUDIENCE

create a birthday greeting card for an eight year old girl named Laura who lives in Boston, loves Dora the Explorer, trains, and has a Golden Retriever named Flux. For the front of the card, create an image showing her dog wearing a Chilean hat and riding a train through the Torres del Paine. For the inside of the card, write a funny limerick about everything she can look forward to when she is nine years old. The poem should be at a fourth grade reading level. Make sure to include Boston, Laura, and Flux in the limerick.

Text conditioning + detailed instructions

GENERATED IMAGE

✦ Happy Birthday Laura!

☑ Instruction-following : train, Torres del Paine, golden retriever, Chilean hat

GENERATED TEXT

Inside the card:

You're 8 today, that's super cool
But wait till you're 9, you'll break every rule!
You'll ride the T all by yourself,
With Flux by your side on a fuzzy toy shelf.
Boston's your oyster, there's so much to see,
Happy birthday, dear Laura, from me!

☑ Instruction-following: Limerick, Boston, exploration

☒ Instruction-following error : Limerick rhyme scheme should be AABBA, not AABCA.

Additional details:

- You can add a personal message to Laura inside the card.

- You can also decorate the card with stickers or other decorations.

Figure 2-3. Creating a greeting card with Gemini.

WRITING A LETTER USING META AI

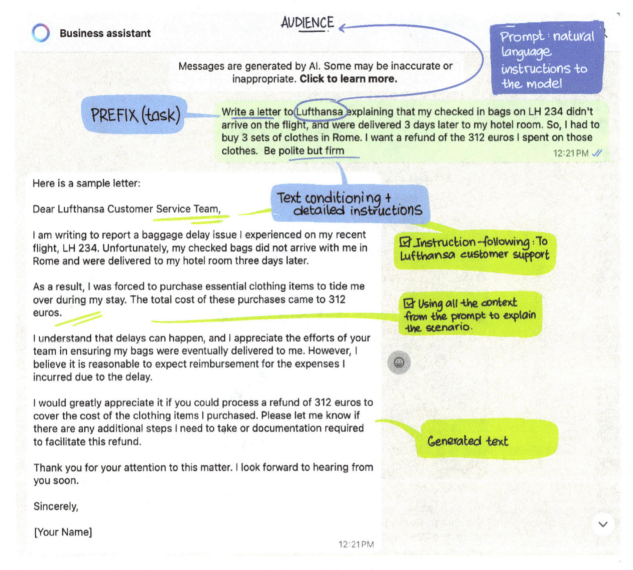

AUDIENCE

○ **Business assistant**

Prompt : natural language instructions to the model

Messages are generated by AI. Some may be inaccurate or inappropriate. **Click to learn more.**

PREFIX (task)

Write a letter to Lufthansa explaining that my checked in bags on LH 234 didn't arrive on the flight, and were delivered 3 days later to my hotel room. So, I had to buy 3 sets of clothes in Rome. I want a refund of the 312 euros I spent on those clothes. Be polite but firm

12:21PM ✓✓

Here is a sample letter:

Dear Lufthansa Customer Service Team,

Text conditioning + detailed instructions

I am writing to report a baggage delay issue I experienced on my recent flight, LH 234. Unfortunately, my checked bags did not arrive with me in Rome and were delivered to my hotel room three days later.

☑ *Instruction-following : To Lufthansa customer support*

As a result, I was forced to purchase essential clothing items to tide me over during my stay. The total cost of these purchases came to 312 euros.

☑ *Using all the context from the prompt to explain the scenario.*

I understand that delays can happen, and I appreciate the efforts of your team in ensuring my bags were eventually delivered to me. However, I believe it is reasonable to expect reimbursement for the expenses I incurred due to the delay.

I would greatly appreciate it if you could process a refund of 312 euros to cover the cost of the clothing items I purchased. Please let me know if there are any additional steps I need to take or documentation required to facilitate this refund.

Generated text

Thank you for your attention to this matter. I look forward to hearing from you soon.

Sincerely,

[Your Name]

12:21PM

Figure 2-4. Prompt for writing a letter using Meta AI, along with the results.

verify that the generated text or image matches your instructions. In the context of a greeting card, these are minor errors and can be ignored.

Even if you can't draw dogs or write doggerel, GenAI lets you create personalized greeting cards. If you can imagine it and describe it, GenAI can draw it and compose it. This is a pretty good card, customized to our niece's interests. She'll be pleased, don't you think?

Writing a Complaint Letter

Let's say that the airline lost your bags on your way to visit Rome for a week, and you had to buy clothes to tide you over until the bags were returned to you. Now, you want to ask the airline to refund you the cost of the clothes you bought. You've got to write a letter. Are you looking forward to writing that letter?

Let's use Meta AI, the AI built into WhatsApp, to create a complaint letter for us:

```
Write a letter to Lufthansa explaining
that my checked in bags on LH 234
didn't arrive on the flight, and were
delivered 3 days later to my hotel
room. So, I had to buy 3 sets of
clothes in Rome. I want a refund of the
312 euros I spent on those clothes.  Be
polite but firm.
```

Meta AI generates a letter (Figure 2-4) that we can send Lufthansa.

The letter is nicely formatted and professional. It'll do. But shouldn't we add more details? How will the airline know we really were on that flight

and had bags that were not delivered? I asked Meta AI a follow-up:

```
Is there any additional information i
need to provide? do you have an address
for where I can send this to?
```

Meta AI responds with details of what to attach and an address to send it to, as shown in Figure 2-5.

Is the information correct, though? When it comes to factual details like this, it is always a good idea to verify. Because they are just next-to-ken predictors, GenAI tools have a tendency to "fill in the blanks" with likely-looking text that may not be accurate. This is called *hallucination*. We should definitely verify that the list is complete and that the address is correct. Some GenAI tools (such as Gemini) provide a way to immediately fact-check the response, but it's not too difficult to do a web search and verify that the address and list of items to include are correct.

Searching for "lufthansa lost baggage compensation" brings up a host of advice from other passengers and a web form, but no mailing address. Where did Meta get this address? Searching the web for "P.O.Box 80502" and "60546 Frankfurt am Main" doesn't return anything. It appears that Meta hallucinated this address. Good thing we checked!

As we did with instruction-following and Gemini, we'd like to caution that hallucination is endemic to all GenAI models, not just to Meta AI.

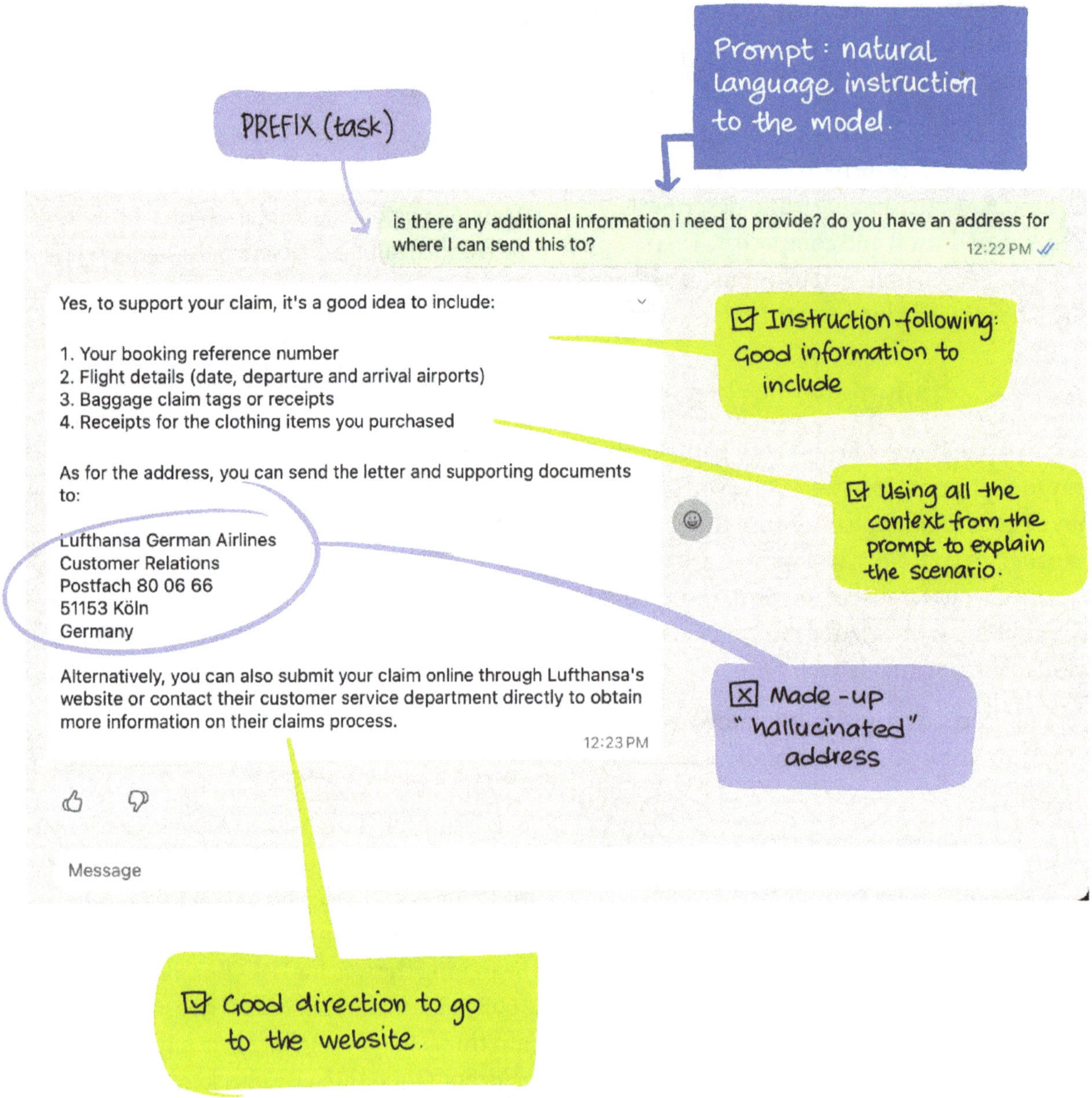

Figure 2-5. Requesting follow-up information from the model.

CREATING A PACKING LIST USING CHATGPT

AUDIENCE

PREFIX (task)

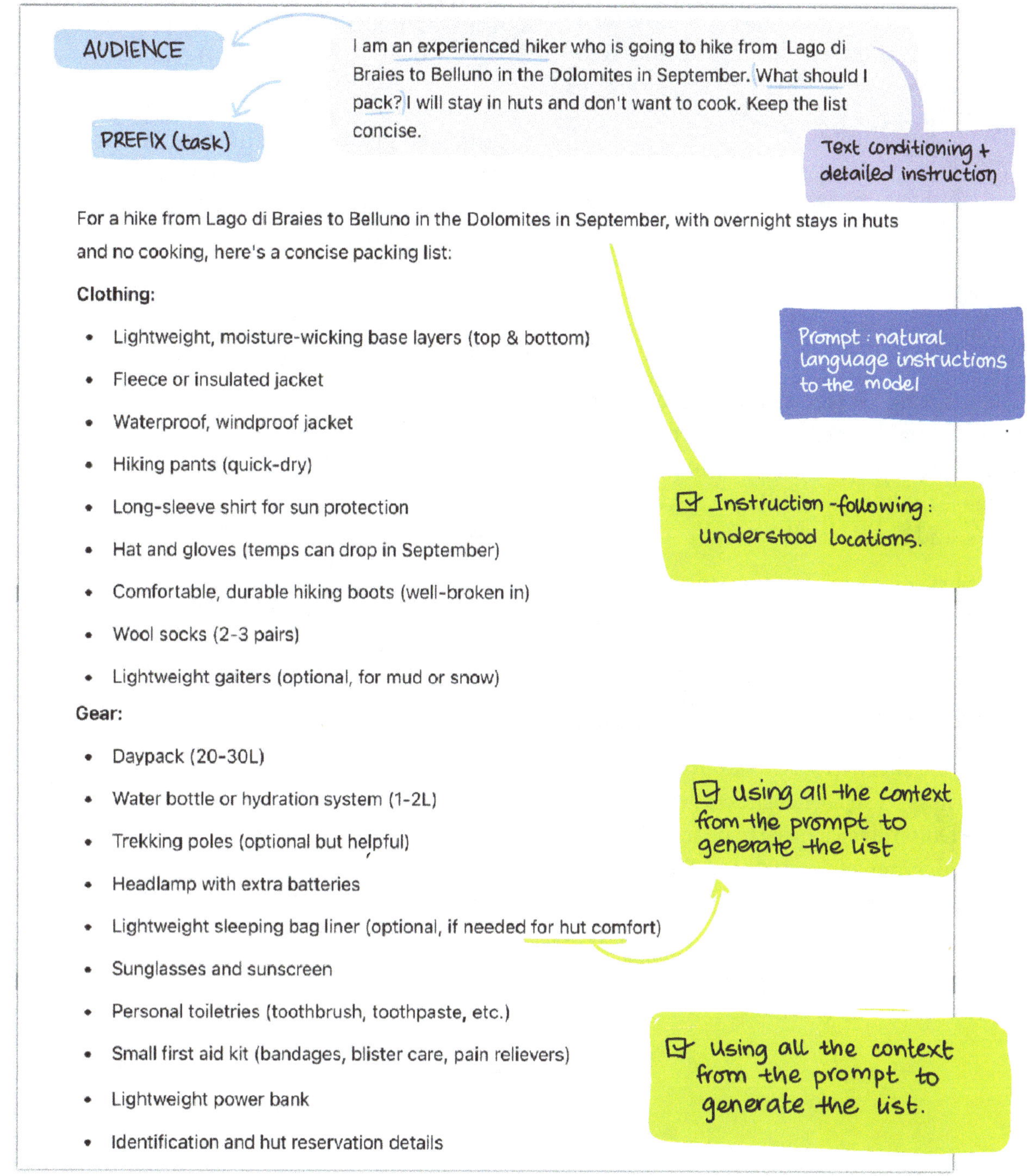

I am an experienced hiker who is going to hike from Lago di Braies to Belluno in the Dolomites in September. What should I pack? I will stay in huts and don't want to cook. Keep the list concise.

Text conditioning + detailed instruction

For a hike from Lago di Braies to Belluno in the Dolomites in September, with overnight stays in huts and no cooking, here's a concise packing list:

Clothing:

- Lightweight, moisture-wicking base layers (top & bottom)
- Fleece or insulated jacket
- Waterproof, windproof jacket
- Hiking pants (quick-dry)
- Long-sleeve shirt for sun protection
- Hat and gloves (temps can drop in September)
- Comfortable, durable hiking boots (well-broken in)
- Wool socks (2-3 pairs)
- Lightweight gaiters (optional, for mud or snow)

Gear:

- Daypack (20-30L)
- Water bottle or hydration system (1-2L)
- Trekking poles (optional but helpful)
- Headlamp with extra batteries
- Lightweight sleeping bag liner (optional, if needed for hut comfort)
- Sunglasses and sunscreen
- Personal toiletries (toothbrush, toothpaste, etc.)
- Small first aid kit (bandages, blister care, pain relievers)
- Lightweight power bank
- Identification and hut reservation details

Prompt: natural language instructions to the model

☑ Instruction-following: Understood locations.

☑ Using all the context from the prompt to generate the list

☑ Using all the context from the prompt to generate the list.

Figure 2-6. Creating a packing list using ChatGPT.

Creating a Packing List

How organized are you when planning for a trip? We are going on a hiking trip and would like a list that we can check off as we pack our travel bags. Let's ask OpenAI's ChatGPT to create one:

```
I am an experienced hiker who is going
to hike from  Lago di Braies to Belluno
in the Dolomites in September. What
should I pack? I will stay in huts
and don't want to cook. Keep the list
concise.
```

The resulting list seems pretty thorough and knowledgeable (see Figure 2-6). It even tells us to pack a sleeping bag liner, cash, and earplugs because the huts provide bare cots, don't take cards, and could be noisy.

Is the list complete? To some extent, the more hiking lists ChatGPT has seen, the better it will be at generating a complete list. However, because of randomness, there is no guarantee that even essential items always make it onto the list.

When the alternative is to be out of luck in the wilderness (even a wilderness as well-trodden as the Dolomites), it helps to be sure. One way to check for completeness is a *multiple generation* approach: alter the prompts slightly, generate multiple lists, and combine the answers. When the authors did this, we found that the list in

Figure 2-6 was missing a few things, including hut reservations, electrolyte tablets, waterproof bags for important documents, permits, and a lightweight daypack for side trips.

In this section, we looked at three examples of ways a layperson might use GenAI: to create a greeting card, to write a complaint letter, and to brainstorm a packing list. For variety, we used a different GenAI foundational model for each one.

With relatively little effort, the GenAI tools produced usable output, saving us a lot of time and hassle. We also discovered that we can't take these tools' responses at face value. It's important to ensure that the tool follows instructions faithfully, does not hallucinate any facts, and provides complete and comprehensive responses.

General-purpose GenAI tools such as Gemini, Meta AI, and ChatGPT can generate good first drafts. However, you should understand their limitations and edit their responses to fit your needs. What's more, if you plan to build applications that use GenAI tools, then you'll need to ensure that your app verifies and validates the LLM responses automatically.

Next, let's look at best practices for crafting text prompts.

PROMPTING GENAI MODELS

In Chapter 1, we described how GenAI models are trained to create text, images, video, etc., in response to text prompts. Even though the prompts appear to be natural-sounding language, any model will work best when the structure of your prompt matches the structures of the prompts employed in training that model. In this section, we describe this prompt structure.

Prompts as Human-Computer Interface

The Holy Grail of user interface (UI) research is to create a computer that understands human language and inputs, rather than needing humans to provide instructions in specified structures.

UI design has evolved to make the process of providing instructions to computers as natural as possible: for example, keyboard terminals were an improvement over punch cards. Point-and-click mice were an improvement over terminals, and touchscreens are more natural than mice. This process has most recently led to voice-enabled speakers like Alexa and Siri. Alongside the improvements in the physical nature of the UI, the logical nature of the UI has also evolved. Punch cards require assembly instructions. Mice click on graphical depictions of real-world metaphors such as buttons and folders. Touchscreens allow the user to become immersed in augmented reality (AR) depictions. Voice-enabled speakers operate timers and lights. UIs have evolved to become more and more aligned to human actions and real-world objects.

A *text prompt* is an interface to the foundational model that lets you tell the computer what you want it to do. It continues this evolution toward more natural human-computer interfaces. Text prompts work because they request tasks (such as rephrasing a piece of text) that the GenAI model has been trained to do. Recall that the initial foundational model is just a next-token predictor. As you learned in the last chapter, the GenAI model you're invoking has been prefix-tuned using human feedback to follow instructions and create human-pleasing text.

General Guidelines

The problem is that the companies that provide foundational models don't publicly disclose the instructions on which they train their models, considering this proprietary information. Even many "open" models such as Llama provide only their weights, not their training data. You'll just have to hope that the task you want the model to do is one of the thousands of tasks it was trained for, or that the model can generalize to the task you want.

Knowing that, which prompt would be better?

- Reword the following paragraph to be more concise

- Rephrase the following paragraph in 2-3 sentences

- Shorten the following paragraph

PROMPTING GENAI MODELS

Figure 2-7. Understanding prompt engineering.

It is unclear which of these variants was part of the model's instruction-training dataset, and which would rely on its generalization capability (and therefore, fare slightly worse). Different models will vary because their training datasets are different! So, prompt engineering to get the best results from a model is more of an art than a science (See Figure 2-7).

Fortunately, there are some publicly available instruction-training datasets we can look at. The Dolly dataset (*https://oreil.ly/51yr0*) was created voluntarily by Databricks employees operating under succinct guidelines about the types of tasks to ask the model to do. These guidelines are a good place for us to start understanding how to phrase our tasks to "hit the training dataset." In Figure 2-8, we explain and demonstrate these guidelines. However, the proprietary models used in large-scale production are likely to be different: in most cases, they were created by paid employees in low-cost locations working under more elaborate guidelines. The model training also continues in production, driven by actual user prompts.

We encourage you to try the example prompts in Figure 2-8 and variations of them, in a GenAI tool. To save you typing, you can find the text of the prompts in our GitHub repository *(https://oreil.ly/vga_ch02prompts)*. The best way to develop an intuition of how a GenAI model works is to do such iterative exploration.

Always keep in mind that LLMs are token generators, and there is no guarantee that the generated text is accurate. If you happen to ask the model for information or a task that it has not been trained on, the results could be nonsensical. For example, Figure 2-9 shows a hallucinated response from Gemini. The response is supposed to be an encrypted form of the provided input, but asking the model to decrypt that same passage proves clearly that this is not the case. In some cases, you may get nonsensical answers even for questions and tasks that are within the training frontier. Always check the responses you get from generative models.

Prompt Structure

The general guidelines in the previous section will suffice in a large number of cases. To get better results, it helps to understand that training datasets often contain multiple possible responses to the same prompt. These might be because they are written from the perspectives of different roles, are targeted at different audiences, or appear in different formats. An accountant, a lawyer, and a journalist would each write a different paragraph when asked to explain a tax law. The explanation will also be different depending on whether the intended reader is a student earning below the minimum wage, a worker earning the median wage, or an executive earning far more than the average. The prose style might vary depending on whether it's a newspaper article, a letter to the editor, or an article submitted to a law journal. Specifying these constraints in the prompt is important to getting the results you want (see Figure 2-10), and this section offers some instruction on how to do so.

What happens if the training dataset doesn't contain any paragraphs written by an accountant to a student in the form of an email? This is where LLMs' ability to mix-and-match comes into play: the model will be able to merge the

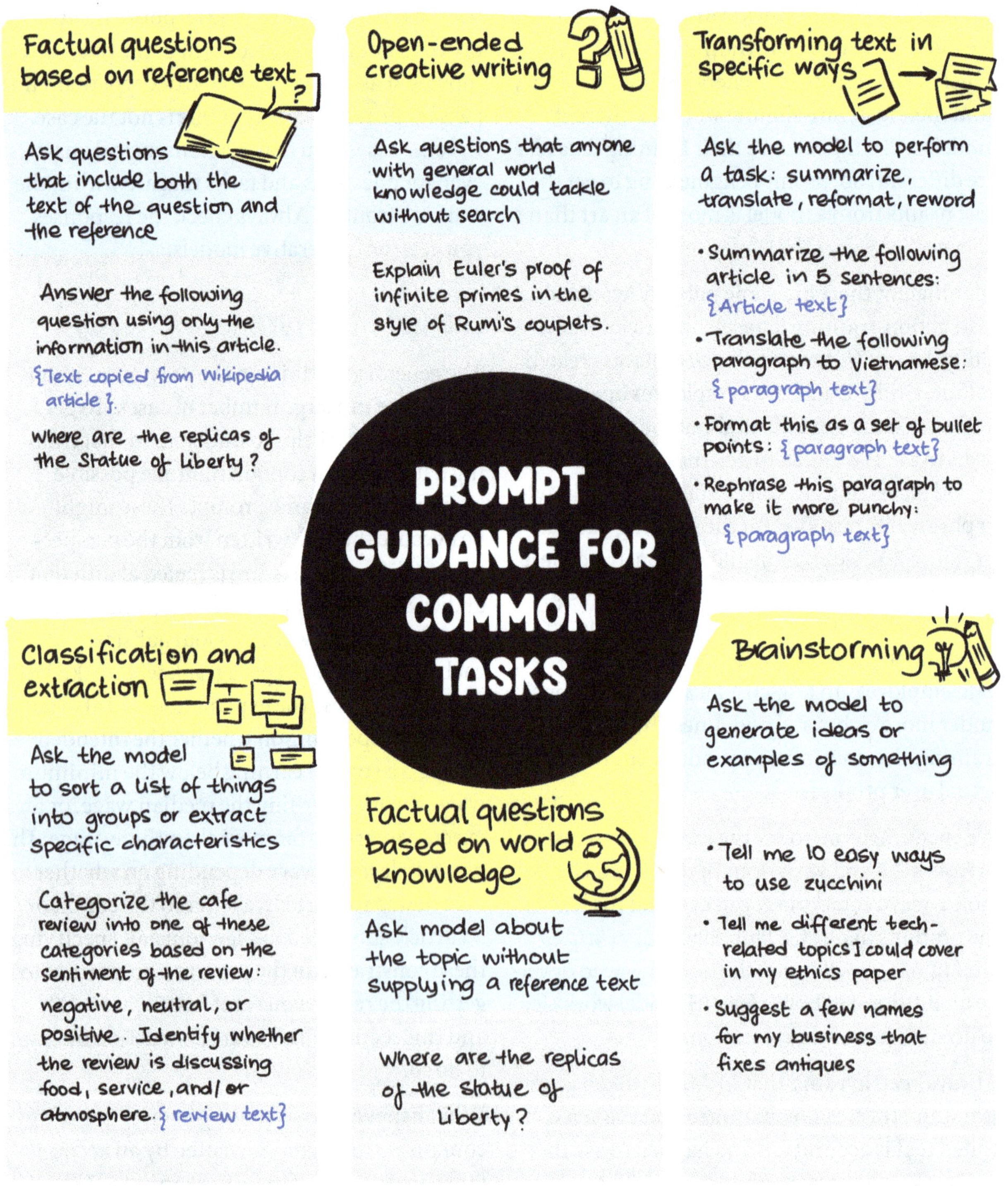

Factual questions based on reference text

Ask questions that include both the text of the question and the reference

Answer the following question using only the information in this article. {Text copied from Wikipedia article}

where are the replicas of the Statue of Liberty?

Open-ended creative writing

Ask questions that anyone with general world knowledge could tackle without search

Explain Euler's proof of infinite primes in the style of Rumi's couplets.

Transforming text in specific ways

Ask the model to perform a task: summarize, translate, reformat, reword

- Summarize the following article in 5 sentences: {Article text}
- Translate the following paragraph to Vietnamese: {paragraph text}
- Format this as a set of bullet points: {paragraph text}
- Rephrase this paragraph to make it more punchy: {paragraph text}

PROMPT GUIDANCE FOR COMMON TASKS

Classification and extraction

Ask the model to sort a list of things into groups or extract specific characteristics

Categorize the cafe review into one of these categories based on the sentiment of the review: negative, neutral, or positive. Identify whether the review is discussing food, service, and/or atmosphere. {review text}

Factual questions based on world knowledge

Ask model about the topic without supplying a reference text

where are the replicas of the Statue of Liberty?

Brainstorming

Ask the model to generate ideas or examples of something

- Tell me 10 easy ways to use zucchini
- Tell me different tech-related topics I could cover in my ethics paper
- Suggest a few names for my business that fixes antiques

Figure 2-8. Prompt guidance for common tasks.

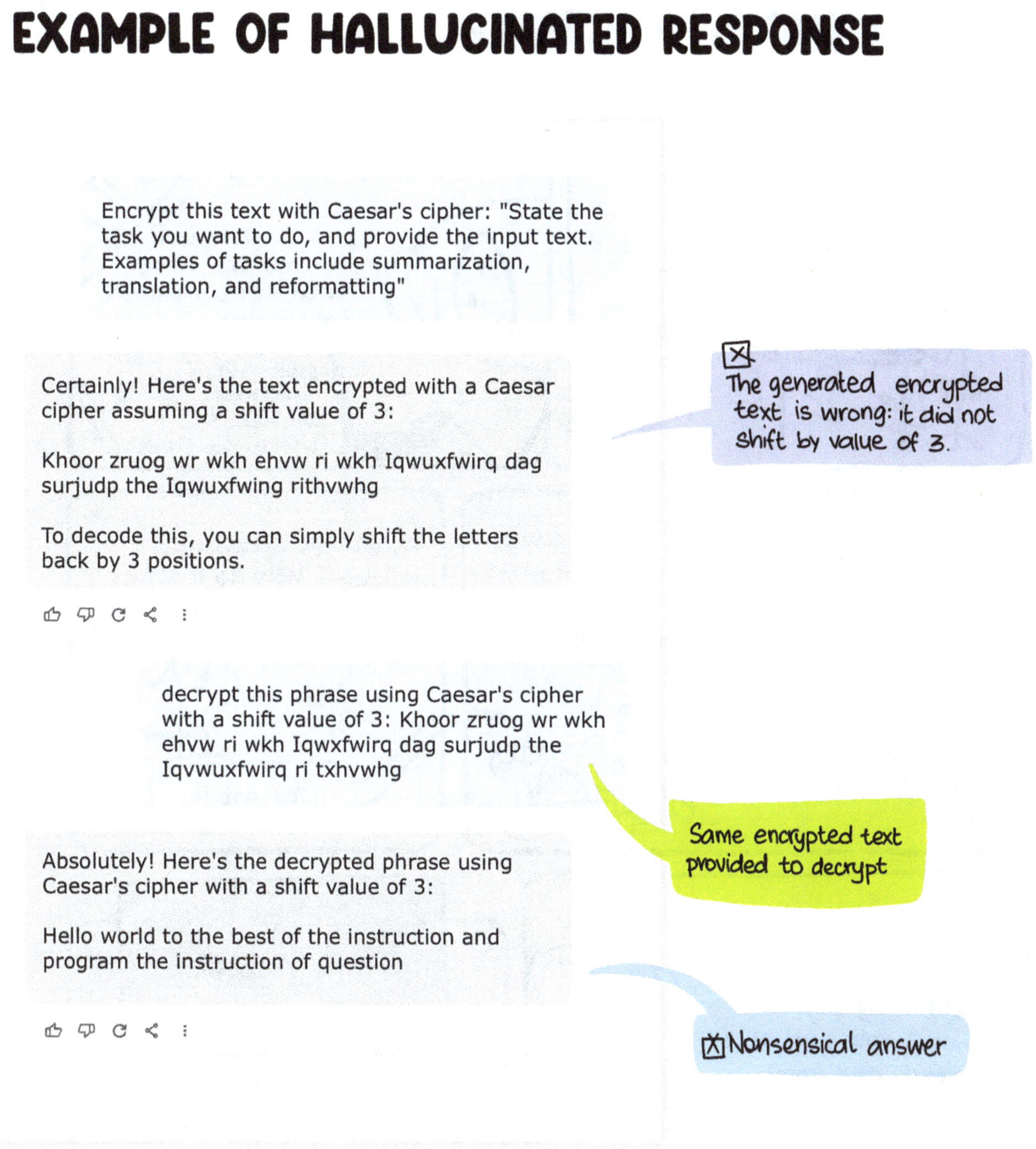

EXAMPLE OF HALLUCINATED RESPONSE

Encrypt this text with Caesar's cipher: "State the task you want to do, and provide the input text. Examples of tasks include summarization, translation, and reformatting"

Certainly! Here's the text encrypted with a Caesar cipher assuming a shift value of 3:

Khoor zruog wr wkh ehvw ri wkh Iqwuxfwirq dag surjudp the Iqwuxfwing rithvwhg

To decode this, you can simply shift the letters back by 3 positions.

👍 👎 C ⤴ ⋮

☒ The generated encrypted text is wrong: it did not shift by value of 3.

decrypt this phrase using Caesar's cipher with a shift value of 3: Khoor zruog wr wkh ehvw ri wkh Iqwxfwirq dag surjudp the Iqvwuxfwirq ri txhvwhg

Absolutely! Here's the decrypted phrase using Caesar's cipher with a shift value of 3:

Hello world to the best of the instruction and program the instruction of question

👍 👎 C ⤴ ⋮

Same encrypted text provided to decrypt

☒ Nonsensical answer

Figure 2-9. Example of a response hallucinated by Google's Gemini model in April 2024.

PROMPTING STRUCTURE

Figure 2-10. A good prompt should trigger characteristics of how training datasets are segmented and clearly specify role, audience, and format.

necessary information and the appropriate style to create an apt response. Such mix-and-match is what makes LLMs generalize, and so even if it occasionally goes awry, it's considered a desired feature, not a bug.

A good prompt should try to "trigger" these characteristics of how training datasets are segmented by clearly specifying the role, audience, and format:

Role

Who is doing the writing? This is the role the LLM plays: for example, writing from an accountant's perspective.

Audience

Who is the intended reader for this text? For example, is this paragraph meant to explain a tax law to a student earning below minimum wage?

Format/style

How should the response be formatted: for example, as an email?

What do we mean by triggering? Recall that GenAI models are transformers that use an attention mechanism. We hope that when the transformer attends to specific words in our role, audience, and format descriptions, we will get output text that better mimics the segment of the training data that meets these criteria.

In addition, follow the general guidelines in the previous section for the different task categories. If asking a factual question, for example, it can be helpful to provide a reference text to ground the response, as in the following first example.

Finally, as you add these preambles, your prompts will get longer, and it can be easy for the model to lose track of the exact question you want answered. It can be helpful to repeat the question at the end of your prompt. Another way is to end the prompt with the start of the answer—if you end the prompt with a hint such as: **Summary** and the model generates tokens to continue the prompt, the result will be to complete the desired task.

Here is a simple prompt that does not follow the recommended structure:

```
Answer the following question using
only the information in https://
en.wikipedia.org/wiki/Replicas_of_
the_Statue_of_Liberty: Where are the
replicas of the Statue of Liberty?
```

Here is the same prompt rewritten to follow the recommended structure:

```
You are a trivia host creating
questions for a nighttime TV show. You
want to show an image of a replica
of the Statue of Liberty and ask the
contestants where it is.  Complete
the following response using only the
information in https://en.wikipedia.
org/wiki/Replicas_of_the_Statue_of_
Liberty:  The most unusual, but famous
location where you can find a large
replica of the Statue of Liberty is __.
```

Here is the result we got from Gemini:

```
The most unusual, but famous location
where you can find a large replica of
the Statue of Liberty is Cadaqués,
Spain. This replica is unusual because
it has two arms and two torches!
```

THE DIFFERENCE BETWEEN A GOOD PROMPT AND A BAD ONE

uHHH!

> tell me 10 easy ways to use zucchini squash

Not very descriptive. It's missing who the recipes are for, who is making them (a novice or a chef), and in what format.

✦ Zucchini is incredibly versatile! Here are 10 easy ways to use it:

- 1. Sautéed Zucchini:
    - Slice or dice zucchini and sauté it with olive oil, garlic, and your favorite herbs. It's a simple and delicious side dish.
- 2. Grilled Zucchini:
    - Slice zucchini lengthwise, brush with olive oil, and grill until tender and slightly charred. This brings out its natural sweetness.
- 3. Zucchini Noodles (Zoodles):
    - Use a spiralizer to turn zucchini into noodles. Sauté them or use them as a low-carb pasta alternative.

Describes the role ←

Describes the audience ←

Describes the format ←

> You are a famous chef who is known for serving comfort foods in a glamorous way. You know that many home gardeners end up with way too many zucchini squash in summer. Write an Instagram post titled "10 delicious ways to use up your zucchini".

☑ **Followed format** ←

✦ Alright, my darlings, gather 'round! Chef [Your Chef Name] here, and let's talk about that glorious, abundant, sometimes overwhelming gift from the garden: ZUCCHINI! 💚 We've all been there, haven't we? Suddenly, you're swimming in a sea of green, wondering, "What in the world am I going to do with all this?" Fear not! I'm here to transform your summer surplus into culinary masterpieces. ✨

10 Delicious Ways To Use Up Your Zucchini!

1. **Zucchini Blossom Tempura:** Delicate, crispy, and oh-so-chic. Serve with a yuzu dipping sauce. 🌸

2. Zucchini & Ricotta Stuffed Blossoms: A creamy, savory delight. Perfect for an elegant appetizer.

   ⋮

10. **Zucchini Relish with Pickled Shallots:** A bright, tangy condiment that adds a touch of summer to any dish. 🥒

Don't let those zucchinis go to waste, my lovelies! Get creative, get cooking, and remember: even comfort food can be glamorous. 😉 #ZucchiniRecipes #SummerCooking #ChefLife #GlamComfortFood #GardenToTable #SeasonalEating #HomeCooking #Foodie #Delicious #RecipeIdeas

✦ Much better suggestions, after a prompt describing the role, audience and format.

Figure 2-11. The difference between a good prompt and a bad one.

Similarly, instead of simply asking the model, "Tell me 10 easy ways to use up zucchini squash," you could prompt the model in a more structured way (see Figure 2-11):

```
You are a famous chef who is known for
serving comfort foods in a glamorous
way.  You know that many home gardeners
end up with way too many zucchini
squash in summer. Write an Instagram
post titled "10 delicious ways to use
up your zucchini".
```

You can follow this prompt structure to create images, too:

```
You are a food photographer. Create a
high-resolution photo of a table with
three zucchini dishes: zucchini bread,
zucchini boats, and zucchini alfredo.
The dishes should be garnished and
shown in an appealing Iberian-style
serving container. The table should be
outside and bathed with warm afternoon
light.
```

Compare the results in Figure 2-11 of the original and enhanced prompts. Do you see an improvement?

Workarounds to Common Problems

Here are some workarounds to common GenAI problems:

The result is correct, but isn't what you wanted.

> Try being more specific by specifying the role, audience, and/or format in the prompt.

You would like the model to show you better ideas.

> GenAI tools do not provide deterministic responses. Therefore, we recommend rerunning the query or looking at other drafts if you are not happy with the first response you get. In some cases, the tools cache previous responses, and so you will have to modify the query slightly to get a different response.

When you ask a new question, the model responds as though it's answering your previous question.

> All the tools mentioned in this section maintain session state. So, they use your previous questions in the same session as part of the context when generating a response. If you are starting a new topic, clear the session or start a new chat.

You aren't sure whether the facts in the responses you're getting are accurate.

> Use GenAI responses in conjunction with tools that allow you to look at the source content. Because GenAI tools are next-to-ken generators that have been tuned using human feedback, they will generate a likely response that uses the right jargon and tone. Therefore, you should always verify the accuracy of any factual information from a GenAI tool: for example, by using a web search. This capability is built into tools such as Bing Copilot and Gemini. Note, however, that citations are not a panacea. They can be (and often are) hallucinated as well! If a tool

BUILDING PRODUCTS WITH GENAI

Figure 2-12. Building products with GenAI components.

provides a citation, examine the cited text to make sure that the citation is to an existent source and actually contains the material being quoted.

The response contains hallucinations.

You can reduce the incidence of hallucination when looking for factual information by providing one or more trusted reference texts to ground the model's response.

Sharing and Monetizing Prompts

Once you have a prompt that works for you, wouldn't it be great to share it with your colleagues? Maybe even deploy it as a web application and monetize its use? GenAI frameworks increasingly offer users the ability to share and monetize prompts and prompt libraries. OpenAI calls these shareable prompts GPTs (*https://chatgpt.com/gpts*) and Google calls them Gems (*https://oreil.ly/51wJG*). Anthropic has a Prompt Library (*https://oreil.ly/Ur9zZ*). LangChain allows for prompt sharing through LangChain Hub (*https://oreil.ly/VhqOT*).

Find out which of these are supported by your organization, browse the prompts that have been contributed by your colleagues, and follow the instructions provided by your organization to use them in your own work.

BUILDING PRODUCTS WITH GENAI CAPABILITIES

Products with built-in GenAI functions are rapidly being adopted for use with photos, emails, and meetings and in coding, customer support, marketing, and sales. These products are inspiring even more product managers and software developers to imagine and build products infused with GenAI (**Figure 2-12**).

Adobe Sensei uses GenAI to provide image-creation capabilities, while Google Photos' Magic Eraser tool provides easy-to-use photo editing capabilities. Gmail and Microsoft Outlook use GenAI to suggest replies to emails. Workspace and Office provide AI assistance when creating slides or writing documents. Zoom, Microsoft Teams, and Google Meet offer AI-powered video transcriptions and meeting summaries. GitHub Copilot, Replit, and Tabnine use GenAI to provide coding assistance. ServiceNow and Zendesk employ GenAI to offer assistance when resolving tickets. Jasper and Typeface use GenAI to create marketing content. Salesforce employs GenAI to help sellers customize their emails to prospective customers.

Figure 2-13 illustrates four ways you can guide GenAI models into producing the kind of content you need within your products. You can call out to a pretrained model using its API. Secondly, you could add information to the context of the prompt before making the call. Thirdly, you could train a custom model for your task using fine-tuning or distillation. Finally, you customize pretrained models by combining any of the previous three approaches.

In the remainder of this chapter, we'll look at how you can use these approaches to build GenAI-infused products.

4 WAYS TO BUILD GENAI-INFUSED PRODUCTS

INVOKING GENAI APIS

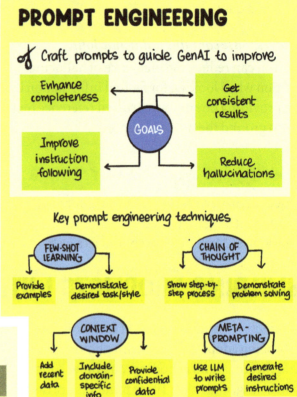

1. GET API KEY
2. HERE'S YOUR API KEY
3. RESPONSE
4. INVOKE API

GenAI provider
- Meta
- ChatGPT
- Gemini

AGENT FRAMEWORK: LANGCHAIN, AUTOGEN, etc.

PROMPT ENGINEERING

✂ Craft prompts to guide GenAI to improve

GOALS
- Enhance completeness
- Get consistent results
- Improve instruction following
- Reduce hallucinations

Key prompt engineering techniques

FEW-SHOT LEARNING
- Provide examples
- Demonstrate desired task/style

CHAIN OF THOUGHT
- Show step-by-step process
- Demonstrate problem solving

CONTEXT WINDOW
- Add recent data
- Include domain-specific info
- Provide confidential data

META-PROMPTING
- Use LLM to write prompts
- Generate desired instructions

FINE-TUNING & DISTILLATION

1. PREFIX TUNING

WHAT: Train a task-specific set of weights (change prefix weights) on additional small dataset

USE CASE: Show how to perform a desired set of tasks

2. ADAPTER TUNING

WHAT: Add extra layer of weights (trained on a new dataset) on top of pretrained models.

USE CASE: Emphasize parts of the original dataset. Often employed to match style, tone, etc.

CUSTOMIZING PRETRAINED MODELS

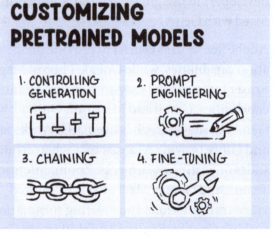

1. CONTROLLING GENERATION
2. PROMPT ENGINEERING
3. CHAINING
4. FINE-TUNING

Figure 2-13. Four ways to build products that are infused with GenAI capabilities.

Invoking GenAI Through APIs

So far in this chapter, we have discussed how to employ general-purpose GenAI tools. You've learned how to use these tools to perform a variety of tasks, from information retrieval to text transformation, using well-structured prompts.

The web frontends for ChatGPT and Gemini are convenient, but you'll often want to embed GenAI tools within a software program. For example, you might want to create a program that can automatically process reviews that appear on your company's website and react to the negative ones. This would require your app to send the user review directly to a GenAI tool and then process its response. The way to programmatically access GenAI tools is through their APIs.

Getting an API key

In order to invoke the models from software, you'll need a billing key from the GenAI provider. You then send that API key with every request, so that the provider can charge you. This charge is usually based on the number of tokens you provide as input and the number of tokens the service responds with.

GenAI tools often have a free tier, which should be sufficient to reproduce the calls that we make as you follow along with this book. However, since pricing changes frequently, we recommend that you read the terms and restrictions carefully before entering your credit-card details. Also, as discussed in Chapter 1, the API to a specific GenAI tool could be reaching an ecosystem that includes a foundational model as well as tools such as web search tools, toxicity filters, and so

on; this is different from the API that reaches only the foundational model. Read the documentation associated with the API endpoint to know what you are getting.

To follow along with us, you can find our sample code in this book's GitHub repository (*https://oreil.ly/vga_ch2*). Clone that directory and install the necessary packages using pip:

```
python -m pip install --user -r
requirements.txt
```

Next, fire up your favorite Python programming environment and create a file named *keys.env* with the following structure:

```
OPENAI_API_KEY=sk-...
GOOGLE_API_KEY=AI..
GROQ_API_KEY=gsk_…
ANTHROPIC_API_KEY=sk-ant-...
```

For one or more of the providers above, create an account, obtain an API key, and set the key value in the *keys.env* file. At the time of writing, the API keys can be created at the following links:

- OpenAI Platform (*https://oreil.ly/dkmJS*)
- Gemini: API Key in Google AI Studio (*https://oreil.ly/gIHNu*)
- Groq (for open models such as Llama 3 and Mixtral): API Keys (*https://oreil.ly/WqkzG*)
- Anthropic Console (*https://oreil.ly/6TpXO*)

Now, make sure that you can load these keys using the code stored in the repository, in the file *invoke_llm.py*:

```
from dotenv import load_dotenv
import os
```

```
load_dotenv("keys.env")
print("OPENAI_API_KEY:",
os.getenv("OPENAI_API_KEY"))
```

Invoking the API

While each of the four providers has a Python API, the APIs are all slightly different. To make it convenient to try out all four (and avoid getting locked into any one), we'll use the Python package LangChain in this section. The requirements file installs the necessary packages: `langchain-openai`, `langchain-google-genai`, `langchain-groq`, and `langchain-anthropic`.

You can create a `langchain` LLM as follows, depending on which one you want to use:

```
llm = ChatOpenAI(model_name="gpt-3.5-
turbo",
openai_api_key=os.getenv("OPENAI_API_
KEY"))
llm = GoogleGenerativeAI(model="gemini-
pro",
google_api_key=os.getenv("GOOGLE_API_
KEY"))
llm = ChatGroq(model_name="mixtral-
8x7b-32768",
groq_api_key=os.getenv("GROQ_API_KEY"))
llm = ChatAnthropic(model="claude-3-
sonnet",
api_key=os.getenv("ANTHROPIC_API_KEY"))
```

With the LLM created, you can send it a prompt (the code and full prompt are on GitHub; *https://oreil.ly/vga_ch02invoke*) and get a response back:

```
prompt = "Categorize the restaurant
review below into …"
response = llm.invoke(prompt)
print(response)
```

Regardless of the provider, you'll use the `llm` object the same way.

We got the following response back from Google Gemini (as always, your response may vary because GenAI models are not deterministic):

```
**Sentiment**: Positive
**Aspects Discussed**: Food and Service
```

On the other hand, Groq-Mixtral gave us this:

```
content='Category: Positive\n\nThe
review is discussing both the food
and service. The reviewer expresses
positive sentiment towards the hot
temperature of the food, the "wok hei"
taste, and the friendly and quick
service. They also mention that they
plan to visit again, indicating a high
level of satisfaction.' response_
metadata=...'
```

Because the response objects and formats are different, it would be difficult to simply swap one LLM out for the other in our hypothetical review-processing application.

To become truly agnostic to the LLM being used, you'll need to employ higher-level abstractions in LangChain. Let's look at that next.

Prompt template and chain

Look carefully at the structure of the prompts in **Figure 2-14**. Imagine you are writing an application that needs to create recipes on demand, or an application that needs to classify thousands of reviews. Will the prompt change completely for each input?

Typically, much of the prompt will remain the same, and a small part of the prompt will change each time. For example, the review-classification prompt consists of a fixed part (the instruction to the model on what to do) and a dynamic part (the review text) that will change for each review. We can set up a PromptTemplate in LangChain as follows, setting up a template for the review text (see Figure 2-14):

```
prompt = PromptTemplate.from_
template("""
Categorize the restaurant review below
into one of three categories based on
the sentiment of the review: Negative,
Neutral, Positive and identify whether
the review is discussing food, service,
and/or atmosphere.

**Review**:
{review_text}
""")
```

Also, since some LLMs return strings and others return messages with multiple parts, let's ask LangChain to parse the output and extract just the response string:

```
output_parser = StrOutputParser()
```

We can then construct a chain as follows:

```
chain = prompt | llm | output_parser
```

To invoke the LLM, we supply a dictionary that contains each of the templated variables that the chain requires:

```
review = "A real gem of …"
response = chain.invoke({
        "review_text": review
    })
```

The way this works is that the dictionary gets passed into the chain, which involves sending it to the prompt template, where the review text

gets replaced. This string prompt is sent to the LLM, which responds with a message. The parser then parses the message and outputs a string (see Figure 2-15).

With the use of a chain that includes a parser, we always get a string object, although the format of the strings differs by LLM. Gemini returns exactly what we specified, while Mixtral is more verbose. Even if we don't change LLMs, we don't know if we will get the exact response structure each time, because LLM responses are not deterministic. Is this a problem?

Prompt signature

If response structures vary too much, they become hard to automate within software programs. What we want here are outputs that are structured in a prespecified way that matches a desired data schema. Modern LLMs support structured outputs that match a provided schema, but the way you provide the schema to be matched varies from LLM to LLM.

A framework that ensures structured inputs and outputs is DSPy (*https://oreil.ly/iI6Jm*). The goal of DSPy is to abstract away a lot of prompt engineering and make it possible to use LLMs from different providers in a standardized way. It does this by asking the programmer to specify desired inputs and outputs (which are, together, termed the task's *signature*).

For our review-classification task, the signature might be this:

```
context, review -> sentiment, topics,
explanation
```

INVOKING GENAI THROUGH API PROMPT TEMPLATES AND CHAINING

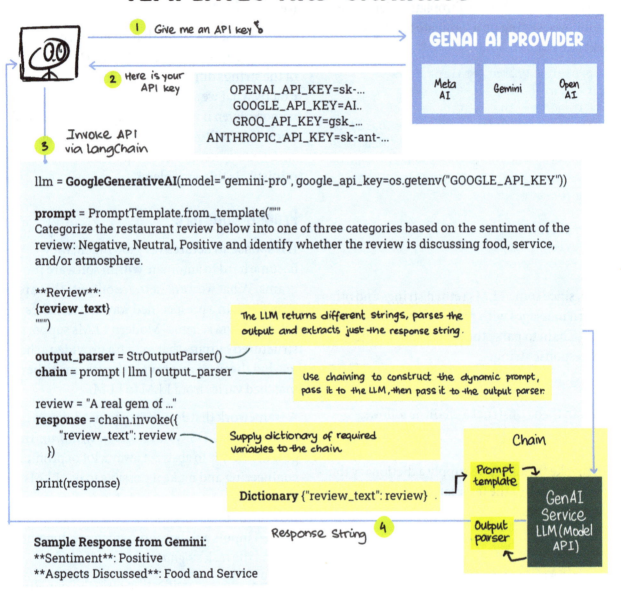

Sample Response from Gemini:
Sentiment: Positive
Aspects Discussed: Food and Service

Figure 2-14. Workflow for invoking GenAI through prompt templates and chaining.

RESPONSE STRING

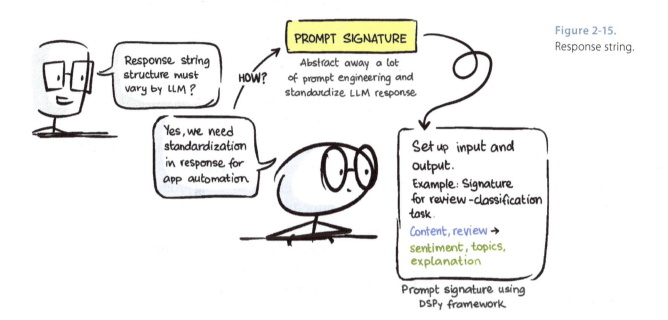

Figure 2-15.
Response string.

Here, context and review are the inputs; sentiment, topics, and explanation are the desired outputs.

In our case, the context is the plain-language task definition, "Categorize the restaurant review below…," and the review is the input to the model: "A real gem of Cantonese cooking. Food was…."

This is wired together as follows (see *prompt_signature.py* in the GitHub repository of this book for the full code; *https://oreil.ly/vga_ch02prosig*):

1. Create a `dspy.Predict` object with this signature:

```
prog = dspy.Predict("context, review ->
sentiment, topics, explanation")
```

2. Create an LLM object. DSPy, like LangChain, supports many providers. For example, we can do any of the following:

```
llm = dspy.OpenAI(model="gpt-3.5-turbo",
    api_key=...)
```

```
llm = dspy.Google(model="models/
    gemini-1.0-pro", api_key=...)
```

```
llm = dspy.GROQ(model="mixtral-
    8x7b-32768", api_key=...)
```

```
llm = dspy.Claude(model="claude-3-
    sonnet", api_key=...)
```

3. Invoke the `Predict` object within the context of the LLM and pass in the inputs and obtain a response object:

```
answer = self.prog(context="Categorize
the restaurant …", review="A real gem …")
```

4. The answer object contains fields that we can use in subsequent code:

```
answer.sentiment,
answer.topics, answer.explanation
```

In this way, the DSPy framework can be used to abstract away:

- the text processing involved with creating the prompt

- the LLM provider

- the invocation API with user-defined parameters

- the text processing involved in extracting the response

Because these are regular Python objects, setting up a prompt chain is intuitive—simply pass the result of one call as an input to the next.

Finally, the framework also allows you to utilize an on-device, or *local*, model instead of invoking a cloud-deployed model using its API. To do that, you'd create the LLM using a model whose weights are open and can be downloaded:

```
llm = dspy.OllamaLocal(model='mistral')
```

Or:

```
llm = dspy.HFModel(model='meta-llama/
    Llama-2-7b-hf')
```

In the previous code, we are using either Ollama or Hugging Face to retrieve the model weights and telling it the name of the model whose weights we want downloaded. In Chapter 5, we'll discuss how to select the GenAI model that is most appropriate for your use case.

Customizing Pretrained Models

In the previous sections, we used GenAI models as-is through their APIs. In this section, we will discuss different ways to customize *pretrained* models, by which we mean obtaining a response different from the response we'd get back from the API without training a GenAI model from scratch (see Figure 2-16).

You can customize a pretrained model by controlling the generation, by using prompt engineering, by using prompt chaining, or by fine-tuning the model. In this section, we will look at each of these approaches and how to choose between these approaches. The discussion is summarized and some specific techniques in each category are shown in Figure 2-16.

Controlling generation

The simplest way to get a different response from a pretrained model is to take advantage of some of the "knobs" provided by the LLM providers. These knobs allow you to specify a nondefault value for various parameters that control how LLMs generate text. To understand these parameters, we'll need to revisit how GenAI tools use foundational language models to generate text, so let's look at the next-token prediction problem in a bit more detail than we did in Chapter 1.

Next-token prediction

Remember that foundational language models are *next-token predictors*, which means that, given the previously generated text, they return a probability distribution for the next token to be generated. For simplicity, let's think of it as a

CUSTOMIZING PRETRAINED MODELS

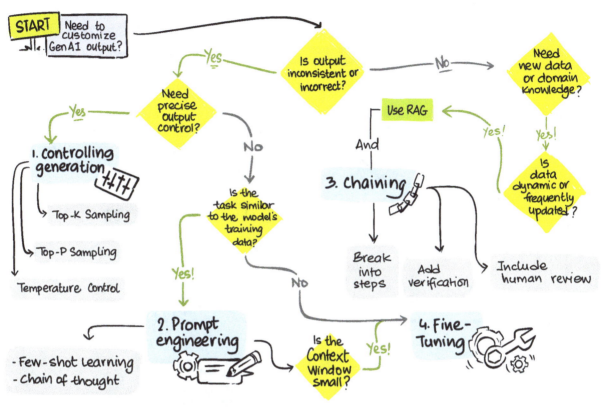

CUSTOMIZATIONS

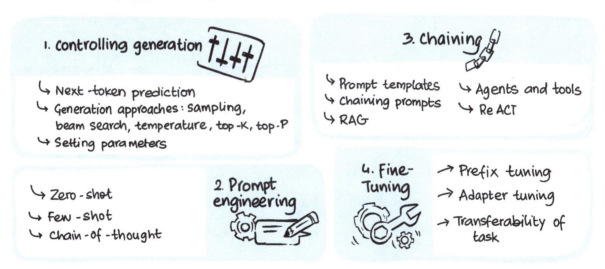

Figure 2-16. Another way to build a GenAI-infused product is to customize a pretrained model.

CONTROLLING PRETRAINED MODEL OUTPUT

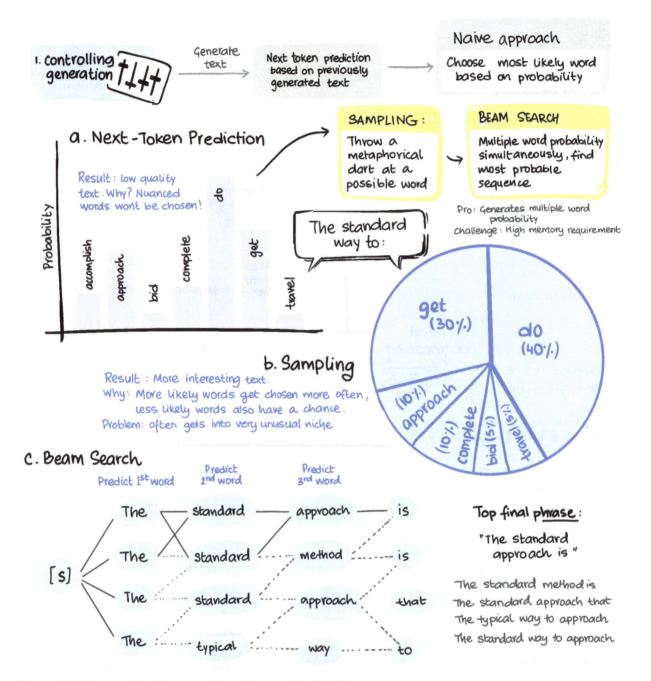

Figure 2-17. You can control the generation using a variety of techniques.

problem of predicting the next word. Suppose the text so far is the following:

```
The standard way to
```

The returned probability distribution might look something like what's shown in Figure 2-17.

How does the GenAI tool use the foundational model's response to construct phrases, sentences, and paragraphs? The naive way to choose among the possible continuations would be to pick the most likely word, which is *do* in this case. Then the LLM asks the foundational model to predict the next word to complete, "The standard way to do" and so on. Perhaps the most likely word is now *this*.

The problem with the naive approach of always choosing the word with the maximum likelihood is that sophisticated or nuanced words are almost never chosen. Therefore, this approach leads to low-quality text. Only toy LLMs employ this method.

Generation approaches

The decoder in the LLM's transformer architecture employs one or more approaches (they are not mutually exclusive) to generate higher-quality text and exposes the parameters to help you control how the decoding works. These approaches include sampling, beam search, temperature, top-K, and top-P. Let's consider them one by one.

Sampling

Instead of always choosing the most likely word, in *sampling*, the LLM throws a metaphorical dart at a dartboard containing all the possible continuations. The more likely words still get chosen more often, but less likely words also have a chance. Even if *do* is chosen on the first (it's the most likely, after all), the next word could be *calculations*. This makes the generated text more interesting.

The problem with a pure sampling approach is that the generated text often gets into very unusual niche topics. That's because, while the chances are low of an esoteric word being chosen at a specific point in the sequence, the chances of one esoteric word being chosen *somewhere* in the sequence are quite high. If the esoteric words together add up to a probability of 0.2, then the chances of an esoteric word occurring somewhere in a five-word phrase are $1 - (1 - 0.2)^5$ or about 67%!

Beam search

Instead of choosing one word, fixing it, and then predicting the next word, a tool using *beam search* can generate possible continuations, for say, three possibilities at each step, and compute the overall probability of the resulting four-word phrases. That would produce a tree similar to the one shown in Figure 2-17.

If we keep track of five possibilities for each word, we will have 25 two-word phrases, 125 three-word phrases, 625 four-word phrases, and 3125 five-word phrases! So beam search leads to exponential memory requirements. Because of this, it also requires pruning strategies to keep the resulting tree relatively small. The intractable computational complexity of beam search prompted engineers to search for other approaches.

TEMPERATURE

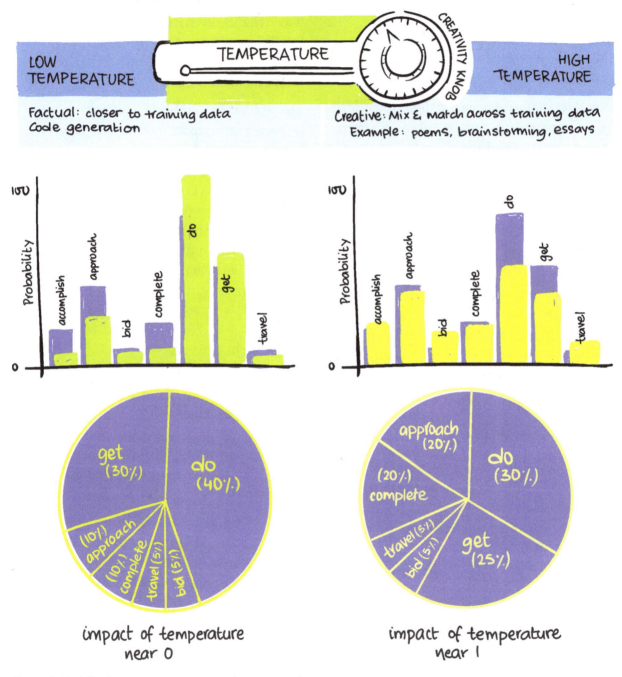

Figure 2-18. Adjusting temperature to control text generation.

Temperature

Now that we have looked at the text generation technique, let's look at parameters like temperature and top-K that can be used to control the text generation (Figure 2-18).

One way to handle the problem of esoteric continuations in sampling is to lower the probabilities of either the most likely words or the most unlikely words using a correction factor called *temperature*. In our example, even though *do* and *get* are the most common continuations, there is a very long tail of words that could fit, and together, they add up to a large probability.

If we want to suppress unlikely continuations, we can reduce the temperature to near zero. This will suppress the small probabilities (because the overall probability has to be equal to one) and make the likely continuations even more likely. Use a low temperature (such as 0.1) for tasks where you want to stick closely to the training data, such as for generating code or providing factual information.

On the other hand, to make things more "creative," we could *increase* the temperature. This suppresses the likelihood of the most common continuations and makes the unlikely ones more likely. Use a high temperature (such as 0.8) for tasks where you desire a lot of mixing and matching from across the training data, such as brainstorming or literary output, such as essays and poems.

Adjusting the temperature is useful if you want the GenAI tool to use the full spectrum of words, but give slight favor to familiar phrases or to get creative.

Top-K

Often, you'll want the tool to be creative and go beyond the first one or two most likely continuations, but not to venture *too* far out into weird combinations. Temperature adjustments don't help here—a low temperature will suppress unlikely words, but not make their probabilities zero so that they are never selected.

In such cases, it can be helpful to set an upper limit on the number of words that the tool can consider. This is called *top-K generation*. If you set *k* to 4, you are telling the GenAI model to limit its generation to the four most likely continuations at each step (see Figure 2-19). It will choose from among these four words in proportion to their probability. It's as if you've removed all the unlikely words like *bid, travel*, etc., and redivided the dashboard based on the relative shares of the likely continuations.

The top-K approach works well only in situations where the probability distribution is peaked and there are only a handful of good continuations. Mostly, you'll tune the temperature and top-P, which is covered next. Top-K is most commonly used as a guardrail to remove odd words in situations where the risk of untested combinations would be too high.

Top-P

Consider a phrase such as "We are going to __," as shown in Figure 2-20. The number of potential next words is large, and what's more, many of the words (*walk, talk, hang, sit, …*) are all somewhat equally likely. Artificially limiting the generation to the five most likely words would be problematic for sentences like this. Increasing the *k* fails to solve the problem of weird and

TOP-K (word limit)

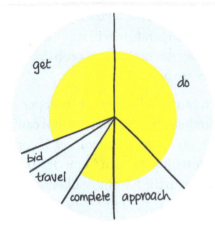

Limit number of words that can be considered for generation

K=4, Limit generation to 4 most probable words

Example text:
The standard way to...

Pick the most probable four choices. This approach works when you have a few very likely continuations, and a long tail of rare words that will sound odd.

Figure 2-19. Top-K is a technique to limit the number of words the model can consider.

unlikely words leaking through when you have a peaked distribution.

One way to address this is to set the threshold not on the number of words, but on their cumulative probability. This is formally called *nucleus sampling*, or informally, *top-P sampling*. If you set `top_p` to 0.8, you are asking the GenAI tool to choose the smallest list of words that together cover 80% of the dartboard, and discard the rest.

The top-P approach works for both flat and peaked distributions. In cases of flat distributions, there will have to be a lot of words on the dartboard to reach the 80% cutoff. In a peaked distribution, you could hit the 80% limit with just two or three words. In this way, top-P provides the benefits of both the temperature and the top-K settings.

It is possible to use temperature and top-P together. The temperature readjusts the relative areas that the words occupy, and

the top-P discards the most unusual candidate continuations.

The various concepts of text generation and the parameters that control it are shown in Figure 2-21. Figure 2-22 gives an example of how the parameters would affect the continuation of a simple sentence.

Setting parameters

Some general-purpose GenAI tools allow you to specify parameter settings, but most often, you'll only get access to the LLM settings when invoking them through the API.

If you are using DSPy, for example, you can set the following parameters on the LLM object you use to make API calls:

```
llm = dspy.OpenAI(model=..., api_
    key=.., temperature=0.3, top_
    p=0.8, top_k=3)
```

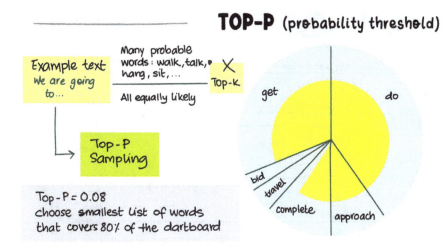

TOP-P (probability threshold)

Example text
We are going to…

Many probable words: walk, talk, hang, sit, … ✗ Top-k
All equally likely

Top-P Sampling

Top-P = 0.08
choose smallest list of words that covers 80% of the dartboard

get   do
bid
travel
complete   approach

Figure 2-20. Top-P is a technique for sampling the most likely next words.

EXAMPLES OF TECHNIQUES TO CONTROL PRETRAINED LLM OUTPUT

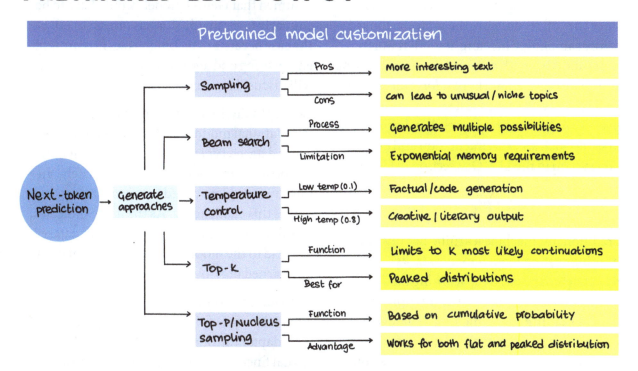

Pretrained model customization

Next-token prediction → Generate approaches →

Sampling
- Pros → More interesting text
- Cons → can lead to unusual/niche topics

Beam search
- Process → Generates multiple possibilities
- Limitation → Exponential memory requirements

Temperature control
- Low temp (0.1) → Factual/code generation
- High temp (0.8) → Creative/literary output

Top-k
- Function → Limits to k most likely continuations
- Best for → Peaked distributions

Top-P/Nucleus sampling
- Function → Based on cumulative probability
- Advantage → Works for both flat and peaked distribution

Figure 2-21. Summarizing how to control text generation by pretrained LLMs.

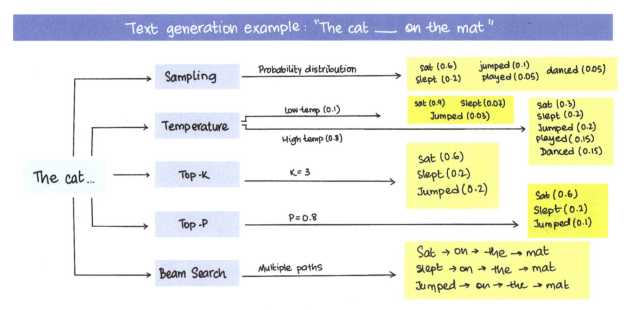

Figure 2-22. How different techniques generate a next word.

The parameters all interact with each other, since they all reconfigure the same dartboard before sampling. Therefore, it is often worth experimenting with different parameter settings and choosing what works best for your problem. To do that, you'll need a test suite and an objective way to measure responses. We discuss how to set up such an experimentation and evaluation system in the LLMOps section of Chapter 6.

Fine-Tuning and Distillation

Traditionally, machine learning has involved training custom models for new tasks and to reflect new datasets. Deep learning models introduced the idea of transfer learning, which is a way of training a foundational model on a generic task on an extremely large dataset and then fine-tuning that foundational model on a very small dataset for a specific task. When GenAI models were introduced, many people assumed that GenAI models would have to be similarly fine-tuned. This has proven to not be the case because of techniques such as prompt engineering and agent frameworks, which we will discuss later in this chapter.

Conceptually, in fine-tuning, you train the foundational model for a few more iterations on a new dataset, typically one that shows it how to perform a brand-new task. Unfortunately, an unsolved problem called *catastrophic forgetting* makes this challenging. As the name indicates, continuing to train a model on a small dataset can lead to the model forgetting much of what it has learned previously.

Therefore, customizing a foundational model often takes one of three approaches: prefix tuning, adapter tuning, or knowledge distillation. Actual fine-tuning would involve changing all the billions of weights of the foundational model and is rarely done.

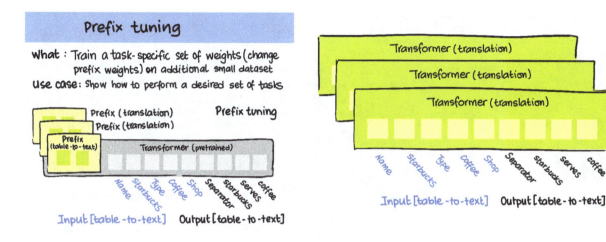

Figure 2-23. Fine-tuning a pretrained model with prefix tuning.

Prefix tuning

The idea behind *prefix tuning*, introduced in a 2021 paper (*https://oreil.ly/kyi3I*) by a pair of Stanford researchers, is to freeze the pretrained foundational model's parameters and optimize only the prefix parameters for the set of tasks you care about (**Figure 2-23**).

However, prefix tuning tends to be a viable solution only for models whose weights are published, such as T5 or Llama 3. You won't have access to the postprefix portion of the weights of foundational models available through their APIs.

Adapter tuning

Another type of fine-tuning is to add an extra layer of weights on top of the pretrained model. The weights of this extra layer are trained on a new dataset and used to adapt the foundational model's weights on the fly to produce a response. *Adapter tuning* tends to be sufficient to emphasize parts of the original dataset, and is often employed to make a GenAI model match a desired style (**Figure 2-24**).

Adapter tuning is particularly well-suited for cloud deployments. Because it doesn't modify the foundational model at all, you can continue using the provider's API. The only weights you modify are your own, which you can keep confidential in your cloud project. The cloud provider takes on the hard task of running the enormous foundational model, and you take on the relatively simpler task of running the tiny adapter layer.

Distillation

In *knowledge distillation*, a model with fewer parameters is trained on the responses of a larger foundational model (**Figure 2-25**). Its training dataset consists of the smaller set of tasks or queries that the GenAI model is expected to encounter in practice. The distilled model can be much smaller than the foundational model while having the same accuracy (*https://oreil.ly/bMp3W*).

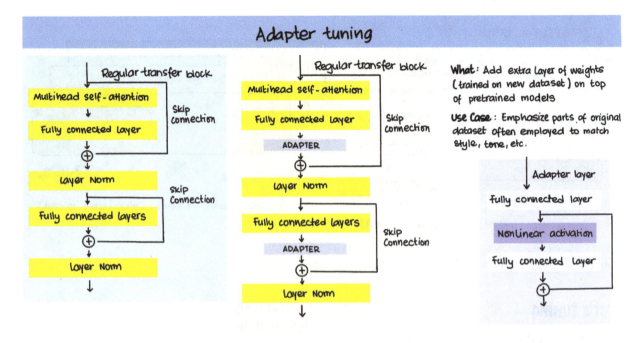

Figure 2-24. Fine-tuning a pretrained model with adapter tuning.

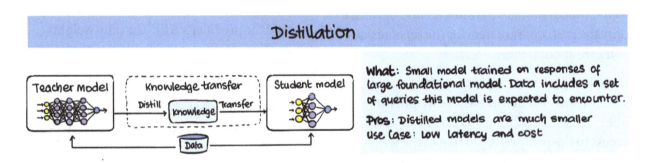

Figure 2-25. Fine-tuning a pretrained model with distillation.

In some cases, the distilled smaller model also uses smaller data types (8-bit instead of 32-bit numbers, for example) and/or specialized hardware that provides a further speed boost. You can use distillation to create smaller models in situations where you need low-latency or edge deployments. You can also use it to create models with the lowest cost for a given quality.

Adapter tuning and distillation are sophisticated ways to use GenAI. We will look at how to use these techniques in more detail in Chapter 4.

Prompt Engineering

So far in this chapter, we have limited ourselves to providing just instructions to the GenAI model, without including any examples or hints. This approach, called *zero-shot learning*, is completely dependent on whether the model has been trained on a task similar enough to the one you are asking it to do. While you can fine-tune a model to learn a new task, this turns out to be unnecessary in many cases. In this section, we will look at ways to address problems with instruction-following, hallucination, and completeness while continuing to use the pretrained model as-is (**Figures 2-26** and **2-27**).

There are three ways to get a pretrained model to go beyond its original training, as depicted in **Figure 2-28**. In *few-shot learning*, you demonstrate a desired task or style by showing the model a few examples. In the *chain-of-thought* approach, you demonstrate the steps to solve a new problem or task. And with the *context window* approach, you provide the model with data that will help it answer the question.

In addition to teaching the GenAI model new tasks or new data, these techniques can help you get consistent results from a GenAI model. Try them if you are finding that the GenAI model is not following instructions faithfully or if its results are too variable. Let's look at each of these three techniques.

Few-shot learning

In few-shot learning, you provide a few examples of the task being correctly performed, and then ask your question. Here's a prompt demonstrating this technique:

```
You are a physics tutor. I will tell
you a real-life situation and you will
tell me the physics principle involved.

** Example 1**:
Situation: A ball is thrown in the air.
It comes back to the ground.
Physics principle: Gravity or Newton's
law of universal gravitation

** Example 2**:
Situation: You are walking on ice and
suddenly stop. This causes you to slip
and fall.
Physics principle: Inertia or Newton's
first law of motion

** Question **:
Situation: When you push harder on
a bicycle pedal, the bicycle moves
faster.
```

Posing this prompt to OpenAI ChatGPT, we get this:

```
Physics principle: Newton's second law
of motion (F = ma, where force equals
mass times acceleration).
```

How many examples do you need? What kinds of examples should you choose? In general, it is helpful to have the examples cover the kinds of inputs the model is likely to face, with more examples for the more likely kinds of queries.

That said, since calls to the model APIs are priced based on the number of tokens you send to them, there is a practical limit to how many examples you can include. One common trick is to choose specific examples to match the task. While *retrieval-augmented generation* (RAG) is commonly used to add data to the context, it can also be used to add the most appropriate examples. We'll cover RAG in detail in Chapter 4.

PROMPT ENGINEERING

Figure 2-26. Prompt engineering is about crafting prompts to improve consistency.

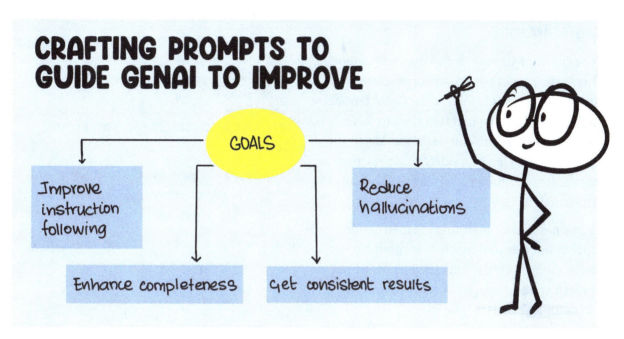

Figure 2-27. Crafting prompts to guide GenAI to improve.

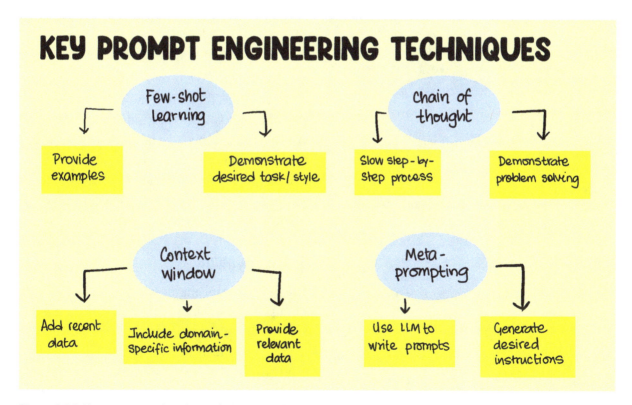

Figure 2-28. Key prompt engineering techniques.

Chain of thought

In the chain-of-thought technique, you demonstrate to the model how to solve a problem by showing it the steps to follow. The GenAI model can then use the demonstrated steps to solve similar problems. This can be particularly helpful because GenAI models tend to be poor at reasoning and problem solving, but excellent at pattern matching.

In some cases, simply adding the instruction "think about this step-by-step" is enough to get more reasoned replies from an LLM. However, in practical situations, it's best to provide the specific logical steps to follow.

Here's an example prompt demonstrating this technique:

```
You are a gardening consultant who
recommends plants to home gardeners.
Follow the steps given in the example
to recommend appropriate plants for the
given location and requirement.

** Example **:
Question: I live in Tucson, Arizona and
want to plant a tree that will provide
shade. What do you recommend?
Steps:
1. Tucson, Arizona is in USDA Zone 8
and has a hot desert climate.
2. Trees that grow well in hot desert
climates include the Mesquite tree,
Palo Verde tree, and the Desert Willow.
3. The Mesquite tree is a good choice
because it is drought-tolerant and
provides good shade.

Answer:
I recommend planting a Mesquite tree in
your garden.
```

```
Question: I live in Portland, Oregon
and want to plant flowers that will
bloom early in the spring. What do you
recommend?
```

Posing this prompt to Google Gemini, we get this:

```
1. Portland, Oregon is in USDA Zone 8 and
   has a mild, temperate climate with cool,
   wet winters and warm, dry summers.

2. Flowers that bloom early in the spring
   in this climate include crocuses, daffo-
   dils, tulips, hyacinths, and primroses.

3. Daffodils and tulips are particularly
   good choices because they are hardy and
   easy to grow. They add a bright splash of
   color to the garden after a long winter.

Answer: I recommend planting daffodils
and tulips in your garden for an early
spring bloom.
```

As you can see, the GenAI model has used our steps as a template for the kind of reasoned analysis to return. If there is a human in the loop, it is easy for that human to catch errors in the logic and correct the recommendation that goes to the user. We'll discuss how to do this in Chapter 5 when we discuss system architectures.

Context window

The third prompt engineering technique we'll discuss is using *context windows*. GenAI models are trained on a corpus of data that was available to model providers at the time that the model was trained. This corpus is unlikely to contain extremely recent data or data that is confidential to your company or specific to your industry.

You can provide such data as context within the prompt, for the model to use when generating its response. The size of this context window used to be quite limited, but starting in 2024, models such as Gemini and Claude have started to allow multimodal context windows in the millions of tokens.

For example, you could teach the model about what's on sale at your local grocery store by passing the image or PDF of weekly ads (see Figure 2-29) to the model as context.

The following prompt instructs the model to use the ads in the flier to create recipes for a week of dinners and a shopping list:

```
You are a frugal and imaginative home
cook. I will give you a flier for a
local grocery store that has a sale on
ingredients. You are planning to make a
meal for your 4-person family. You want
to make a meal that is both delicious
and healthy. Make a weekly recipe plan
and shopping list based on the flier.
```

You don't need to extract text from the PDF of the ad brochure. Instead, you can employ a multimodal model such as Gemini or GPT-4o and pass in the pages of the PDF rendered as images. (See the GitHub repository for the complete code; *https://oreil.ly/vga_ch2*.)

```
flyer = []
with tempfile.TemporaryDirectory() as
temp_dir:
    pdf = pdfium.PdfDocument("flyer.pdf")
    for page_num in range(len(pdf)):
        filename = os.path.join(temp_
dir, f"flyer_p{page_num}.png")
        image = pdf.get_page(page_num).
render().to_pil()
        image.save(os.path.join(temp_
dir, filename))
```

```
        flyer.append(genai.upload_
file(filename))
    response = model.generate_
content([prompt] + flyer)
    print(response.text)
```

The result from the model is a weekly recipe plan that takes advantage of the sales, along with a shopping list organized by the section of the store.

Meta-prompts

There are so many considerations behind creating a good prompt. Wouldn't it be great if you could have an expert help you write a good prompt? Where would you find such an expert?

You got it—ask an LLM to help you create a good prompt. Here's an example of asking Gemini to create a good prompt targeting a specific LLM (Claude Haiku):

```
You are a prompt engineer who is an
expert on writing prompts for Anthropic
Claude Haiku. Write a prompt to be
given to Haiku, following the best
practices that Anthropic has published.
The goal is for the LLM to read the
PDF of an article and generate the
following structured information
suitable to create a presentation out
of it:

class Slide(BaseModel):
    title: str
    key_points: List[str]
    audio_script: str

class Lecture(BaseModel):
    slides: List[Slide]
    lecture_title: str
    based_on_article_by: str
```

Figure 2-29. It is possible to pass an image or PDF as part of the context of the prompt.

The result is this:

Task: Transform a PDF article into a structured presentation.

Output Format:

- Lecture:
  - **lecture_title:** A concise title summarizing the article's main theme.
  - **based_on_article_by:** The author(s) of the article.
  - **slides:** A list of Slide objects.

    title: A clear and concise title for each slide.

    key_points: A list of bullet points summarizing the main ideas of the slide.

audio_script: A script for narrating the slide content, including relevant audio cues (e.g., "click here").

Example:

Guidelines:

- Clarity: Ensure the presentation is easy to understand and follows a logical flow.
- Conciseness: Keep slides and audio scripts concise and to the point.
- Relevance: Only include information that directly supports the article's main arguments.
- Engagement: Use engaging language and visuals to keep the audience interested.

This technique is called *meta-prompting*. Meta-prompting is a great way to generate a detailed prompt from just the concept. Note that the suggested prompt requires an example—edit the prompt to include such an example before using it.

ARCHITECTING GENAI APPLICATIONS

While the monolithic recipe-creation prompt seems to have worked, it's hard to be confident about the quality of the resulting recipes and the comprehensiveness of the grocery list. The chicken stirfry doesn't seem to involve actually cooking the marinated chicken at all! And we are not confident that all the recipe ingredients have made their way onto the shopping list.

This is because carrying out complex workflows with a single call to an LLM does not allow us to examine intermediate outputs and take corrective action. For a task as complex as creating a week's worth of recipes and a corresponding grocery list, it's better to have a human verify and validate the individual steps. If we have a database of nutrition data, we'd want to use that database instead of having the LLM potentially hallucinate the calorific content of the recipe (see Figure 2-30).

When it comes to architecting GenAI applications, there are several techniques and capabilities that we can rely on:

Chaining prompts

We could explicitly specify the sequence of actions, or chain of steps, and hardcode them in code.

Agent framework

Instead of hardcoding the steps, we could have the language model itself determine the sequence of actions to take, and then carry those steps out in order. Agent frameworks enable GenAI models to create and execute a chain of actions dynamically.

Tools

Not every step in the chain needs to be done using GenAI—we might want to invoke software tools such as web search and calculators that the chain or agent framework already knows about.

Function calling

We might also make our existing backend systems available through APIs. LLMs are capable of gathering up the inputs to the APIs, calling these functions, and postprocessing the outputs of the APIs.

Retrieval-augmented generation

It is possible to dynamically populate the context of a prompt with information that is relevant to the query.

Let's look at how to solve the weekly recipe planner using these approaches.

Chaining Prompts

One way to break up the task of creating a weekly recipe plan and shopping list is to list the steps involved:

1. Identify items that are on sale.

2. Ideate dinner recipes that involve these ingredients.

3. Gather the ingredients from each recipe.

4. Combine the ingredients into a shopping list.

5. Organize the shopping list by category.

You could implement each of these steps using an LLM, passing the output of previous steps into subsequent ones—a technique known as *prompt chaining* (Figure 2-31).

LangChain simplifies prompt chaining. It also allows you to define Pydantic data structures (see repository at *https://oreil.ly/vga_ch2*; Pydantic [*https://oreil.ly/TLbIa*] is a data validation Python library):

```
class SaleItem(BaseModel):
    name: str = Field(description="item
    name")
    price: str = Field(description=
    "price e.g. $3.97/lb")
    sale_type: str = Field(description=
    "sale type e.g. None, member
    price,...")
```

You can use these structures to retrieve data from the LLM's response:

```
sale_item_parser = JsonOutputParser(
pydantic_object=SaleItem)
```

Figure 2-30. It is possible to architect GenAI applications to get around the limitations of a single LLM call.

You can use this parser object to generate formatting instructions for the LLM:

```
find_sale_items_prompt = """
Parse the weekly grocery ad brochure
and find all the items on sale.
""" + sale_item_parser.get_format_
instructions()
```

The chain for the first step then becomes:

```
find_sale_items_message = HumanMessage(
find_sale_items_prompt + flyer_pages)
prompt = ChatPromptTemplate.from_
messages([find_sale_items_message])
chain = prompt | model | sale_item_
parser
sale_items = chain.invoke(input={}).
text
```

Given the grocery flyer, the output of the previous chain would be something like:

```
[{'name': 'USDA Choice Boneless Beef
Chuck Roast',
'price': '$4.97/lb', 'sale_type':
'Member Price'},
```

Similarly, the second step in the chain defines a Recipe class:

```
class Recipe(BaseModel):
  title: str = Field(description
      ="Recipe title")
  ingredients: typing.List[RecipeItem]
      = Field(description="list of
      ingredients")
  instructions: typing.List[str]
      = Field(description="steps to
      take")
```

The formatting instructions for the recipes are inserted into an LLM prompt:

```
create_recipes_prompt = f"""
You are a frugal and imaginative home
cook.
I will give you a JSON list of
ingredients that are on sale at the
local grocery store.
Plan out 5 delicious and healthy
dinner recipes for a family of four,
prioritizing the use of items that are
on sale.

**Sale Items**
""" + f"{sale_items}\n\n" + recipe_
parser.get_format_instructions()
```

Given the output of the previous step as input, the output of this step will be something like:

```
[{'title': 'Grilled Chicken and Avocado
Salad', 'ingredients':
```

This, in turn, can be passed to the next step of the chain.

Breaking a monolithic prompt into small steps allows humans to verify and edit or validate the results, such as how the weekly recipe plan is built. The resulting software components are also much easier to test and maintain.

Agent Frameworks

Chaining a specific set of prompts is easy for simple situations, but the code that links the LLM calls can get very complex if your use case involves dynamic logic, errors and retries, or human curation:

Dynamic logic

If the logic of choosing between the steps depends on the input (such as if the family includes a vegetarian) or system state (such as

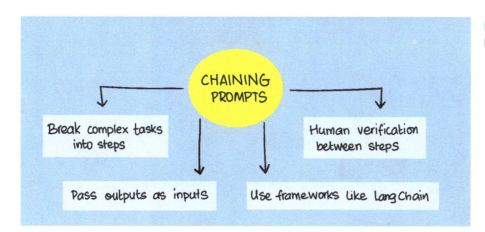

Figure 2-31.
Prompt chaining.

if there is a limit on the total sugar content), the "glue" code that binds the steps becomes rather complicated.

Errors and retries

What happens if any of the steps in the previous LLM chain fail? If we were doing it interactively, we'd look at the error message, modify it, and try again. Retrying is easy in code, but modifying the prompt before retrying is hard to do.

Human curation or correction

Ideally, you'd allow humans to remove sale items they are not interested in or recipes that don't appeal to them, before moving onto the next step. Building in such human interactions makes the code complex.

Agent frameworks (Figure 2-32) provide ways to address these limitations. At the time of writing in 2024, agent frameworks are in a state of flux, with different organizations taking different approaches to orchestration, automation, and human involvement. Two approaches are no-code and low-code agent frameworks.

No-code agent frameworks

Agent frameworks, such as Google Cloud's Vertex AI Agent Builder, let you specify steps by describing them in natural language (see Figure 2-33). The framework then builds the necessary code and deploys it as a pipeline.

First, specify the overall goal of the agent—what you'd ask a monolithic application to do—and then specify the steps one by one, as instructions in natural language. For example, say the second instruction is, "Ask the user if they have specific dietary needs." This instruction gets translated by the agent framework into a human-in-the-loop interaction, and the human input (typically from a staff member) guides the agent through the remainder of the task.

The drawback of no-code agent frameworks is that they are limited to the no-code capabilities built into the framework. While you can extend frameworks using tools and function calls (covered shortly), they tend to be more limited than frameworks that are fully realized by code.

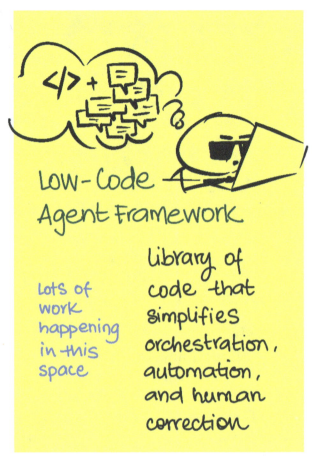

AGENT FRAMEWORKS

ADDRESSES CHALLENGES

Dynamic Logic

Human curation or correction

Errors and retries

No-Code Agent Framework

limited to the no-code capabilities

You specify steps by describing them in natural language, and then the framework writes the necessary code & develops it as a pipeline.

Low-Code Agent Framework

Lots of work happening in this space

Library of code that simplifies orchestration, automation, and human correction

Figure 2-32. Agent frameworks.

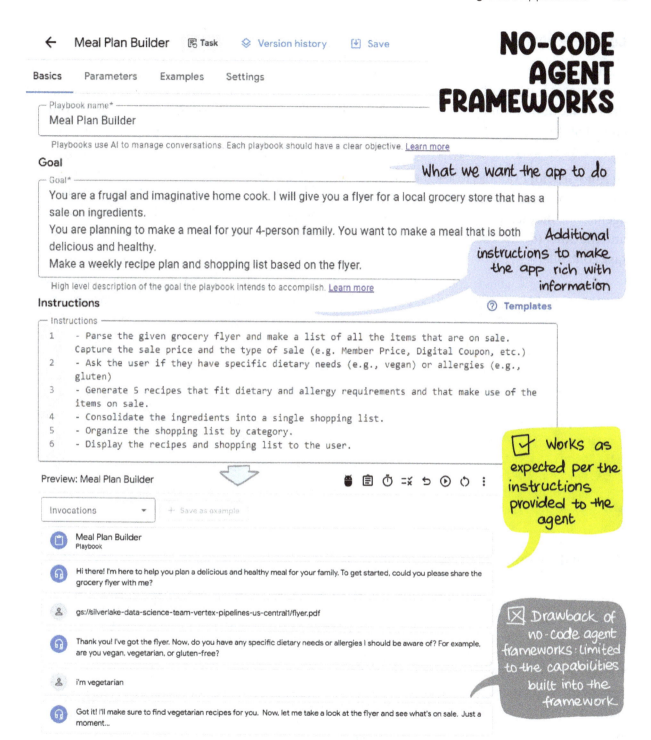

Figure 2-33. No-code agent framework in Vertex AI.

Low-code agent frameworks

Agent frameworks such as AutoGen, an open source agent framework by Microsoft, help address these limitations by providing a library of code that simplifies orchestration, automation, and human correction.

In AutoGen, for example, to ask the human for input on their dietary needs, you'd create two agents, one that acts as a proxy for the human and the other (`recipe_agent`) for the primary task controller:

```
human_proxy = ConversableAgent(
"human_proxy", llm_config=False,
# no LLM used for human proxy
human_input_mode="ALWAYS",
# always ask for human input
)
recipe_agent = ConversableAgent(
"recipe_agent",system_message
="You are a frugal and imaginative … "
llm_config={"config_list":
[{"model": "gpt-4", "api_key":
os.environ["OPENAI_API_KEY"]}]},
human_input_mode="NEVER",
# never ask for human input
)
```

You would then ask the two agents to converse:

```
result = human_proxy.initiate_chat(
recipe_agent, message="Do you have any
specific dietary needs or allergies?",)
```

The human proxy agent carries out its side of the conversation by passing along all the recipe agent's messages to the human and sending the human's messages to the recipe agent.

By creating agents and linking them together, you can see that it's possible to orchestrate complex tasks dynamically.

Tools

Both prompt chaining and agent frameworks can use external tools to carry out specific tasks (**Figure 2-34**). For example, suppose you want to attach nutritional information to each recipe (such as that one serving contains 10 g of protein, 350 kCal, and so on). You can't trust an LLM to generate the nutritional information spontaneously—it's likely to simply hallucinate those numbers.

To get a correct nutritional value, you could write code to look up the nutrition value of each ingredient, sum it all up, and return a result. In AutoGen, this would look as follows:

```
from autogen.coding.func_with_reqs
import with_requirements
@with_requirements(python_packages
=["pandas"], global_imports=["pandas"])
def calculate_nutritional_value(recipe:
Recipe)
-> pandas.DataFrame:
result = pandas.DataFrame.from_dict({
        "type": ["protein", "sugar", …],
        "amount": [0.0, 0.0, …],
}).set_index("type")

for ingredient in recipe.ingredients:
    nutrition_values = look_up_
    nutrition(ingredient)
    result = result.add(nutrition_
    values, fill_value=0.0)
return result
```

To execute this code, and plug in the resulting nutritional values alongside the recipe, you'd need to create a tool capable of running code:

```
nutrition_tool = autogen.coding.
LocalCommandLineCodeExecutor(
functions=[calculate_nutritional_
value])
```

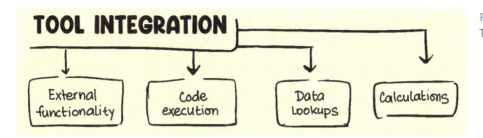

Figure 2-34.
Tool integration.

Then you'd have to pass the tool to the recipe agent:

```
recipe_agent = ConversableAgent(
    "recipe_agent",
    …, # as before
    code_execution_config={
        "executor": nutrition_tool,
    },
)
```

You'd then add instructions to the prompt for the recipe agent, telling it to use the tool to obtain nutrition information for the recipe.

If you're using a low-code framework like AutoGen, you can have it execute code directly, using the `LocalCommandLineCodeExecutor`. As for a no-code agent framework such as Vertex AI, we'll look at how to do that next.

Function Calling

In many cases, the external tool you want to use will be available through a REST API, even if the desired functionality is not. You can wrap any desired code or backend calls (such as the `look_up_nutrition` function in the previous section) behind a REST API or a Model Context Protocol (MCP) interface. MCP standardizes how LLMs invoke external tools by adding in the necessary tool descriptions.

Once you have a REST API or MCP tool for the desired functionality, you can ask the LLM to gather the necessary inputs and invoke the API. For example, you could give a Vertex AI agent the open API spec of a REST service and tell it when to invoke it, as shown in **Figure 2-35**.

In this way, function calling bridges the gap between GenAI tools and existing enterprise software.

Retrieval-Augmented Generation

As discussed in the section on prompt engineering, one way to improve the freshness and accuracy of generated results is to incorporate relevant information into the prompt's context window using a RAG architecture (**Figure 2-36**). The RAG can retrieve relevant information from a knowledge base and stuff it into the prompt context. This is such a widespread need that most agent frameworks ship with a RAG tool.

Using a RAG architecture consists of three phases: creating the knowledge base, finding relevant content within the knowledge base, and including the relevant content in the prompt's context window.

Suppose you're searching for advice on adapting a recipe for vegetarians. A traditional search index won't perform well for this type of search

FUNCTION CALLING

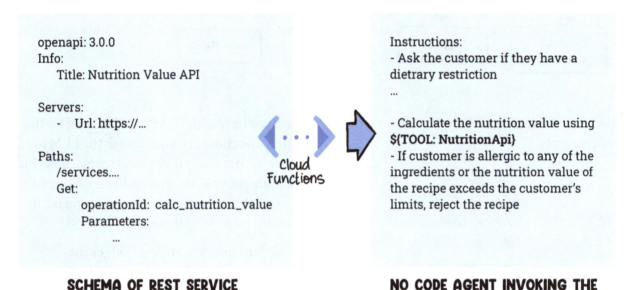

openapi: 3.0.0
Info:
    Title: Nutrition Value API

Servers:
    -    Url: https://...

Paths:
    /services....
    Get:
        operationId: calc_nutrition_value
        Parameters:

            ...

Instructions:
- Ask the customer if they have a dietrary restriction

...

- Calculate the nutrition value using **${TOOL: NutritionApi}**
- If customer is allergic to any of the ingredients or the nutrition value of the recipe exceeds the customer's limits, reject the recipe

Cloud Functions

SCHEMA OF REST SERVICE

NO CODE AGENT INVOKING THE SERVICE AS A TOOL

Figure 2-35. Function calling.

because you are searching not for a keyword, but for an idea. Simply searching for keywords like *vegetarian* is unlikely to yield meaningful results—most of the results will be for vegetarian recipes. Instead, look for sentences that are semantically close to the idea of adapting a recipe for vegetarians. Language models make such semantic searches relatively easy to implement.

Suppose, instead, that you have access to articles and recipes published in food magazines and cookbooks (maybe this is proprietary because you are the publisher, or you have purchased this content from the publisher). The first task in creating the knowledge base is to take the existing sentences in our articles and represent their meanings as vectors. A vector that represents the meaning of a fragment of text (or image or video) is called an *embedding*. The ability to create an embedding turns out to be a byproduct of training a language model, because such models need to compress all the knowledge they see into their parameters. Even an LLM with billions of parameters has far fewer parameters than the number of words it sees, so it can't memorize them all.

Once the embedding of a sentence is created, that embedding and the corresponding plain-text sentence are stored in a *vector database*. There are many vector databases available now, including open source ones (Chroma, Faiss), proprietary ones (Pinecone), and vector capabilities built into traditional databases (such as pgvector in Postgres).

ARCHITECTING GENAI APPLICATIONS WITH RAG

Semantic search of a knowledge base — Dynamically populate the context of a prompt with information relevant to the query

RAG Architecture

1. Create the knowledge base
2. Find relevant content in the knowledge base
3. Prompt the LLM, including the relevant content in the prompt
4. Task: Advice for adapting a recipe to be vegetarian

❌ Traditional keyword search won't work: "Vegetarian" keyword will lead to vegetarian recipes

✅ Semantic search works because we are looking for the idea of adapting a recipe for vegetarians

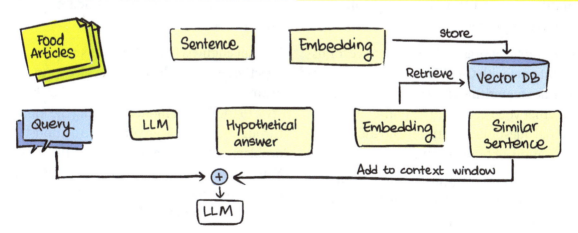

Figure 2-36. Retrieval-augmented generation (RAG).

In the second phase, when you need to find relevant sentences, you can give the LLM a zero-shot learning prompt: "How can you adapt the following recipe to make it suitable for vegetarians?" You can then take its answer (which is probably wrong) and look for similar sentences in the knowledge base. These answers are probably correct because we [should] have vetted the data we put into the knowledge base by having all knowledge base articles tested in real kitchens—if you are a publisher who has been doing this all along, you now have a market opportunity selling your content to AI model providers. You can then take the explanation of

how to adapt the recipe for vegetarians, add it to the prompt context, and reprompt the LLM to generate a vegetarian-friendly recipe.

The RAG approach has proven extremely powerful in practice. Besides using it to find accurate information, it can be used to provide fresh data to LLMs without having to constantly retrain them. You can also use the RAG approach to find relevant examples for few-shot or chain-of-thought prompting—in this case, you'd start by storing vetted answers or list of steps in the vector database. We will look at RAG in a lot more detail in Chapter 4.

SUMMARY

In this chapter, we discussed how generative AI is being used by consumers and developers. Consumers use GenAI products such as ChatGPT and Meta AI as a general-purpose tool for tasks such as brainstorming, writing, and art creation. While these GenAI tools can generate usable output, it's important to recognize their limitations in instruction-following, hallucination, and completeness.

Text prompts serve as a natural interface for users to interact with GenAI models. We discussed guidelines for writing effective prompts based on whether you need creative writing, answers to factual questions, text transformation, text classification, or brainstorming.

You can utilize foundational models through their APIs to integrate GenAI functionalities into existing products. However, LLMs by themselves have several limitations such as knowledge-cutoff, inability to plan or reason,

and inability to act on the environment. You can use agents, programs that interact with GenAI models and external tools, to extend the capabilities of LLMs. You can also use parameters such as temperature, top-K, and top-P sampling to control the selection of next tokens in text generation. More advanced customization methods include prefix tuning, adapter tuning, and distillation.

Prompt engineering techniques are quite effective. Few-shot learning involves providing examples to demonstrate the desired task or style to the GenAI model. Guiding the model through a step-by-step process to demonstrate problem-solving is called chain-of-thought. You can incorporate relevant data, including images and PDFs, into the prompt's context for enhanced accuracy and relevance.

GenAI applications often involve more than a single call to an LLM. Instead, they often accomplish complex tasks by chaining prompts, by breaking down complex tasks into smaller steps, each implemented using an LLM, with outputs passed as inputs to subsequent steps. You can orchestrate complex workflows using agent frameworks. You can also integrate external tools (e.g., web search, calculators, custom functions) into GenAI workflows. In particular, you can use serverless functions and REST APIs to bridge GenAI tools with existing enterprise software.

A very popular architecture for GenAI applications is retrieval-augmented generation (RAG). This architecture involves dynamically populating the prompt context with information from a knowledge base to improve accuracy and provide up-to-date data. The information is retrieved from the knowledge base by performing semantic search on embeddings of user queries and information chunks.

In the next chapter, we will look at enterprise use cases of GenAI.

## Chapter 3

GENERATIVE AI USE CASES

So far in this book, we have looked at how to use GenAI. But what can you use it for? One common criticism of GenAI, at the time we are writing this book, is that it is a lot of hype without much in the way of practical use cases. This is not true! In this chapter, we will showcase practical use cases that have proven valuable.

We hope to show you that GenAI has the potential to reshape industries and redefine possibilities. This chapter explores the profound impact that GenAI is already having across diverse domains by delving into detailed examples that illuminate its potential to revolutionize customer support, code review and generation, marketing and advertising, data analysis and visualization, and enterprise search (**Figure 3-1**).

GenAI, in essence, transcends traditional AI models by not merely analyzing existing data, but creating novel content, designs, and solutions. In customer support, it empowers virtual agents with the ability to craft personalized responses, anticipate customer needs, and streamline interactions, ultimately enhancing customer satisfaction and operational efficiency. Within the realm of software development, generative AI is a game-changer, automating code review processes, generating code snippets, and suggesting innovative solutions to complex programming tasks, making developers more productive and efficient.

Marketing and advertising have also witnessed a paradigm shift because GenAI is driving down the cost of rich media and personalization. In these areas, GenAI fuels the creation of captivating ad copy, generates eye-catching visuals, and tailors campaigns to individual preferences with precision. In data analysis and visualization, it empowers users, even those without deep technical skills, to uncover hidden patterns, glean actionable insights, and communicate complex information through intuitive visualizations. Enterprise search, too, has been

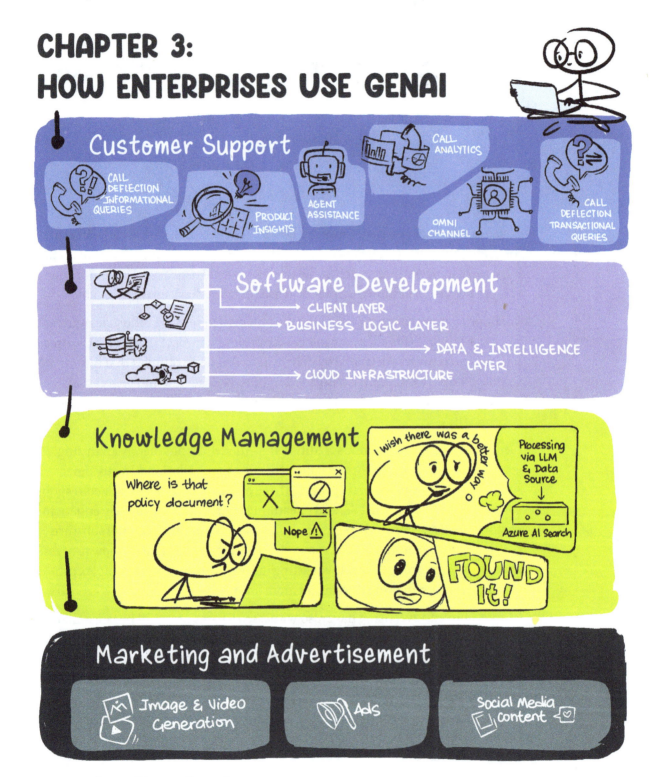

Figure 3-1. What you'll learn in Chapter 3.

transformed, with GenAI extracting meaning- ful knowledge from vast datasets, facilitating informed decision making and propelling em- ployee efficiency and innovation (Figure 3-2).

In Chapter 2, we looked at consumer use cas- es for GenAI. We pointed out that GenAI is great for creating first drafts, and that busi- ness-to-consumer (B2C) AI products are successful if they can reduce friction, increase accuracy, improve scalability, and/or add efficiency. In this chapter, we will look mostly at enterprise use cases for GenAI. Business- to-business (B2B) software has to address the needs of the buyer, not just the user. Buyers, for the most part, are interested in scale and effi- ciency. Across customer support, engineering, knowledge management, and marketing, the lens that buyers look through when adopting GenAI is focused on whether nontechnical users can do things that used to be reserved for technical users (scale) and whether tasks that used to require manual effort can be done automatically (efficiency).

We believe that this focus on scale and efficiency can be somewhat short-sighted. It is possible to use GenAI to affect the business metrics associ- ated with even non-AI products. For example, it is possible to reduce the friction associated with using complex software using agentic systems (we will cover agentic systems in Chapter 4). By endowing agents with tools, it is possible to in- crease the accuracy with which enterprise tasks are carried out. However, this is an area that is still in flux at the time we are writing this chap- ter (early 2025). Even in enterprise use cases, we

encourage you to go beyond scale and efficiency. Consider how you can reduce the friction and increase the accuracy with which your enter- prise products are being employed.

In this chapter, we'll examine real-world case studies and practical implementations to shed light on the tangible benefits and transformative potential of generative AI across these diverse fields. We will explore how organizations are leveraging this technology to achieve operation- al excellence, enhance customer experiences, streamline workflows, drive innovation, and ultimately gain a competitive edge in the dig- ital age. By the end of this chapter, we hope to convince you that generative AI is not merely a technological advancement but a catalyst for change, with the potential to reshape industries, redefine processes, and unlock new possibilities. More importantly, we hope that this detailed examination helps you look at your own domain of expertise with new eyes, and to recognize the potential of GenAI to drive a transformational change in your own business.

At the same time, it is important to realize that GenAI is not a panacea—the shortcomings we discussed in Chapter 1 do exist. Therefore, successful use cases of GenAI will have to be designed around the problems of nondeter- minism, limits of the training data, hallucina- tion, toxicity, and bias. Additionally, taking a methodical, selective approach to AI adoption, focused on well-defined problems with clear success metrics, is often more effective than broad implementation.

1. CUSTOMER SUPPORT

Improving customer satisfaction with AI-powered assistance

- Real-time help
- Issue Resolution

2. CODE GENERATION

Accelerating development with AI-powered coding

GenAI wrote this!

3. KNOWLEDGE MANAGEMENT

Finding information across enterprise system

Exactly what you need from your enterprise data.

GENAI ENTERPRISE USE CASES

4. DATA ANALYSIS

Democratizing insights with conversational analytics

Natural-language data queries

5. MARKETING & ADVERTISING

Scaling personalized content creation

AI-generated ad copy

AI-generated image

6. ENTERPRISE INTEGRATION

Connecting enterprise systems with intelligent automations

GenAI

TRANSFORMING ENTERPRISES THROUGH GENERATIVE AI

Figure 3-2. Enterprise use cases for GenAI.

CUSTOMER SUPPORT

In this section, we explore how generative AI revolutionizes customer support, transforming it from a reactive, often frustrating experience into a proactive, personalized, and efficient one. We'll show you how companies harness GenAI's ability to understand and generate human-like language, empowering them to automate mundane tasks, enhance agent performance, and elevate customer satisfaction.

Startups such as Cresta (*https://cresta.com*) and Sierra AI (*http://sierra.ai*) are leading the way in building and validating GenAI capabilities in the call center. More traditional providers of telephony software are also catching up, so by the time you read this book, these capabilities may be widespread across the industry.

Cresta shared some fascinating insights with us about how AI-enhanced customer support drives product adoption, which in turn fuels revenue growth. We'll explore how enterprises can leverage GenAI in clever ways, from real-time agent assistance and automated ticket routing to sentiment analysis and personalized recommendations.

Now, let's dive into the exciting capabilities that GenAI brings to customer support. We'll show you how combining natural language understanding, high-quality voice generation, and accurate AI-enabled retrieval unlocks several exciting use cases, as illustrated in Figure 3-3.

Call Deflection

It has long been possible to handle a large subset of calls automatically using AI (this is called call deflection). As early as 2018, Marks & Spencer, a UK retailer, saw a 50% reduction in call volumes to stores after they began routing calls through an AI tool (*https://oreil.ly/znlTy*). Until about 2022 (*https://oreil.ly/Uj_-Q*), Marks & Spencer did call deflection by transcribing the calls ("speech-to-text"), classifying the intent using text classification models, and either routing the calls to live agents or answering the questions directly and voice encoding the answer ("text-to-speech"). Because of this cumbersome process, the latency involved with call deflection was high. The only calls that could be deflected involved informational queries such as store hours that did not involve follow-up questions.

The advent of GenAI has changed the landscape of what's possible. Newer deployments of voice AI that are based on GenAI can use AI agents to gather inputs from the users and invoke backend APIs. The newer voice models operate "live" or in streaming mode and even allow users to interrupt the bot and change the topic. ADT, a home security company, has used GenAI from Sierra AI to automate its handling of many customer requests, even those that go beyond merely asking for information. For example, its AI agent can help a customer troubleshoot why their alarm is beeping (*https://oreil.ly/Hb6no*). By November 2024, the AI agent was handling around two million inquiries per month. This frees up human agents to handle time-sensitive life- and property-threatening security incidents.

Because of their reliance on text classification and predesigned conversational flows, early versions of voice AI required engineers to anticipate

Figure 3-3. A capabilities matrix for GenAI-powered customer support use cases, graphed to show difficulty level with respect to value created.

users' every possible utterance and design conversational flows starting from each of these utterances. This was of course an impossible demand since there are so many ways to phrase any request. The resulting bots' inability to understand user requests led to customer frustration and destruction of brand value. In 2016, for example, the *Wall Street Journal* deployed a bot that made it impossible for users to unsubscribe (*https://oreil.ly/vLW9d*). However, now GenAI-based agents can understand natural language and respond in a comprehensive and informative way, even to unforeseen prompts and questions. This allows for more natural conversations, leading to a more engaging and productive customer experience.

The limitations of this technology, however, go beyond the need for more natural conversation flows and for supporting many different ways of asking a question. Today's customers also expect seamless interactions across multiple channels—something many businesses struggle to provide. For example, they may expect to be able to reach customer support via WhatsApp or text responses during a voice call to avoid painfully spelling out product/model IDs or street names. We often see customers become frustrated when transitioning between channels. They might start an application online but need to complete it with an agent, or find that their information doesn't carry over from one touchpoint to another. This disjointed approach leads to repetitive interactions, increased customer effort, and lower satisfaction.

Generative AI streamlines these hybrid or omnichannel customer journeys by integrating data gathered from text, call, web, and social media interactions to create a unified view of each customer's journey. For instance, when a customer starts an application on the web and later connects with an agent, the AI provides the agent with a comprehensive summary of the customer's previous interactions and current needs summary (more on that later in this section). It can then dynamically generate personalized scripts and recommendations for human agents, ensuring continuity across channels. GenAI-based call deflection helps with automatic resolution if possible (see Figure 3-4), and then escalates to humans, passing along gathered information, and helps analyze sentiment, prioritization, and routing effectively.

Call Analytics

Call centers often struggle to efficiently evaluate human agent performance and identify areas for improvement across large volumes of customer interactions. Traditionally, managers have had to manually review calls. Since there is a limit to how many calls a manager can review, it's difficult to gain a comprehensive view of call quality and agent effectiveness.

As illustrated in Figure 3-5, GenAI solutions for conversational use cases can apply advanced natural language processing (NLP) and machine learning techniques to call transcripts, automatically identifying crucial metrics, such as key performance indicators (KPIs) and leading indicators, across entire call datasets. These tools can also monitor calls in real time for leading indicators, which might include proper greetings, adherence to scripts, and successful upsell attempts. The AI models slice these metrics by individual agent and by workload type, providing granular insights into performance patterns.

HOW DOES CALL DEFLECTION WORK?

 VOICE    CHAT    SOCIAL   WEB

GenAI Processing

Natural Language Processing

Processes the natural language query from user

Context Analysis

Understands context pertaining to the question

Intent Recognition

Understands the question's intent

Auto-Resolution

Information Queries

Troubleshooting

Status Checks

Resolve queries automatically using AI

Automated Tasks

Call Notes

CRM Updates

Documentation

Makes automatic updates to backend systems

Hand off to Human Agent

Complex Issues

Escalations

High Priority

Queries that cannot be handled automatically by AI are sent to human agent

Figure 3-4. Call deflection resolves issues automatically if possible; if not, it escalates to humans, passing along the information it has gathered to support the customer efficiently.

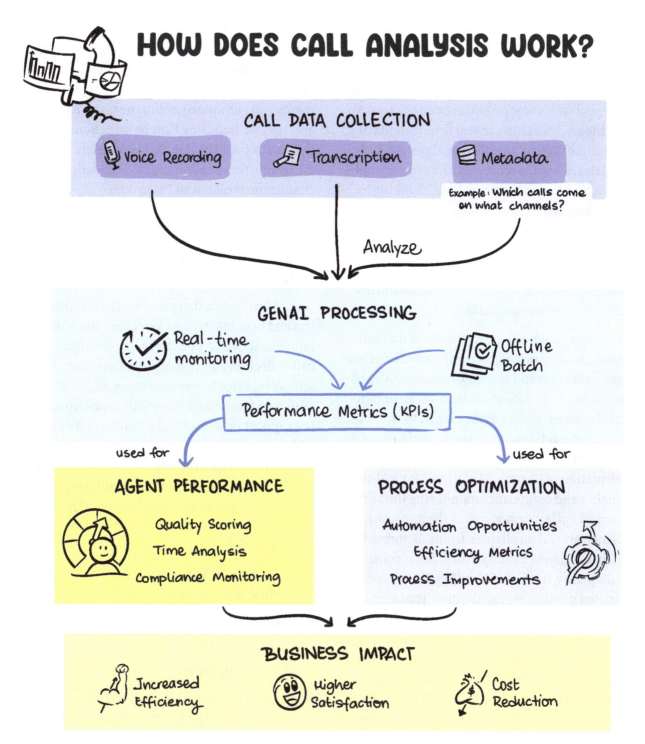

HOW DOES CALL ANALYSIS WORK?

CALL DATA COLLECTION

Voice Recording · Transcription · Metadata

Example: Which calls come on what channels?

Analyze

GENAI PROCESSING

Real-time monitoring · Offline Batch

Performance Metrics (KPIs)

used for · used for

AGENT PERFORMANCE

Quality Scoring
Time Analysis
Compliance Monitoring

PROCESS OPTIMIZATION

Automation Opportunities
Efficiency Metrics
Process Improvements

BUSINESS IMPACT

Increased Efficiency · Higher Satisfaction · Cost Reduction

Figure 3-5. By using AI to analyze call transcripts for key performance indicators, call center operations can improve their operations, ensure compliance, and improve customer satisfaction.

The process can be broken down into a few steps: In call analytics, voice recordings and transcripts are analyzed to extract performance metrics. You also look at metadata such as which types of calls come on what channels. You can do the analysis either in real time (monitoring) or offline (batch). In either case, you get KPIs, which are used to score agents, ensure compliance, and understand how long it's taking to handle specific types of calls. The KPIs can also identify automation opportunities to deflect calls and to improve performance and efficiency metrics. As a result, call centers can improve their operations, ensure compliance, and improve customer satisfaction.

Ping Wu, CEO of Cresta, points out that call analysis often provides an impetus to improve call deflection and task automation by identifying which subtasks or call intents can be handled automatically. Cresta uses AI to streamline those interactions, boost agent efficiency, and drive revenue growth. Snap Finance's implementation of Cresta's AI platform for real-time quality and compliance monitoring (*https://oreil.ly/3gSDg*) demonstrates the impact of Generative AI on all three fronts. Before using GenAI, Snap's challenges included inconsistent call quality, inefficient handling times, and limited monitoring capabilities. Traditional random sampling for quality assurance was inadequate. Cresta's solution provided real-time assistance to Snap's agents, ensuring consistent language and compliance and allowing for comprehensive performance evaluation. By utilizing GenAI, Snap Finance enhanced its call deflection, task automation, and call analytics,

resulting in better customer experiences, improved operational metrics, and increased employee satisfaction. Based on AI analysis of 100% of calls, Snap achieved operational improvements and automated mundane tasks, reducing average call-handling time by 40%. Some of these calls could be handled completely by the AI agent—these calls increased the deflection/containment rate from 7% to 30%.

According to Wu, using GenAI has improved operational efficiency and employee satisfaction at Snap Finance, as shown by its Net promoter and engagement scores.

It's not just Cresta that provides these capabilities and benefits. Weight Watchers' implementation of Sierra's AI platform demonstrates that call deflection can enable more customers to self-serve. Prior to implementing AI, Weight Watchers faced challenges with time-consuming support processes and a limited ability to scale customer interactions about its weight-loss program. Weight Watchers deployed GenAI to handle its specialized product terminology and customer interactions. Based on initial results (*https://oreil.ly/wpSft*), the AI system accomplished the following:

- Achieved a 70% case-handling rate within the first week of deployment

- Maintained customer satisfaction scores above 4.6 out of 5

- Significantly reduced average handle times

- Successfully managed nuanced program-specific language, like the "Points" system

- Met security and compliance requirements

The AI solution provided consistent responses across multiple customer touchpoints, leading Weight Watchers to plan broader deployment across their support operations and deflect calls to AI where needed.

Product Insights

When companies fail to gain timely, actionable insights from customer interactions, they miss opportunities to address emerging issues and improve their products. Traditional methods of gathering product feedback move slowly, require intensive labor, and often overlook subtle trends or infrequent but significant problems.

Generative AI solutions can aid in generating insights about trending issues and emerging patterns in product usage and customer satisfaction. They analyze vast amounts of customer interaction data from calls, chats, and surveys, detecting subtle linguistic cues and sentiment shifts that might escape human analysts, to highlight potential product flaws or areas for enhancement.

As Figure 3-6 shows, GenAI helps companies build product improvement flywheel by flywheel, by detecting problematic patterns in customer interactions, prioritizing them by impact and frequency, identifying and making improvements to the product to address these problems, and validating that the changes fix the original problem.

Agent Assistance

So far, we've noted a few ways that GenAI tools can help human call center agents provide quick, accurate, and personalized responses to customer inquiries. Their jobs often require them to navigate multiple information systems, recall extensive product knowledge, and maintain a consistently high level of service quality across numerous interactions, often while dealing with complex issues or unfamiliar topics.

For example, United Airlines faced persistent challenges with customer wait times and operational inefficiencies in its chat support system. The airline partnered with Cresta to implement their Agent Assist platform, which leverages generative AI to provide real-time support to service agents. The system offers immediate behavioral guidance, smart compose capabilities, and contextual response suggestions, helping agents navigate customer interactions more effectively (see Figure 3-7). The results were significant: within just 45 days of implementation, United saw a 15% improvement in agent response time while simultaneously reducing average handle time by 15% (*https://oreil.ly/JJVKA*). The impact extended beyond operational metrics, with 90% of agents reporting positive experiences and an impressive 97% employee satisfaction rate. Additionally, the platform enhanced supervisory capabilities, increasing coaching efficiency by 30%. This transformation demonstrates how generative AI, when thoughtfully implemented in agent assist tools, can simultaneously enhance operational efficiency, employee satisfaction, and customer experience in large-scale customer service operations.

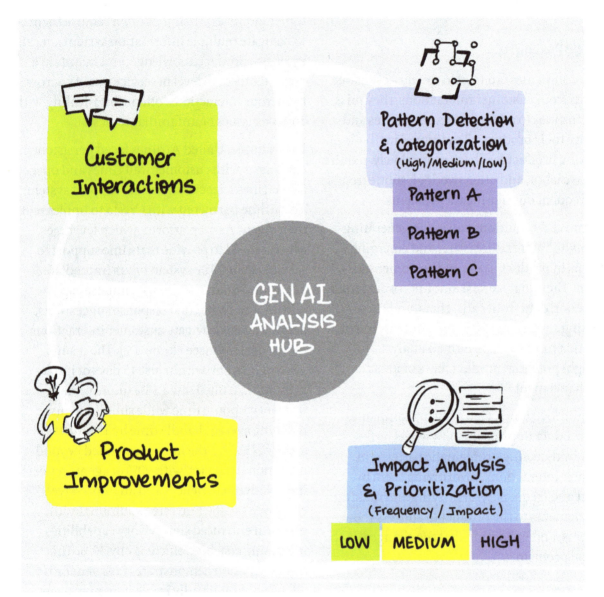

Figure 3-6. How GenAI powers the product insights flywheel, from customer interactions to pattern detection, impact analysis, and finally product improvements.

AGENT ASSISTANCE: CRESTA'S PLATFORM

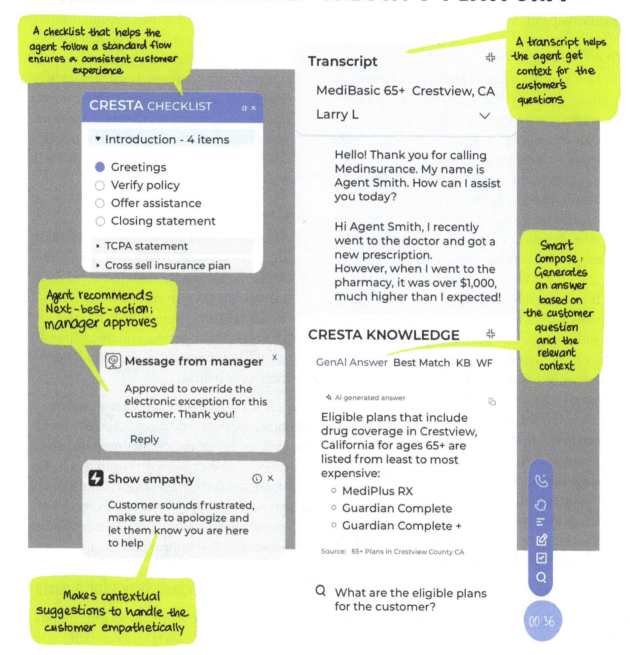

A checklist that helps the agent follow a standard flow ensures a consistent customer experience

CRESTA CHECKLIST

▼ Introduction - 4 items

● Greetings
○ Verify policy
○ Offer assistance
○ Closing statement

‣ TCPA statement
‣ Cross sell insurance pian

Agent recommends Next-best-action; manager approves

👤 **Message from manager**   ✕

Approved to override the electronic exception for this customer. Thank you!

Reply

⚡ **Show empathy**   ⓘ ✕

Customer sounds frustrated, make sure to apologize and let them know you are here to help

Makes contextual suggestions to handle the customer empathetically

Transcript

MediBasic 65+ Crestview, CA

Larry L   ⌄

A transcript helps the agent get context for the customer's questions

Hello! Thank you for calling Medinsurance. My name is Agent Smith. How can I assist you today?

Hi Agent Smith, I recently went to the doctor and got a new prescription. However, when I went to the pharmacy, it was over $1,000, much higher than I expected!

CRESTA KNOWLEDGE

GenAI Answer Best Match KB WF

✦ AI generated answer

Eligible plans that include drug coverage in Crestview, California for ages 65+ are listed from least to most expensive:

○ MediPlus RX
○ Guardian Complete
○ Guardian Complete +

Source: 65+ Plans in Crestview County CA

🔍 What are the eligible plans for the customer?

Smart Compose: Generates an answer based on the customer question and the relevant context

00:36

Figure 3-7. An example of Cresta's Agent Assistance screen with a fictional healthcare customer.

There are several areas where GenAI systems can have a significant impact on business operations:

Intelligent suggestions

GenAI systems can act as real-time copilots during calls, analyzing customer queries and conversation context to suggest relevant responses, ranging from simple phrases and sentences to complete paragraphs, tailored to the inquiry and the conversation history. They can also evaluate the agent's performance in real time, offering suggestions for improving their tone, empathy, or problem-solving approaches. (See the section on "Quality assurance and coaching.") Vendors of agent assistance solutions claim that agents appreciate AI suggestions as a safety net, especially when dealing with complex queries or during high-stress moments. It helps them feel more confident knowing they have backup. Less experienced agents often find real-time suggestions particularly valuable for learning proper phrasing and tone, helping them ramp up more quickly. However, we must consider the flip side of these suggestions, too: agents might feel distracted by pop-ups while trying to focus on customers, struggle to maintain their authentic communication style, or find suggestions unnecessary when they're already experienced.

Knowledge base integration

AI assistants can automatically pull related documents, policies, and product information from vast knowledge bases, presenting agents with the most pertinent details at the right moment. This reduces the agents' need to search for information manually, reducing response times and ensuring that customers receive accurate and up-to-date answers. One agent from a Fortune 500 financial services company says (*https://oreil.ly/p5kKy*), "It truly helps me quickly glimpse to see if the content matches my needs without adding time to my call by having to look for relevant resources! Also, having the ability to share why a resource wasn't helpful is beneficial so that improvements can be made to tailor the responses we're given."

Next-best-action recommendations

AI assistants can also recommend the best action for an agent to take next. This could involve escalating the issue to a supervisor, transferring the customer to a different department, or offering a specific product or service, depending on the customer's needs, the agent's expertise, and the company's policies.

The impact of real-time agent assistance on customer support is profound. Agents now have the tools and information they need to deliver exceptional service quickly, resulting in higher customer satisfaction and loyalty. Additionally, this technology improves agent efficiency and reduces the need for extensive training, leading to cost savings and improved scalability.

Automating mundane tasks for agents

GenAI's biggest strength is automating mundane, repetitive tasks of the sort that have traditionally burdened customer support agents, like updating backend systems and the customer relationship management (CRM) system, taking notes, routing tickets, and drafting email responses:

Call notes and summaries

AI-powered tools can automatically transcribe and summarize customer interactions, extracting key information and insights. This eliminates the need for agents to manually take notes, saving them valuable time and ensuring that they don't overlook crucial details. This not only improves accuracy but also ensures that all pertinent information is documented for future reference. Brinks Home reported after-call tasks have drastically decreased, saving more than 600 hours of typing time due to auto-notetaking (*https://oreil.ly/R3Nl8*).

Updating the CRM system

AI tools can automatically update CRM systems with information gleaned from interactions. This helps ensure that customer data remains up-to-date and readily accessible.

Ticket routing

AI can intelligently route customer inquiries to the most appropriate agent or department based on the nature of the issue, the customer's history, and the agent's expertise. This streamlines workflows and reduces resolution times.

Smart Compose

AI can generate draft responses to customer inquiries, which agents can then review and customize. This can significantly speed up response times, especially for routine queries.

These tasks, while essential, often consume significant time and energy, leaving agents with less capacity to focus on building rapport with customers and resolving complex issues. By automating these mundane tasks, you can improve not only customer service, but also agents' job satisfaction and help reduce burnout. From an organizational perspective, automating mundane tasks enables companies to handle a higher volume of inquiries without sacrificing quality or increasing headcount. Automating data entry and documentation also minimizes the risk of human error.

As Cresta's Wu aptly puts it, "With AI reaching an inflection point, companies across industries are trying to navigate the hype and determine how to use this technology to drive more business efficiencies." Snap Finance, United Airlines, and Weight Watchers all exemplify how companies can use generative AI to empower agents with real-time guidance, turning every customer interaction into a learning opportunity.

The benefits of real-time agent assistance extend beyond immediate interactions. By capturing and analyzing conversation data, generative AI identifies patterns and trends that companies can use to improve training programs, refine knowledge bases, and optimize overall customer support strategies. This continuous learning and improvement cycle ensures that customer support remains agile and adaptable in an ever-evolving landscape.

Quality assurance and coaching

Using generative AI in quality assurance (QA) and coaching in call centers shifts the paradigm from reactive, sample-based evaluations to proactive, comprehensive analysis of every customer interaction. Manually reviewing a limited number of calls is time-consuming, resource-intensive, and prone to human bias and oversight. The limited sample means that such reviews often miss critical insights and fail to provide a holistic view of each agent's performance.

Because generative AI tools can process vast amounts of data and identify patterns at scale, they remove that limitation by analyzing every interaction. This helps it uncover subtle trends, recurring issues, and areas where agents excel or struggle at a granular level, helping QA teams identify coaching opportunities and tailor their training programs to address specific needs.

The benefits of this data-driven approach to QA and coaching are manifold. Automating the evaluation process also reduces the burden on QA analysts and ensures greater consistency in scoring and feedback. Agents receive more targeted and actionable feedback, so they can develop their skills and improve their performance faster. Organizations can identify and address systemic issues more effectively, ensuring consistent service quality across all customer interactions. In terms of coaching, GenAI solutions such as Cresta Coach (*https://oreil.ly/NoNKC*) and Gong (*https://www.gong.io*) can discover agent behaviors, connect them to business outcomes to pinpoint what really matters, and surface specific coaching actions for every agent.

As AI models become more adept at understanding nuanced conversations and identifying subtle emotional cues, they will play an increasingly important role in enhancing the quality and effectiveness of customer support interactions.

Holiday Inn, for example, transformed its contact center operations by implementing a GenAI solution to address coaching and support challenges (*https://oreil.ly/Fp6Z8*). The AI tools enabled managers to monitor multiple calls simultaneously and provided agents with real-time assistance through hints and suggested responses integrated with the company's knowledge base. The results were substantial: bookings per day increased 42%, conversion rates rose 30% (despite reduced call volume), employee satisfaction improved from 47% to 70%, and agent attrition dropped from 120% to 60%.

The Future of Generative AI in Customer Support

As AI models grow increasingly sophisticated, we anticipate a range of transformative advancements that will redefine how businesses engage with and serve their customers. Conversational AI agents, already common in many customer support settings, will navigate intricate dialogues, decipher nuanced language, and provide solutions to multifaceted problems with increasing skill. Generative AI will also normalize personalized self-service options, such as intelligent chatbots and virtual assistants, so customers can find answers and resolve issues independently. Perhaps most excitingly, data analysis will allow generative AI to identify patterns that help it proactively anticipate and address customers' potential issues or questions before they arise. This capability will enable businesses to reach out to customers with preemptive solutions, personalized offers, or relevant information, enhancing their satisfaction and loyalty.

In the next section, we'll move from customer support to software development, looking at how GenAI is changing how developers work.

CODE REVIEW AND GENERATION

The second area where there is quite a bit of evidence emerging on the usefulness of GenAI is in software engineering. In a study conducted with Accenture (*https://oreil.ly/ySKea*), 67% of respondents reported using GitHub Copilot, a GenAI-powered coding assistant, at least five days per week.

Amazon CEO Andy Jassy stated in a LinkedIn post (*https://oreil.ly/YtuNc*) that Amazon migrated 30,000 applications from Java 8/11 to Java 17. This reduced the time to migrate an application from 50 developer-days to just a few hours, thus saving the company 4,500 developer-years of development work. Airbyte 10x-ed the speed of building connectors to their platform by enabling an AI to build API integrations to their platform, starting from the documentation of the API to be integrated (*https://oreil.ly/P_mPe*). Microsoft published a research study that claims that developers who used GitHub Copilot completed a given programming task 55% faster than developers who didn't use the tool (*https://oreil.ly/13QyQ*). In its October 2024 earnings call, Alphabet CEO Sundar Pichai claimed that 25% of code at Google was being written by AI (*https://oreil.ly/K_9ur*).

Take these anecdotes with a grain of salt, though. It is unlikely that the 4,500 developer-year savings that Andy Jassy attributes to the project were all driven by AI. Klaus Häuptle notes that the project also used OpenRewrite, an open source code refactoring tool and that, in his experience, 80% of the reported savings were likely achieved using deterministic recipes (*https://oreil.ly/hiBOW*). The OpenRewrite

recipe for Java 17 migration is the result of active development (*https://oreil.ly/o76JC*). The Airbyte use case, which uses Fractional AI, is a very narrow use case that requires generating the code to call an already-existing API to land data into a known system. But even this very narrow use case required several months of effort and a highly skilled team. The AI works, but only because it was *carefully built* to handle many edge cases. Code generation is not plug-and-play, let alone code generation when the requirements are not as clear-cut. Programmers do more than just code—they solve problems, so improvements on a well-defined programming task such as that described in the study by GitHub do not capture the actual improvement in productivity. Anonymous Google engineers claimed that the 25% figure attributed code completion, even of a single line of code, wholly to AI. If Google is launching products 25% faster, it is not readily apparent. Google has not been reducing the number of engineers working on its high-priority products.

That said, it is clear that GenAI does improve programming. Both authors of this book have been using GenAI coding assistants in their work and find that they enter an "in the flow" stage more often, and for longer, when using GenAI. The use of GenAI coding assistants, such as GitHub Copilot built into VS Code and PyCharm, has greatly reduced the number of times we have to read documentation or refer to Stack Overflow. That said, AI-generated code is not ready to use as-is. Instead, as we discussed in Chapter 2, GenAI provides great first drafts.

GENAI-POWERED CODE GENERATION & REVIEW

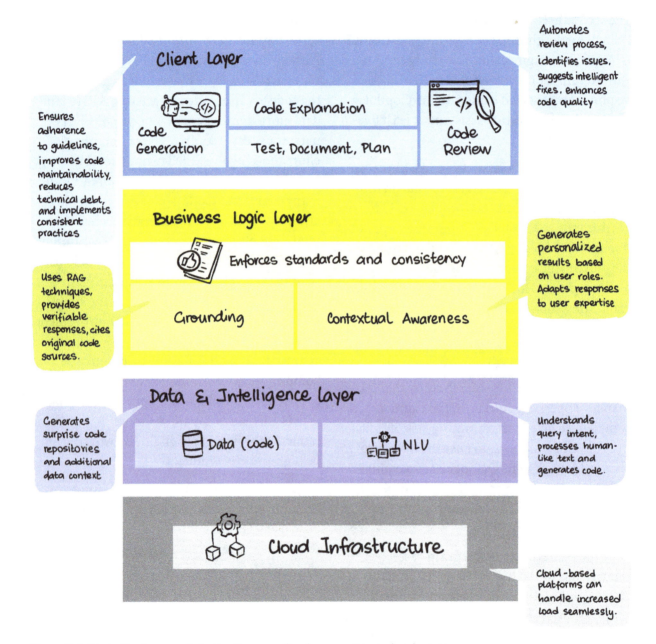

Figure 3-8. Illustrative framework for GenAI-powered code generation and code review.

Harvard Business School carried out a two-year study of 187k developers by examining their activity logs (*https://oreil.ly/wouQO*). The researchers found that developers using AI shifted task allocation toward their core work of coding, and away from noncore tasks such as project management—programmers using AI spent 12% more time on technical coding work, with junior developers benefiting the most.

Developers are using agentic coding assistants like Anthropic's Claude Code to streamline code reviews, automate code generation, and enhance overall efficiency. Industry giants like Microsoft, with its Copilot tool, and Google, with Gemini Code Assist, are vying to lead this charge, but a multitude of innovative startups and smaller players such as Windsurf (formerly Codeium), Tabnine, Replit, CodeRabbit, Augment, Cursor, and Sourcegraph are also emerging, each contributing its own distinct flavor to this rapidly evolving space. There have also been well-publicized fiascos. For example, Cognition Labs has been accused of fabricating a compelling demo of a coding assistant named Devin (*https://oreil.ly/dDejs*).

We spoke to Brandon Jung of Tabnine and Harjot Gill of CodeRabbit to separate fact from fiction. When we asked them how developers harness their GenAI coding assistants, they mentioned the ability to automate repetitive tasks, bolster code quality, and slash development time.

As summarized in Figure 3-8, a GenAI-powered code generation and review illustrative framework consists of four interconnected layers that enable intelligent software development. It is built on a robust cloud-based infrastructure layer that provides scalable computing resources to handle increased workloads seamlessly. Above this foundation sits the data and intelligence layer, which combines a comprehensive code database that integrates with enterprise repositories with natural language understanding (NLU) capabilities to process queries and generate human-like text responses.

The business logic layer builds upon these capabilities by implementing grounding techniques and maintaining contextual awareness to enforce enterprise-specific coding standards and consistency. This layer is crucial for ensuring code maintainability, reducing technical debt, and delivering personalized results based on user roles and expertise. It employs RAG techniques to provide verifiable responses with proper citation of original code sources.

At the topmost level, the client layer serves as the interface for developers, offering key functionalities including code generation, code explanation, testing, documentation, planning, automated code review, and more. This layer streamlines the development process by automatically identifying potential issues, suggesting intelligent fixes, and ultimately enhancing overall code quality through systematic review processes.

Getting Started with a Coding Assistant

Getting started with a coding assistant typically involves a few key steps that are common across most platforms. First, developers need to set up a subscription or account with the chosen coding assistant service. Once access is secured, the next step is to install the appropriate extension or plugin for their preferred integrated development environment (IDE). This usually involves navigating to the IDE's extension marketplace, searching for the coding assistant, and installing it. After installation, users typically need to authenticate their account within the IDE and configure any necessary settings for projects and access. After the setup, developers can begin using the coding assistant directly in their workflow. As you code, the assistant will provide suggestions or autocompletions, or generate code snippets based on context and comments. Some assistants also offer a chat interface, natural language interaction with the code, and editing the files via chat. To maximize the benefits of a coding assistant, it's important to write clear comments, review generated code carefully, and use the tool to enhance productivity rather than replace critical thinking. We also showcase the steps to get started with a coding assistant in Figure 3-9.

Automated Code Generation

At its core, code generation builds on what we've already learned about generative AI as a next-token predictor. However, there's something special about code that makes it particularly well-suited for AI generation compared to natural language text.

When generating natural language, there are countless valid ways to express the same idea, so the AI must choose between many possible correct continuations at each step. But with code, there are typically fewer valid ways to implement a given functionality. The syntax must be precise, the logic patterns are often standardized, and common programming tasks tend to follow similar structures across different projects.

This more constrained nature of code, combined with the vast amount of open source code available for training, helps explain why AI excels at code generation. The models can learn common patterns, idioms, and best practices from millions of real-world examples (Figure 3-10).

Tabnine, which was one of the first AI coding assistants, offers an AI-powered code-completion tool that integrates into existing workflows and provides real-time suggestions, effectively automating the creation of repetitive code snippets. As Brandon Jung, head of product marketing, explained to us, "The simplest boilerplate stuff such as setup and config, common data operations, standard programming patterns, etc., is taken off of the developer's plate so they can do the most complicated stuff."

AI-powered coding assistants address three key areas: data, models, and UI/UX. The goal is to deliver the right code suggestion to the right developer at the right time. This targeted approach particularly benefits newer and junior developers, empowering them to become more productive and write code with greater ease and confidence.

Companies like Tabnine have built on these fundamental capabilities to create practical developer tools. The platform starts by providing intelligent code suggestions and autocompletion all the way to explain, refactor, test, and review code. It leverages open source models, which Tabnine then fine-tunes with a proprietary customer codebase. The code recommendations are highly personalized due to bespoke models trained on the customers' codebase. A personalization service sits in the middle between the Tabnine AI models and the query from the

GETTING STARTED WITH A CODING ASSISTANT

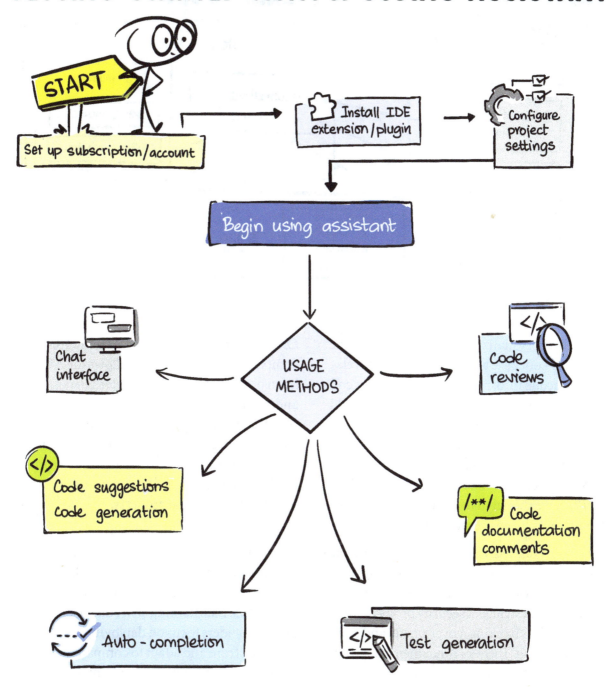

Figure 3-9. General steps to get started with a coding assistant tool.

HOW DOES THE AI-POWERED CODING ─── EXPERIENCE WORK?

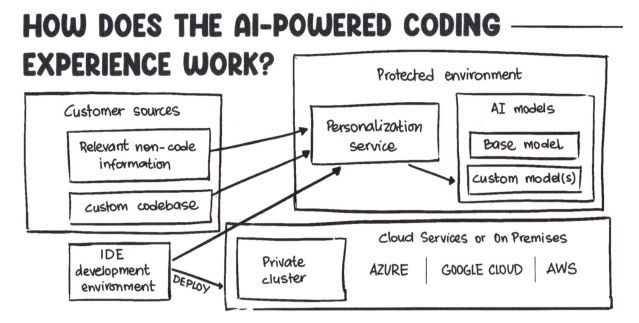

Figure 3-10. How does the AI-powered coding experience work?

user. This personalization service taps into the customer codebase and also dips into the relevant noncode information to map it to the code recommendations that came from Tabnine AI models. This approach ensures that the generated code is both relevant and reliable. This translates into tangible benefits for businesses: studies by NTT, Accenture, and CIT (*https://oreil.ly/xxfFJ*) have shown that Tabnine can increase productivity by an average of 17.5%.

In general code assistance, GenAI solutions also work across industries, tailoring code suggestions to meet the needs of specific organizational standards and stringent security protocols in sectors such as banking, government, and chip manufacturing. There's a fundamental tension in enterprise AI code assistance: companies want the benefits of AI-powered coding tools but are deeply protective of their proprietary codebases.

On the one hand, training an AI model on a company's specific codebase allows the AI to learn organization-specific patterns, standards, and best practices, potentially making developers significantly more productive. On the other hand, companies are increasingly concerned about their code being used to train general-purpose AI models that could benefit competitors or compromise their intellectual property.

As Figure 3-11 illustrates, this has created an opportunity for specialized AI providers who can thread this needle by offering solutions that can be trained or fine-tuned on private codebases while maintaining strict data isolation. These providers focus on deploying models that can learn from and adapt to company-specific patterns without exposing sensitive code to broader training sets. This approach is particularly appealing to industries with heightened

WHAT'S SO SPECIAL ABOUT CODE GENERATION?

What's the foundation of code generation?

Next-token prediction!

That's true for any text generation. What's so special about code generation?

Unlike natural language, with code, there are typically fewer valid ways to implement a functionality.

Ah, because the syntax is precise and the logic patterns are standardized.

Yes, exactly! Plus, there is lots of OSS code available that makes for a great training dataset.

Figure 3-11. GenAI-powered code generation is a special case: LLMs are architected to achieve enterprise-specific coding outcomes.

security requirements and valuable intellectual property, such as financial services, defense contractors, semiconductor manufacturers, and government agencies.

Smaller, specialized AI companies like Tabnine are carving out this niche by prioritizing data privacy and security while still delivering the productivity benefits of AI-assisted coding. Their solutions typically include features like on-premises deployment, isolated training environments, and compliance with industry-specific security protocols—addressing both the technical and compliance requirements of security-conscious enterprises.

Code Reviews

Code reviews are a linchpin of the software development process, in which developers meticulously scrutinize one another's code for errors, vulnerabilities, and adherence to best practices. However, developers often find reviews time-consuming and error-prone. Generative AI automates several processes involved in code review, identifying potential issues and suggesting fixes. This approach accelerates development cycles and helps ensure a higher standard of code quality and consistency (Figures 3-12 and 3-13).

WHY AI-POWERED CODE REVIEWS?

How is that code review coming along?

Three hours in, and I'm still not sure I caught everything. These security checks are killing me!

I can't wait to get AI powered code reviews to flag security issues and style problems automatically.

After missing that SQL injection bug last week.... that actually sounds perfect!

Figure 3-12. Why GenAI-powered code reviews that are architected to achieve enterprise-specific outcomes are getting traction.

CodeRabbit (*https://www.coderabbit.ai*) is an advanced code review platform leveraging generative AI and machine learning to provide automated, intelligent code analysis. The solution employs fine-tuned language models that continuously adapt through user feedback loops and configurable review policies. At its core, CodeRabbit performs differential analysis with file-level granularity, providing semantic understanding of code changes ranging from single-line modifications to complete feature implementations. The platform integrates real-time bidirectional communication for review discussions while combining traditional static analyzers, security scanners, and AI-powered reasoning to achieve optimal signal-to-noise ratios in its recommendations.

The technical architecture incorporates continuous model refinement through supervised learning on user interactions, automated feature extraction from code diffs, and dynamic policy updates based on repository-specific patterns. This is complemented by an extensible integration framework supporting major Git providers (GitHub, GitLab, Azure DevOps) through open authorization (OAuth) authentication, along with connections to popular issue tracking systems like Jira and Linear. The platform operates on a zero-infrastructure software-as-a-service (SaaS) model, featuring automatic updates and horizontal scaling capabilities.

Implementation is straightforward: after installing the CodeRabbit app via your Git platform's marketplace, you configure authentication scopes and optionally define review policies and external integrations. The system automatically triggers on pull request creation or updates, executing a comprehensive pipeline that includes differential analysis, static code review, security scanning, and AI-powered review generation

HOW AI-POWERED CODE REVIEWS WORK

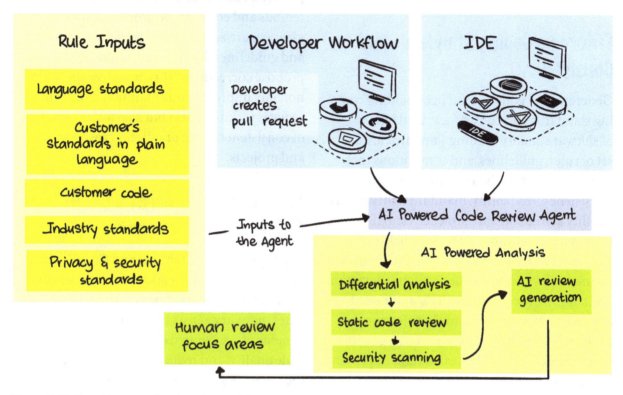

Figure 3-13. How AI-powered code reviews work.

before posting consolidated feedback. This managed service approach eliminates DevOps overhead while maintaining enterprise-grade reliability and security standards, allowing development teams to focus on code quality rather than infrastructure management.

CEO Harjot Gill explains, "We provide AI-driven tooling to help developers improve code quality and streamline code reviews. The AI understands the intent behind code changes better than static analysis tools and can provide contextual fixes." This deeper understanding of context allows CodeRabbit's AI to offer more accurate and relevant suggestions. Its AI-driven

tooling empowers developers to improve code quality and streamline the review process by understanding the intent behind code changes.

Gill adds that "AI can help with higher-level reviews, flagged by AI beforehand," focusing human reviewers' attention where it matters most. He quotes a Fortune 500 financial-services customer as saying, "After implementing CodeRabbit, our code review process was transformed. Time to first review dropped from five days to two, and merge times decreased from four days to just thirteen hours. Most impressively, we saw our team's velocity increase by 36% while reducing forced merges—a rare case of simultaneously improving both speed and quality."

Enforcing Coding Standards and Consistency

Generative AI is also useful in upholding coding standards and consistency, vital pillars of software quality. Coding standards are a set of rules, guidelines, and conventions that developers follow when writing code to ensure consistency, readability, maintainability, and reliability across software projects. GenAI-based code generation and code reviews help enforce automatic analysis of code for adherence to predefined rules and guidelines, flagging deviations and suggesting corrections. This automated approach not only saves time but also ensures a higher level of consistency across large codebases, reducing the risk of errors and improving overall code quality.

AI-powered code review tools can quickly scan vast amounts of code, identifying potential issues, style violations, and security vulnerabilities that human reviewers might overlook. These tools learn from historical data and best practices, continuously improving their ability to recognize patterns and anomalies in code. By leveraging generative AI in both code generation and review processes, development teams can maintain a more uniform coding style, reduce complexity, and accelerate the development cycle while upholding high standards of code quality. This not only improves the maintainability and scalability of software projects but also facilitates easier onboarding of new team members and promotes a culture of excellence in the development team.

As the example in Figure 3-14 shows, AI-powered code reviews automate the often tedious and error-prone process of code review, ensure adherence to predefined rules and guidelines, identify deviations, and even propose corrections. This proactive approach not only improves code maintainability and reduces technical debt but also fosters a culture of consistent coding practices across teams and projects.

The Future of Generative AI in Software Development

The experiences of Tabnine and CodeRabbit underscore the universal appeal of generative AI in software development. While specific use cases may vary across industries, the underlying benefits of accelerated development, improved code quality, and reduced costs resonate across the board. A Harvard Business School working paper by Hoffmann et al. (2024), "*Generative AI and the Nature of Work*" (*https://oreil.ly/uxcwT*), offers a nuanced perspective on the impact of generative AI on software developers' work patterns. The study, which examined the effects of *GitHub Copilot* on open source software developers over a two-year period, revealed significant shifts in task allocation and work approaches. Developers with access to Copilot increased their engagement in core coding tasks while reducing their involvement in project management activities. This change was accompanied by two key mechanisms: an increase in autonomous work and a shift toward more exploratory activities.

CODE REVIEW WITH GENAI: AUTOMATING CODING STANDARDS AND CONSISTENCY

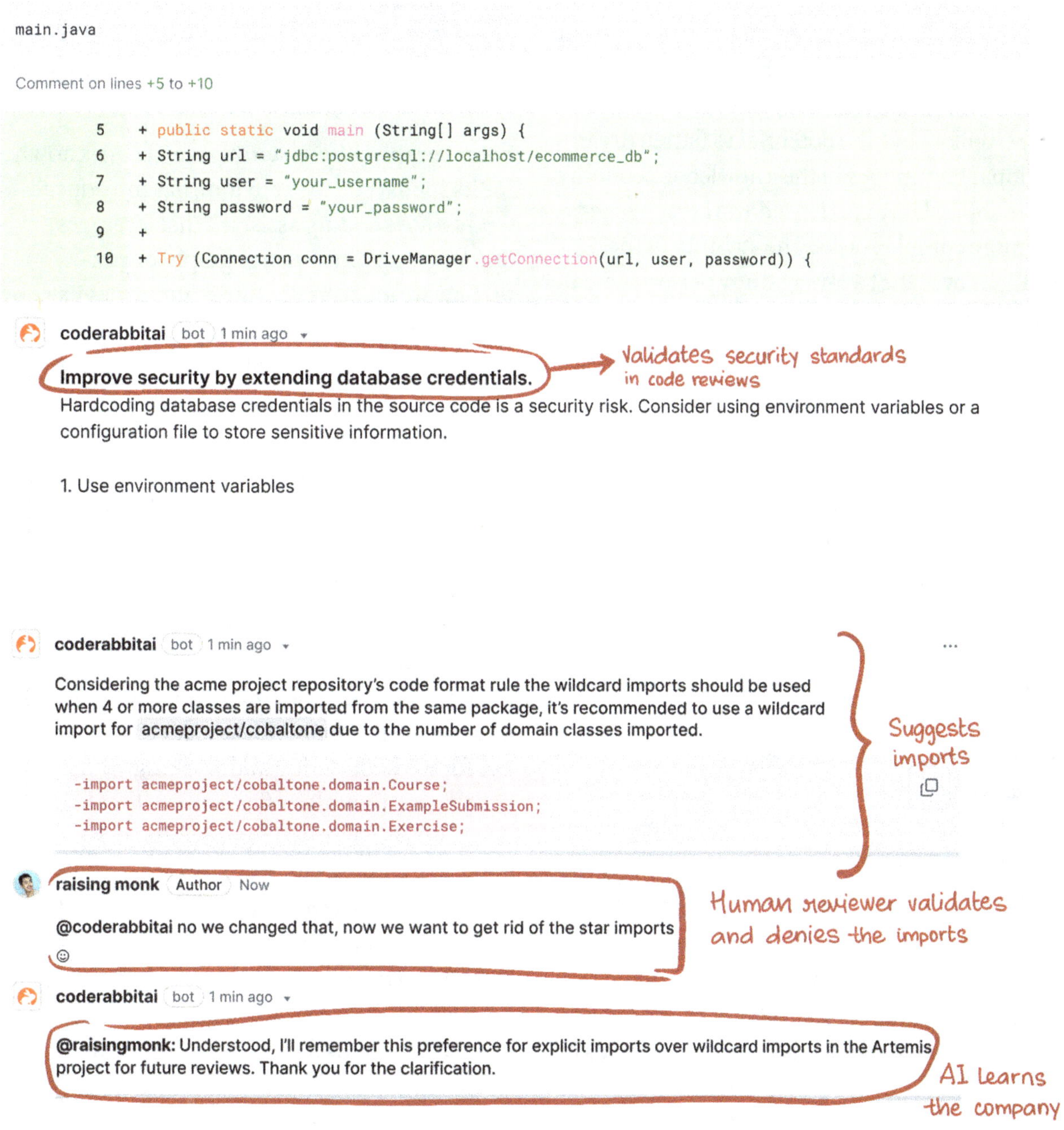

`main.java`

Comment on lines +5 to +10

```java
5  + public static void main (String[] args) {
6  + String url = "jdbc:postgresql://localhost/ecommerce_db";
7  + String user = "your_username";
8  + String password = "your_password";
9  +
10 + Try (Connection conn = DriveManager.getConnection(url, user, password)) {
```

coderabbitai `bot` 1 min ago ▾

Improve security by extending database credentials. *(Validates security standards in code reviews)*

Hardcoding database credentials in the source code is a security risk. Consider using environment variables or a configuration file to store sensitive information.

1. Use environment variables

coderabbitai `bot` 1 min ago ▾   ...

Considering the acme project repository's code format rule the wildcard imports should be used when 4 or more classes are imported from the same package, it's recommended to use a wildcard import for `acmeproject/cobaltone` due to the number of domain classes imported.   *(Suggests imports)*

```
-import acmeproject/cobaltone.domain.Course;
-import acmeproject/cobaltone.domain.ExampleSubmission;
-import acmeproject/cobaltone.domain.Exercise;
```

raising monk Author Now

@coderabbitai no we changed that, now we want to get rid of the star imports ☺   *(Human reviewer validates and denies the imports)*

coderabbitai `bot` 1 min ago ▾

@raisingmonk: Understood, I'll remember this preference for explicit imports over wildcard imports in the Artemis project for future reviews. Thank you for the clarification.   *(AI learns the company)*

Figure 3-14. AI-powered code reviews include validating security standards and integrating company-specific learnings from the codebase and from human feedback.

Interestingly, the study found that these effects were more pronounced among lower-ability developers. When given access to Copilot, these developers showed a greater increase in coding tasks accomplished and a more substantial decrease in project management tasks required compared to their higher-ability counterparts. This finding suggests that generative AI tools like Copilot have the potential to flatten organizational hierarchies in the knowledge economy by enabling less experienced workers to take on more complex tasks. The stability of these changes over the two-year study period indicates that the impact of such AI tools on work patterns may be long-lasting and transformative.

As generative AI continues to evolve, several startups have emerged to challenge the dominant players such as GitHub Copilot. Among these, Augment (*https://www.augmentcode.com*) stands out by offering a unique approach to AI-assisted coding. Augment's AI is trained on code that adheres to best practices, ensuring higher-quality output. It integrates multiple language models, both proprietary and open source, allowing for rapid adaptation to advancements in AI technology. Augment also enhances team collaboration through a Slack chat interface embedded within IDEs and provides inline suggestions for code improvement, even generating entire pull requests when needed.

Cursor (*https://www.cursor.com*), another notable entrant in this space, offers a standalone AI-powered code editor that builds upon the familiar Visual Studio Code interface. It excels in transforming ideas from natural language into functional code and intuitively predicts code edits with smart cursor prediction and multiline suggestions. Cursor's ability to process up to 200k tokens enables it to handle large codebases effectively. Additionally, its privacy mode ensures that code remains secure on the user's machine, addressing significant security concerns.

Sourcegraph (*https://sourcegraph.com*), known for its robust code search tool, has introduced Cody, an AI coding assistant that leverages Sourcegraph's knowledge graph for context-aware answers. Cody distinguishes itself by searching and navigating entire company codebases rather than just individual files or repositories. It integrates seamlessly across various IDEs and Sourcegraph's Code Search engine, and incorporates data from other developer tools such as Jira, Notion, and Linear to enhance its capabilities further.

These startups and their approaches offer distinct advantages. Many developers use multiple tools. Augment's specialized training on vetted code aims for superior quality output. Cursor and Sourcegraph provide enhanced capabilities for understanding and working with larger codebases. They also offer features that facilitate team collaboration and ensure data security—key considerations in modern software development. As the field continues to evolve, we can expect innovative companies to continue expanding the possibilities of AI-assisted development, offering developers more choices and tailored solutions for their specific needs.

KNOWLEDGE MANAGEMENT AND SEARCH

Enterprise knowledge management and search represent one of the most pervasive challenges—and opportunities—in today's business environment. In virtually every enterprise process, from HR to procurement to customer service, employees spend considerable time searching for information across various systems and documents. As Figure 3-15 demonstrates, whether it's a new hire trying to understand benefits policies, a procurement specialist onboarding a supplier, or a sales representative looking for case studies, the ability to quickly find and leverage organizational knowledge is crucial for operational efficiency.

Current State of Enterprise Search

Traditional enterprise search solutions, exemplified by platforms like Elasticsearch (*https://oreil.ly/RsIW7*), have served as the backbone of organizational knowledge retrieval. These solutions typically work by indexing content across various enterprise systems and allowing keyword-based searches. However, they face several significant challenges:

Unstructured data complexity

Most enterprise information exists in unstructured formats—emails, documents, presentations, chat messages, and video recordings. Traditional search systems struggle to effectively index and retrieve information from these diverse formats.

Indexing overhead

Organizations must carefully plan and maintain their indexing strategies, including defining fields, maintaining taxonomies, and regularly updating indices. This requires significant ongoing technical expertise and resources.

Search versus answers gap

Traditional search returns documents or pages that might contain the answer, but users still need to sift through results to find specific information. This distinction between finding documents and finding answers represents a significant productivity burden.

Context understanding

Keyword-based systems often miss relevant results because they don't understand the semantic meaning or context of queries. A search for "supplier onboarding process" might miss a relevant document titled "vendor registration procedures."

These limitations have led to the emergence of new approaches, particularly those leveraging Generative AI. While we'll explore RAG in detail in Chapter 4, it's worth noting that RAG represents a fundamental shift in how enterprises can approach knowledge management and search.

WHY AI-POWERED KNOWLEDGE MANAGEMENT?

Figure 3-15. AI-powered knowledge management gives enterprises an opportunity to make data accessible across multiple systems.

The Evolution of Enterprise Search Solutions

Today's enterprise search landscape is being transformed through three distinct approaches, each catering to different organizational needs and capabilities. The first approach centers on open source solutions, which we'll explore in detail in Chapter 4. Frameworks like LlamaIndex (*https://www.llamaindex.ai*) and LangChain (*https://www.langchain.com*) provide flexible building blocks for custom search solutions, making them particularly attractive for organizations with strong technical teams and specific customization requirements.

The second approach comes from major cloud providers, or hyperscalers, that have developed enterprise search solutions. Google Cloud's Vertex AI Search (*https://oreil.ly/3EgrQ*), Amazon Bedrock (*https://oreil.ly/KkFzB*), and Azure AI Search (*https://oreil.ly/jVExA*) represent this category, offering integrated, scalable platforms that combine traditional search capabilities with advanced AI features. These solutions excel at automated content understanding across multiple languages and formats while maintaining enterprise-grade security and compliance features. Their tight integration with existing cloud infrastructure makes them particularly attractive for organizations already invested in these platforms. They provide comprehensive features, including automated content understanding and indexing, robust multilanguage support, built-in security and compliance controls, and integration with other cloud services.

The third approach involves fully managed solutions from specialized providers like Glean (*https://www.glean.com*), who offer end-to-end knowledge management platforms. Figure 3-16 shows an illustrative architecture of specialized AI-powered knowledge search. The solutions stand out for their comprehensive approach to enterprise search, providing pre-built connectors for common enterprise systems, sophisticated role-based access controls, customized ranking algorithms, and detailed analytics about knowledge usage. They're designed to offer a complete solution that can be implemented with minimal technical overhead while still providing advanced features and customization options.

We spoke with representatives from the Glean team about how GenAI can enhance knowledge management and search capabilities to improve employee productivity, decision making, and overall organizational efficiency.

Stages of the Journey

Leveraging GenAI in knowledge management and search typically unfolds in several distinct stages, each building upon the previous one to create an increasingly sophisticated system:

- The first stage often involves *implementing a basic search and knowledge management solution*. This lays the groundwork by centralizing information and providing rudimentary search capabilities. Organizations at this stage may still be dealing with information silos and limited search accuracy.

HOW AI-POWERED ENTERPRISE KNOWLEDGE SEARCH WORKS

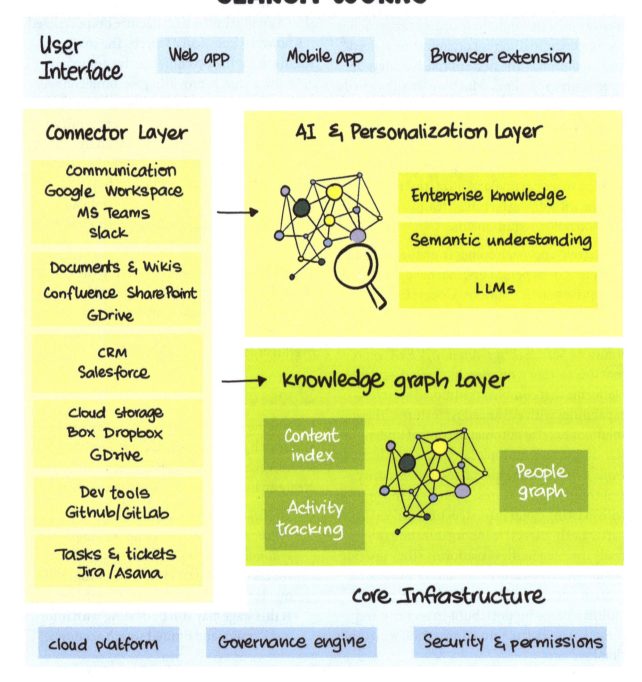

Figure 3-16. Components of AI-powered knowledge search.

- The critical phase of *integrating multiple data sources and systems* brings together disparate information from enterprise applications such as CRM systems, project management tools, and communication platforms. This integration provides a more comprehensive view of the organization's knowledge base, although search capabilities may still be primarily keyword-based.

- *Implementing advanced search techniques* marks a significant leap forward. This is where vector search and embeddings come into play, giving the GenAI model a more nuanced understanding of search queries so that it can deliver more relevant results. At this stage, organizations generally begin to see marked improvements in search accuracy and user satisfaction.

- *Introducing GenAI-powered natural language interfaces* allows users to interact with the knowledge management system by asking questions in everyday language. The system's ability to understand context and intent dramatically improves, making information retrieval more intuitive and efficient.

- *Developing context-aware and personalized search experiences* takes the user's role, previous interactions, and current context into account to deliver highly relevant and personalized results. This stage represents a high level of AI sophistication, where the system not only responds to queries but also anticipates users' needs.

- The final stage is one of *continuous improvement, learning, and expansion*. Organizations at this stage constantly refine their GenAI models, expand use cases across departments, and potentially even extend the system's capabilities to external stakeholders, like customers or partners. The GenAI system becomes an integral part of the organization's operations and decision-making processes.

While these stages provide a general roadmap, the journey is not always linear. Organizations may focus on different aspects simultaneously or revisit earlier stages as new technologies emerge or organizational needs evolve. The key is to maintain a flexible, iterative approach to implementation, always keeping the end goal of improved knowledge management and organizational efficiency in sight.

Some GenAI components that show promise in making knowledge management make the solution work are illustrated in Figure 3-17. Those components include the following:

Comprehensive data integration

GenAI models that can understand and process diverse data types make it easier to integrate information from various sources. A large multinational corporation could use a GenAI-powered knowledge management system that integrates data from Salesforce (customer data), Jira (project management), Confluence (internal documentation), Slack (team communications), and SharePoint (file storage). When an employee asks, "What's the status of Project X for client Y?" the system can pull relevant information from all these sources to provide a comprehensive answer.

Secure and permission-aware access

While not directly a GenAI feature, advanced models can understand and respect access controls. For example, in a healthcare organization, a GenAI search system operates across departments. When a nurse queries about a patient's latest lab results, the system provides only information they're authorized to see based on their role. If a billing department employee makes the same query, they receive different results. This aids in governance, ensuring the system adheres to privacy laws and regulations (such as HIPAA, the Health Insurance Portability and Accountability Act, in the US) and internal access policies.

Advanced search

GenAI enables sophisticated vector search and embedding techniques to improve search relevance and accuracy. For example, a large online retailer could implement a GenAI-powered product search system that uses vector search and embedding techniques. When a customer searches for "breathable running shoes for hot weather," the system will understand the concepts rather than just matching the keywords to return more relevant results. Responses could include the following:

- Lightweight mesh running shoes with good ventilation

- Shoes made with moisture-wicking materials

- Running shoes designed for tropical climates

- Footwear with cooling technology or perforated insoles

These search results are all highly relevant, even if the product descriptions don't contain the exact phrases "breathable" or "hot weather." The system might include shoes described as "engineered mesh upper with enhanced ventilation" or "climate control insole technology," understanding that these features align with the customer's needs. It also ranks results based on customer reviews that mention relevant terms like comfort in warm conditions or performance during summer runs, even if these specific terms weren't used in the original query. This advanced search capability significantly improves the customer experience, making it more intuitive and leading to more accurate product recommendations, particularly for complex or nuanced product searches.

Natural language understanding and generation

GenAI excels at processing and generating human-like text, making interactions more intuitive and effective. As we noted in the earlier section on customer support, a customer support representative at an e-commerce company could ask the GenAI system, "How do I handle a return for a damaged item shipped internationally?" The system will understand the query's intent and generate a step-by-step response, pulling from the company's return policies, international shipping guidelines, and best practices for customer satisfaction.

Contextual awareness

Organizations can train GenAI models on user data to understand employees' roles and provide personalized results. For example, in a financial services firm, when a junior analyst asks, "What's our exposure to emerging markets?" the GenAI system, recognizing their role, would provide a high-level overview with basic explanations. When a senior portfolio manager asks the same question, however, the system would provide a more detailed analysis tailored to their expertise and responsibilities, including specific investment positions and risk assessments.

Grounding AI responses

When a GenAI tool pulls information from a knowledge base, it can provide sources and supporting evidence for its responses, to make them more accurate and verifiable. For example, say a marketing team member at a consumer goods company asks, "What were the key factors in our successful product launch last quarter?" The GenAI system can use RAG techniques to pull information from sales reports, customer feedback, and marketing campaign data. It then generates a response that includes specific metrics, strategies used, and customer testimonials, all linked back to their original sources for verification.

Scalable infrastructure

While not exclusive to GenAI, cloud-based AI platforms like Google Cloud Vertex AI provide the necessary infrastructure to support these advanced models, making it far easier to scale up as needed. For example, a knowledge management system for a rapidly growing startup will experience an increased load of queries, data ingestion, and user accounts as the business expands from 50 to 500 employees in a year. The cloud-based infrastructure allows for expansion of resources without any degradation in performance.

What sets this era of GenAI apart in knowledge management and search is a convergence of technological advancements that significantly enhance user experience and system capabilities. The leap in NLP allows for more nuanced and human-like interactions, while the improved ability to grasp context and user intent leads to more accurate and relevant results. GenAI systems now integrate diverse data sources, creating a more comprehensive knowledge base, and implementing RAG techniques has notably reduced hallucinations. All these improvements culminate in substantial efficiency gains.

The Future of Generative AI in Knowledge Management Systems

The implementation of GenAI in knowledge management and search has yielded impressive results. Arvind Jain, CEO of Glean, claims that one of the most significant impacts of their enterprise search product has been on employee productivity, with users reporting time savings of two to three hours per week. He calls these time savings a significant boost to productivity and attributes the improvement to employees being able to focus on high-value tasks rather than searching for information.

Webflow (*https://oreil.ly/Ss8BV*), for example, faced challenges with information sprawl after rapid growth, leading to productivity issues as employees struggled to find content across multiple systems. To address this, Webflow implemented Glean's AI-powered search solution, which connected over 20 different sources and centralized access to information.

The implementation of Glean significantly improved employee efficiency and knowledge management. It enhanced the onboarding experience for new hires, reduced reliance on tenured employees, and improved overall productivity. Glean also provided unexpected benefits in security and permission governance by offering a single view into all security and permissions across Webflow's documentation.

The success of Glean's implementation at Webflow is evident in several key metrics. About 65% of Webflow employees now regularly use Glean for knowledge discovery. The company collectively saves over 300 hours monthly using Glean search to uncover critical information. Webflow achieved a 3× return on investment from the time collectively saved by leveraging Glean. Furthermore, the improved onboarding

experience allowed new hires to become productive team members more quickly, and Glean enhanced Webflow's ability to identify potential risks as they scaled.

According to Jain, one customer reported a staggering $20 million in savings after deploying a GenAI-powered knowledge management solution. The customer attributed this cost reduction primarily to improved case-resolution times in customer support. Here, Arvind Jain commented, "The ROI our customers are seeing goes beyond our initial projections. It's not just about finding information faster; it's about fundamentally transforming how organizations operate and make decisions."

Arvind Jain concluded by saying, "The frequency of use we're seeing indicates that GenAI-powered knowledge management is becoming an indispensable tool in the modern workplace. It's not just a nice-to-have; it's becoming a core part of how people work."

DATA ANALYSIS AND INSIGHTS

In today's data-driven business landscape, enterprises are grappling with an unprecedented volume of information. The global datasphere is projected to grow from 33 zettabytes in 2018 to 175 zettabytes by 2025 (*https://oreil.ly/0VdwF*), a staggering 61% compound annual growth rate. This exponential increase in data volume presents both opportunities and challenges for organizations seeking to derive actionable insights. Traditionally, extracting value from this data has been a complex, time-consuming process, often restricted to those with specialized technical

skills. However, the advent of generative AI is revolutionizing this paradigm, democratizing data access and analysis across entire organizations.

Current State of Data and Analytics

The current data analytics landscape is characterized by several persistent challenges:

Data silos

Many organizations struggle with fragmented data across departments, hindering a comprehensive view of operations. Studies show that 68% of companies report having data silos that impede their ability to make data-driven decisions (*https://oreil.ly/kiJR0*).

Unstructured data

Approximately 80-90% of enterprise data is unstructured (*https://oreil.ly/gZS66*), making it difficult to analyze using traditional methods. This includes text documents, images, videos, and social media content.

Limited accessibility

Data analysis often requires specialized skills, creating bottlenecks. Business leaders find it challenging to get value from the data due to its complexity or difficulty in access.

Time-consuming process

Obtaining insights can be lengthy. For instance, a sales executive's request for regional sales trend analysis might involve multiple teams and take days to complete. On average, *data scientists spend 45% of their time on data preparation tasks alone.*

Data quality issues

According to Gartner, poor data quality costs organizations an average of $12.9 million annually (*https://oreil.ly/ClOsj*). It not only leads to unreliable results but also impacts decision-making and business strategies.

The Evolution of Data and Analytics Solutions

The introduction of GenAI is transforming the data analytics landscape in several significant ways. Natural language interaction (NLI) has made data querying accessible to nontechnical users, leading to better data utilization. Automated insight generation accelerates the decision-making process within companies. Real-time analysis capabilities have improved operational efficiency, allowing business users to obtain instant insights. GenAI can generate synthetic data to balance datasets and simulate various scenarios, enhancing the quality and breadth of analysis. Reports can be tailored to different audiences, with GenAI adjusting the complexity and focus based on the intended reader.

The implementation of GenAI in data analysis is facilitated through various approaches. LLM frameworks like LlamaIndex and LangChain can be utilized for building GenAI applications that integrate existing data with the application. We cover these in the upcoming chapters. Hyperscaler solutions from major cloud providers like Google Cloud (BigQuery and Looker Studio) and Microsoft (Azure Fabric) provide scalable, enterprise-ready GenAI capabilities within their data platforms. For example, in Looker Studio you can ask questions in natural language and get answers in charts on a dashboard. Specialized managed services, such as *fleet.so* and *Defog.ai,* offer fully managed solutions with text-to-SQL capabilities and industry-specific fine-tuned models.

As **Figure 3-17** shows, the framework consists of four integrated layers enabling intelligent data analysis and insights generation. The foundation is a cloud-based infrastructure layer that provides scalable computing resources to handle increased analytical workloads seamlessly. The

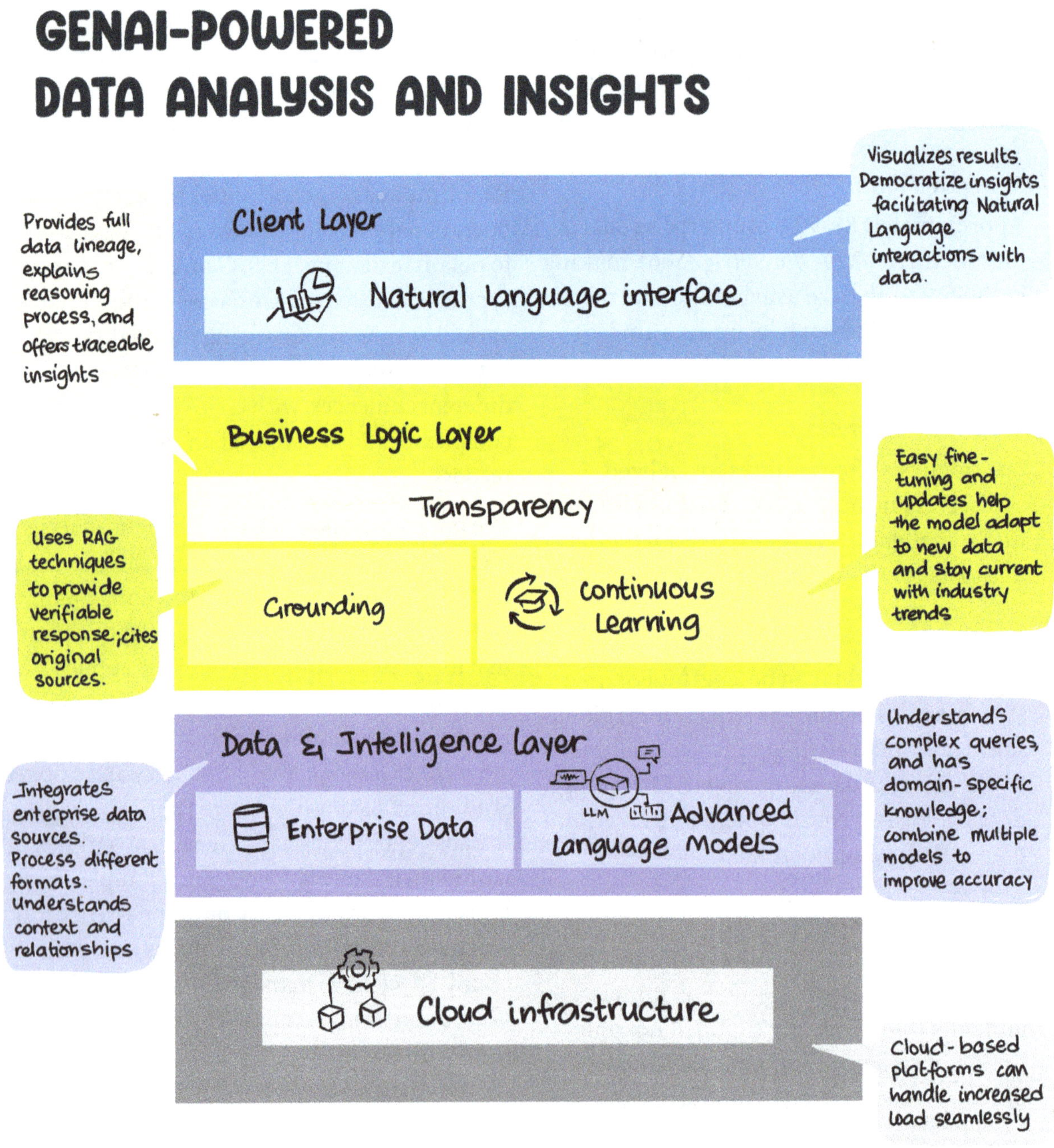

GENAI-POWERED DATA ANALYSIS AND INSIGHTS

Visualizes results. Democratize insights facilitating Natural Language interactions with data.

Provides full data lineage, explains reasoning process, and offers traceable insights

Client Layer

Natural language interface

Business Logic Layer

Transparency

Grounding

Continuous Learning

Uses RAG techniques to provide verifiable response; cites original sources.

Easy fine-tuning and updates help the model adapt to new data and stay current with industry trends

Data & Intelligence layer

Enterprise Data

LLM Advanced Language Models

Integrates enterprise data sources. Process different formats. Understands context and relationships

Understands complex queries, and has domain-specific knowledge; combine multiple models to improve accuracy

Cloud infrastructure

Cloud-based platforms can handle increased load seamlessly

Figure 3-17. What AI-powered data analytics and insights require.

data and intelligence layer above it combines enterprise data sources with advanced language models, enabling complex query understanding and domain-specific knowledge processing for high-accuracy insights.

The business logic layer implements grounding techniques and continuous learning capabilities to ensure transparency and adaptability. This layer employs RAG techniques to provide verifiable responses with citations to original sources, while maintaining transparency in the reasoning process. It enables easy fine-tuning and updates to stay current with industry changes.

At the topmost level, the client layer features a natural language interface that democratizes insights by facilitating intuitive interactions with data. This layer visualizes results and presents insights in an accessible format, allowing users to understand complex data relationships and patterns through NLI. The system integrates enterprise data sources, processes different data formats, and maintains contextual understanding of relationships among data elements to provide comprehensive analytical capabilities.

Stages of the Journey

Implementing GenAI in data analysis and insights involves several interconnected stages, each building upon the last.

Developing robust, domain-specific AI models

This involves fine-tuning existing LLMs for specific industries and use cases. As Fleet founder Nicolai Ouporov told us (*https://www.fleet.so*), Fleet uses "eight to ten models, considering cost, latency, and performance, while benefiting from domain-specific models." This multi-model approach leverages the strengths of each model while mitigating the risks of relying on a single vendor. Fleet takes a unique approach with their headless AI agent, which prioritizes thoroughness over speed. Unlike typical LLMs that provide instant responses, Fleet's solution conducts in-depth research behind the scenes and alerts users when analysis is complete. This research-partner model has proven so effective that customers are specifically hiring analysts to work with Fleet's platform.

Industry-specific adaptations

Different industries require tailored approaches to AI implementations. In the financial sector, AI models need to be fine-tuned to understand complex financial terminology, regulations, and market dynamics. For example, a GenAI model used in financial analysis might be trained on financial reports and statements, market data, economic indicators, regulatory filings, and compliance documents. This fine-tuning enables the model to generate more accurate and relevant insights for financial professionals.

In healthcare, models need to understand medical terminology, drug interactions, and patient data privacy concerns. Fine-tuning might involve the following: training on medical literature and clinical trial data, incorporating knowledge of drug interactions and side effects, and ensuring compliance with HIPAA and other healthcare regulations. For example, when a user mentions a generic variant of a drug, the model should be able to recognize this and provide relevant information about both the brand-name and generic versions, including any differences in efficacy or side effects.

Integrating the AI solution with existing data

Integrating the AI solution with the enterprise's existing data systems is where the rubber meets the road. Defog founder Rishabh Srivastava emphasizes the importance of flexibility here: "We've built something that customers can use in whichever cloud they use." This stage often involves overcoming technical challenges related to data formats, access protocols, and system compatibility. Customers can deploy the solution within their own cloud infrastructure for scalability. For organizations with strict security and compliance requirements, Defog supports on-premises deployment or secure cloud environments with domain-specific models.

Defog (*https://defog.ai*) has achieved accuracy rates up to 99% on customer datasets through its multimodel approach, which combines advanced language models fine-tuned for specific domains. Their focus on text-to-SQL functionality highlights the importance of seamless integration with existing database systems. This capability allows nontechnical users to query databases using natural language, bridging the gap between AI and traditional data storage systems. For instance, in a healthcare setting, a doctor might request, "Show me all patients over 60 who have been prescribed both metformin and lisinopril in the last year." The AI system would need to translate this natural language query into a SQL statement that joins multiple tables (patients, prescriptions, medications) and applies the correct filters. This integration allows

healthcare professionals to access critical information quickly without needing to understand complex database queries.

In the pharmaceutical and healthcare industries, refinement is crucial for handling the complexities of drug information. For example, let's say a user asks, "What are the potential cardiovascular risks of combining Drug X with ACE inhibitors in patients over 65 with a history of hypertension?" The AI system should do the following:

- Recognize the generic name and associate it with brand-name equivalents

- Retrieve information about all variants, including dosage forms and strengths

- Provide up-to-date information on efficacy, side effects, and contraindications

- Provide relevant information from various internal studies, published papers, and regulatory documents

This data lineage and refinement process ensures that healthcare professionals receive comprehensive and accurate information, regardless of how they phrase their queries.

Continuous learning and adaptation capabilities keep the system current with new data and trends. For example, a technology company might use the GenAI system to keep track of emerging technologies and competitor activities. The system could be set up to continuously update its knowledge base with new patent filings, research papers, news articles, and internal reports. When an executive asks about "potential disruptors in our industry," the system would provide up-to-date information, including recent startups or newly announced research that could impact the company's market position.

The key difference between GenAI tools and traditional data-analysis tools is their ability to understand context, handle unstructured queries, and provide human-like analysis at scale. This allows for more intuitive natural language-based interaction with data, faster insight generation, and the ability to handle complex, multidimensional analysis that would be time-consuming or impossible with traditional methods.

The Future of Generative AI in Data Analysis

Both Fleet and Defog report significant efficiency and accuracy improvements among their clients. Ouporov claims that Fleet has seen "a 10×+ improvement in efficiency. Tasks that used to take two to three days in Jupyter Notebooks are now completed in just 45 minutes with Fleet."

Srivastava highlights the substantial time savings Defog's clients report: "When deployed in a 100-person team, we're saving 2500–5000 man-hours per month. We're avoiding back-and-forth

and complex SQL queries, allowing teams to focus on higher-value tasks." He also notes that, without fine-tuning, Defog's model "achieves 94% accuracy, compared to GPT-4's 84%." This high level of accuracy is crucial for building trust in AI-generated insights and ensuring reliable decision support. Both founders hope to see the field evolve toward more autonomous AI analysts capable of proactively generating insights and anticipating needs independently. Srivastava describes Defog's plans as "Building more 'slow thinkers'. All of our products are currently optimized for giving answers quickly. Building products that can start thinking more slowly (for a few hours) to reflect on their insights and come up with follow-on questions themselves (like a human would) is next on the agenda."

While these examples showcase generative AI's potential to transform data analytics, we're still in the early stages of this revolution. Realizing its full promise will require carefully addressing challenges around data quality, bias mitigation, and responsible model training to ensure these powerful tools enhance, rather than compromise, the integrity of business insights.

MARKETING AND ADVERTISING

In marketing and advertising, businesses are using GenAI technologies to create, optimize, and personalize content, campaigns, and customer experiences. Jasper (*https://www.jasper. ai*) and Typeface (*https://www.typeface.ai*) are AI-powered content creation platforms that are widely used by the marketing teams of many

enterprises. They have distinct focuses and capabilities.

Jasper is an AI-based copywriting software that generates content automatically using artificial intelligence, offering features like rapid content generation, customizable templates, and a modified version of a GPT (generative pretrained transformer) for text production. It's particularly useful for generating ideas, researching, organizing thoughts, and writing various types of content up to five times faster than manual writing. Typeface is an enterprise-focused generative AI platform designed specifically for marketing and brand content creation. It emphasizes brand personalization, multimodal content generation (both text and images), enterprise integration, and high standards of safety and governance.

Typeface offers several tools, such as Arc for curating end-to-end campaigns, Hub for integrated multimodal content, Copilot for faster creation, Blend for personalization at scale, and Safe for ensuring responsible AI use. While both platforms aim to enhance content creation efficiency, Typeface is more focused on enterprise-level brand consistency and marketing applications, whereas Jasper offers a broader range of content generation capabilities for various users.

How GenAI-based Content Creation Works

In the marketing workflow, the content generation process begins with comprehensive input processing. The system analyzes brand guidelines, marketing strategies, and campaign objectives through token-level preprocessing and semantic parsing. This initial stage incorporates customer segmentation data, historical engagement metrics, and market trends to inform the content strategy. The AI system can process vast amounts of customer data, including purchase histories, browsing patterns, and previous campaign interactions, to create highly targeted marketing materials. Companies like Typeface are going beyond just generation and offering integration with campaign publishing platforms such as Google, Salesforce, Meta, etc.

As **Figure 3-18** illustrates, the GenAI-powered marketing and advertising framework consists of four interconnected layers that enable intelligent content creation and campaign optimization. It is built on a robust infrastructure layer (cloud-compute GPUs and the like) that provides cloud-based platforms to handle increased load seamlessly. Above this foundation sits the data and intelligence layer, which combines enterprise data alongside advanced language models. This layer is crucial for understanding complex queries and domain-specific knowledge, and combines multiple models to provide high accuracy in content generation and analysis.

The business logic layer builds upon these capabilities through several key components:

- Grounding techniques that use RAG to understand brand voice and marketing strategies

- Creative optimization that analyzes successful ad campaign patterns and optimizes ad copy, visuals, and targeting

- Automated content generation that creates blog posts, social media captions, and emails, freeing up time for strategy and creative direction

- Personalized content at scale that creates content that resonates with individuals

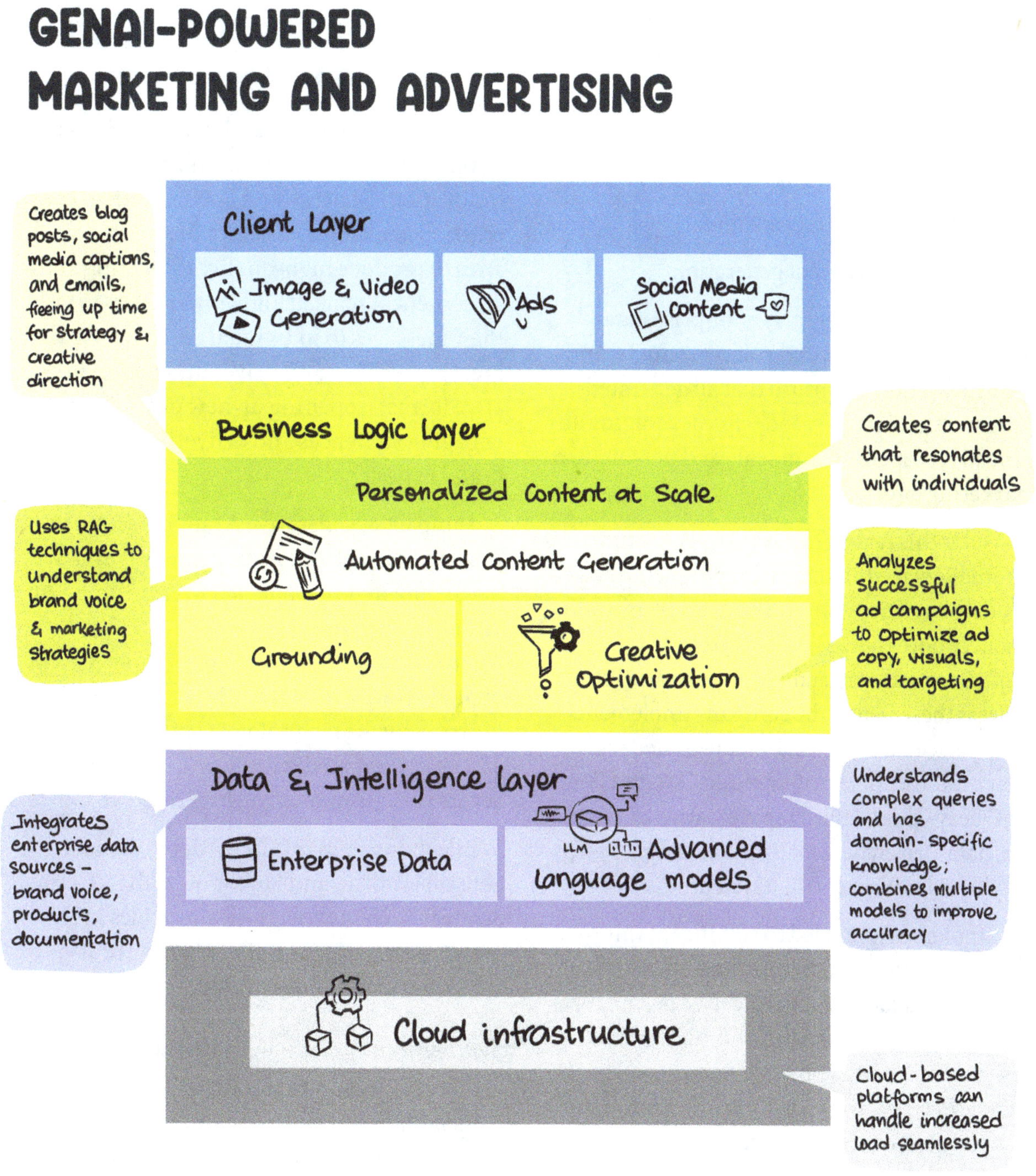

GENAI-POWERED MARKETING AND ADVERTISING

Creates blog posts, social media captions, and emails, freeing up time for strategy & creative direction

Client Layer
- Image & Video Generation
- Ads
- Social Media Content

Creates content that resonates with individuals

Business Logic Layer

Personalized Content at Scale

Automated Content Generation

Grounding

Creative Optimization

Uses RAG techniques to understand brand voice & marketing strategies

Analyzes successful ad campaigns to optimize ad copy, visuals, and targeting

Data & Intelligence Layer

Enterprise Data

Advanced Language models

Integrates enterprise data sources – brand voice, products, documentation

Understands complex queries and has domain-specific knowledge; combines multiple models to improve accuracy

Cloud infrastructure

Cloud-based platforms can handle increased load seamlessly

Figure 3-18. What's needed for AI-powered marketing and advertising.

At the topmost level, the client layer serves as the interface for marketers, offering key functionalities:

- Image and video generation for visual content

- Ad creation and optimization

- Social media content generation

This framework integrates enterprise data sources, including brand voice, products, and documentation, to ensure that all generated content remains on-brand while leveraging advanced AI capabilities to scale and personalize marketing efforts.

Consider this real-world use case. A Fortune 500 automaker faced challenges in producing targeted ads for a major year-end sales event, including resource bottlenecks and limited ability to tailor content for different audience segments. To address these issues, the company implemented Typeface's GenAI solution integrated with their customer data platform and Google Cloud BigQuery. This enabled rapid creation of targeted ads, data-driven personalization, and cost-effective, brand-consistent digital ad production.

The implementation led to significant improvements in content production and efficiency. The automaker quadrupled its creative output, producing over 700 images, including 150 custom designs for specific audience interests (*https:// oreil.ly/PgGLb*). They achieved a 57% productivity savings in content production, resulting in faster time-to-market. The solution enabled the launch of data-driven, personalized display ad campaigns across multiple audience segments and product lines, optimizing content creation for eight unique audience segments.

The Future of Generative AI in Marketing and Advertising

The future of generative AI in marketing and advertising is poised for significant growth and innovation. Generative AI democratizes content creation, making it easier for businesses of all sizes to produce high-quality marketing and ad content at scale. It allows marketers to tailor their messages to individual customers with greater precision and drives innovation in creative formats, opening up new possibilities for engaging audiences and delivering memorable brand experiences.

The impact of generative AI in this sector is substantial, with the global generative AI in marketing market expected to *grow from* $2.6 billion in 2023 to $41.1 billion by 2033, at a robust compound annual growth rate (CAGR) of 31.8% (*https://oreil.ly/GZRWS*). This growth is driven by the technology's ability to enhance efficiency, personalization, and creative output across various marketing functions.

While industry giants like Adobe, with its Sensei platform, and HubSpot, with its Content Strategy tool, make significant strides in this space, startups and smaller players are also emerging with innovative solutions:

Synthesia (https://www.synthesia.io)
   This London-based startup has developed a generative AI platform for creating videos. Users can generate AI-powered videos from text inputs, supporting 120 languages and featuring 125 AI avatars.

Anyword (https://www.anyword.com)

Anyword uses NLP to write copy for blogs, ads, and emails. The platform can be trained to match a company's brand voice and performance predictions and uses results-driven RAG to optimize outputs for business goals, target audiences, and distribution channels.

LOVO AI (https://lovo.ai)

An AI voice generator startup that offers text-to-speech conversion and realistic voice cloning. LOVO's suite of tools includes an online video editor, AI voices in multiple languages, and an AI art generator.

These companies are innovating, addressing various aspects of content creation and personalization in marketing and advertising. As this technology continues to evolve, we can expect to see even more sophisticated applications of generative AI in some other areas:

Hyperpersonalized customer experiences

Already, 54% of businesses use AI to create personalized consumer experiences at scale (*https://oreil.ly/meYKn*).

Real-time content optimization

AI-powered tools will enable marketers to dynamically adjust campaigns based on performance metrics and changing market conditions.

Multimodal content creation

Runway's platform (*https://runwayml.com*) enables marketers to generate video content from text, with their tools being used in hundreds of countries.

Enhanced predictive analytics

Today, 41% of businesses (*https://oreil.ly/PMjDW*) use AI to predict consumer needs and behaviors more accurately.

As the adoption of generative AI in marketing continues to grow, with 69.1% of marketers already incorporating AI into their strategies (*https://oreil.ly/_58QX*), we can expect to see a transformation in how brands connect with their audiences, create content, and measure the success of their marketing efforts.

SUMMARY

In this chapter, we've shown you several practical applications for generative AI across various industries, demonstrating its transformative potential. The chapter covers five key areas where GenAI is making significant impacts.

In customer support, natural language processing and generation are changing the industry with applications that include call deflection, natural conversations, omnichannel customer journeys, call analytics, product insights, and agent assistance. Companies like Cresta use AI to streamline interactions, boost agent efficiency, and drive revenue growth. Benefits include improved customer satisfaction, reduced operational costs, and more personalized experiences.

In software development, GenAI automates code reviews, generates code snippets, and enhances overall development efficiency.

Companies like Anthropic and Cursor offer AI-powered tools for code completion and review assistance. Their benefits include faster development cycles, improved code quality, and freeing developers to focus on complex tasks.

GenAI enhances enterprise knowledge management by organizing, connecting, and retrieving information from various systems. Key components include comprehensive data integration, advanced search capabilities, and natural language interfaces. Companies like Glean report significant productivity gains, with their users saving two to three hours per week on average.

GenAI transforms data analysis by providing more dynamic, accurate, and tailored insights. Companies like Fleet and Defog offer solutions that dramatically reduce the time it takes to perform complex data analysis. Benefits include faster decision making, improved accuracy, and the ability to handle complex queries without extensive technical knowledge.

Finally, we showed you how GenAI is reshaping content creation, campaign optimization, and personalization in marketing and advertising. Key applications in this field include automated, personalized text generation, creative optimization, and image/video generation. Benefits include more efficient content creation, enhanced personalization, and innovative engagement strategies.

GenAI is acting as a catalyst for meaningful transformation across industries. It enables organizations to achieve operational excellence, enhance customer experiences, streamline workflows, and drive innovation. However, success requires a measured approach that acknowledges its current limitations. Organizations must carefully design their AI implementations around challenges like hallucination, bias, and data quality constraints, focusing on targeted use cases where success metrics are clear, rather than rushing toward broad adoption—the power of these tools emerges not from treating them as a universal solution, but from thoughtfully integrating them into existing analytical workflows. Based on this knowledge, the authors of this book encourage readers to consider how GenAI could transform their own domains of expertise and business operations.

## Chapter 4

BUILDING AGENTIC SYSTEMS

Even though LLMs are powerful, there are limits to what you can accomplish with a single LLM call. For example, suppose you are using a foundational model that was trained on data until October 2024, and you ask it a question about chess. Any answer from that model will not reflect who won the World Chess Championship that commenced in November 2024.

Agentic systems provide ways to get around this, and other, limitations of LLMs. We call the software that employs GenAI to automate a single step of a multistep application an agent. We refer to the entire application as being *agentic*. In this chapter, we look into building agentic systems (see Figure 4-1). We discuss how to implement agents that involve multiple steps, then cover two specific types of agents, RAG agents and SQL agents, that are extremely useful in practice. RAG agents allow us to provide LLMs with fresh data that they did not have access to during training. SQL agents allow the LLM to access databases of structured, often confidential, data.

In Chapter 2, we discussed how to use GenAI as a layperson (using the chat interfaces to ChatGPT, Gemini, Meta AI, and the like) and as a software developer (using the API). Toward the end of the chapter, we discussed why a single prompt is not enough for an application, such as a recipe planner. If you are performing a complex task like planning recipes, you will have to break the problem into simpler tasks. Fortunately, you can have the LLM decompose the tasks. In this chapter, we will discuss four agentic architectures—reflection, dynamic planning, tool use, and multi-agent collaboration—that provide different ways of handling task decomposition.

When using these agentic architectures, you will find it necessary to tie together various GenAI capabilities into an end-to-end application. Building an

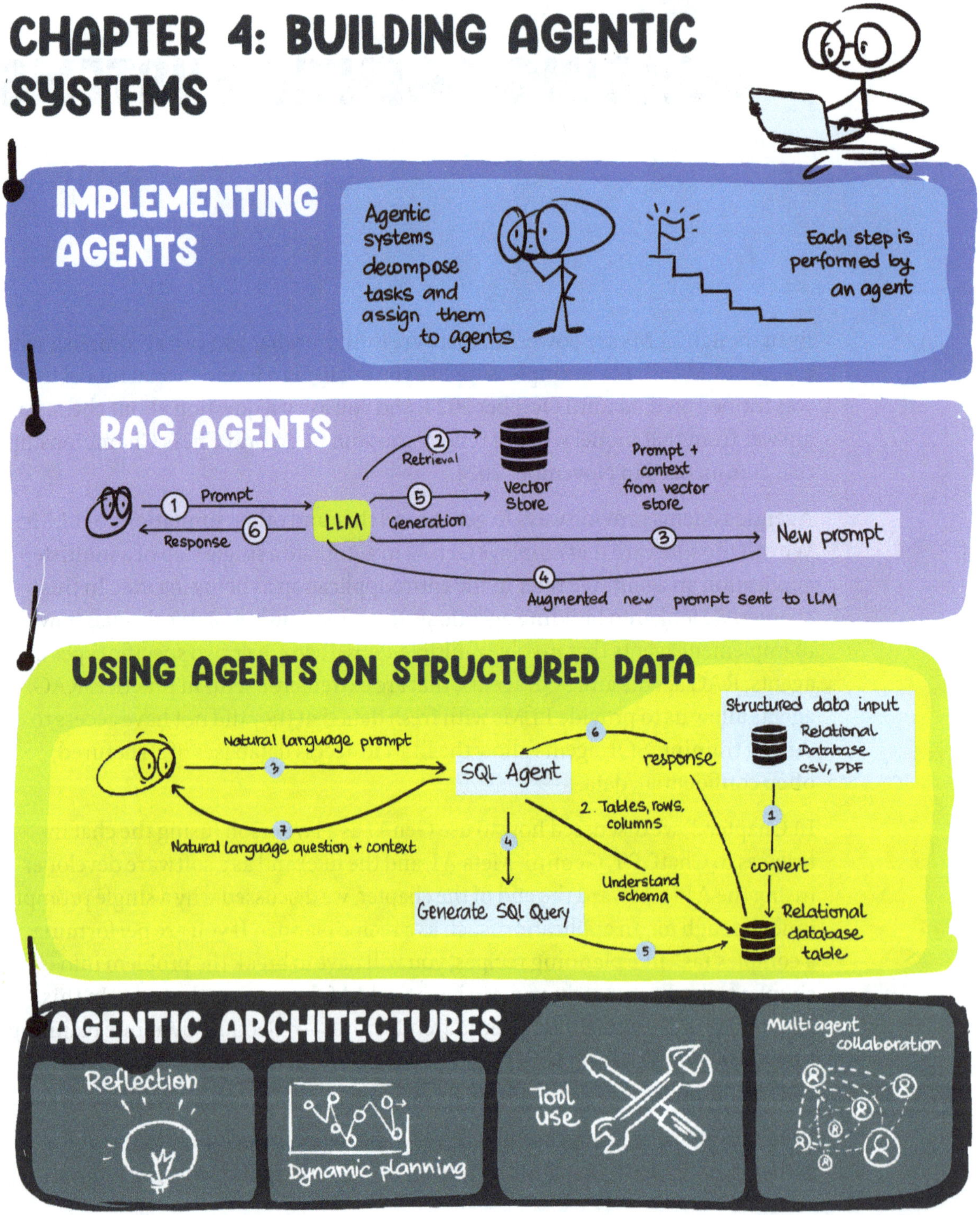

Figure 4-1. Organization of this chapter.

end-to-end GenAI application will require you to build capabilities that are unlike other software applications, because GenAI is non-deterministic and carries unique risks, such as toxicity and bias. In Chapter 6, we cover LLMOps, a fast-developing discipline that provides a framework for the engineering necessary for building these agentic architectures out of unreliable primitives.

WHY AGENTIC SYSTEMS?

Agentic systems provide a way to go beyond the limitations of LLMs (specifically reasoning, math, knowledge cutoff, and the inability to make database updates) and allow enterprises to solve practical problems. It is possible to use specialized agents to obtain custom generative AI outcomes that focus on your specific business need, whether it is math, regulation, industry jargon, database updates, or confidential information.

Breaking Down Complexity

Agentic systems work by breaking down complex tasks into simpler instructions (see Figure 4-2). Some of the instructions are carried out by the LLMs, and other tasks are delegated to SaaS applications' APIs. They provide users of SaaS software with automation capabilities with a very low barrier to entry, through a no-code/low-code approach.

For example, an agentic system will take a user request such as, "I need to make an appointment with Dr. Smith," break it down into a series of smaller tasks, and then execute the tasks by asking the user for pertinent information and invoking APIs on the backend on behalf of the user (Figure 4-3).

The instructions corresponding to the decomposed tasks can be something that GenAI models are natively capable of, like "summarize this email" or "extract the user's address from this text." They could also involve tasks that are beyond the ability of the LLM, such as finding documents relevant to a given query and basing its response on those documents (this is called

Figure 4-2. Understanding agentic systems.

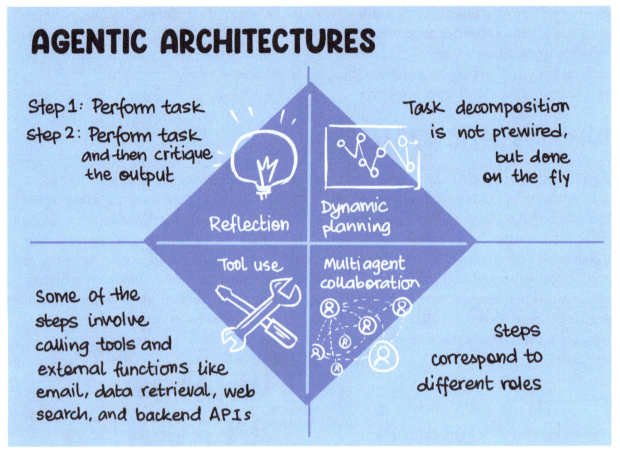

Figure 4-3. An example of how an agentic system assembles a series of tasks and farms out specific actions to solve a problem.

grounding or *retrieval-augmented generation*, shortened as RAG). The foundational model can also call out to an external system by invoking its API (passing in the necessary input values, perhaps extracted from the input document), then grounding its response in the values returned by the API. If there are errors, the agent can respond by iteratively modifying the input or call. Finally, the generated text could be code, such as SQL, that will allow the foundational model to make persistent changes to other systems. We will look at all these possibilities in this chapter.

Agentic systems address the current limitations of LLMs in several ways (see **Figure 4-4**):

Planning and reasoning

They convert complex reasoning tasks into a task of generating a set of steps. For example, suppose the AI application needs to answer the question, "I have 5 toys and 3 kids at a party. How many ways can I distribute these toys?". It's easier to get the LLM to generate

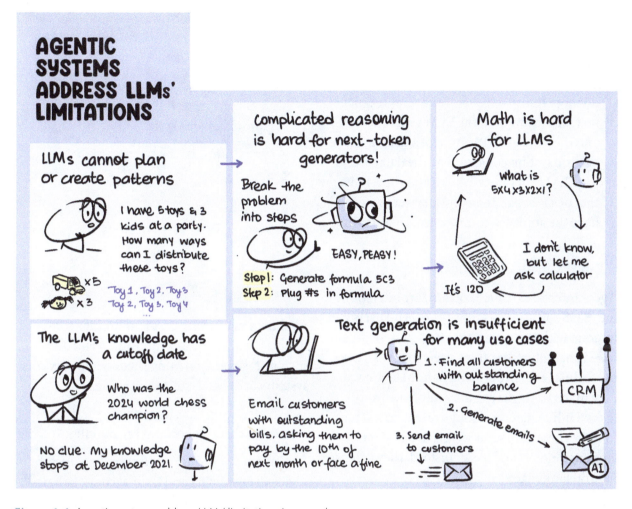

Figure 4-4. Agentic systems address LLMs' limitations in several ways.

the formula $^5C_3$ than to get it to correctly enumerate all the possibilities (which would also require planning what text to output). Another way to get around reasoning and planning limitations is for the user to specify the steps they want done.

Knowledge cutoff

Grounding solves the problem of the foundational model not knowing about recent events or proprietary information.

Math

Once the LLM outputs $^5C_3$, how can the LLM know what the result is? This is a hard problem for a next-token generator. One way around this limitation is for the agent framework to send the text to an external calculator tool that understands factorials. The calculator tool could be available via a stateless API, take a string as input, and return a number back as output.

Capabilities

The tools available via stateless APIs can include company databases, dashboards, and more. Therefore, an agentic system can do more than just generate natural language text. For example, if the LLM generates SQL and the stateless API is that of a database, the agentic system could update the database. If the LLM generates an email and the API is that of `sendmail`, the agentic system would have the ability to communicate via email.

Copilots and Low-code Agents

Agent interfaces (called *copilots*) are often built into SaaS software to simplify how end users can interact with the application (Figure 4-5). Agent-based chat interfaces allow users to invoke the capabilities of the tool using natural language. Like macros, agents can also automate those tasks. Unlike macros, though, users do not have to write the automation scripts in an esoteric language like Visual Basic. Instead, they can use natural language.

One of the first agentic systems built into a SaaS application was Agentforce from Salesforce. Agentforce shipped with copilots and prebuilt agents for common tasks in Salesforce, such as marketing automation. To see the promise of this technology, however, it's important to see the power it gives to a user who wishes to automate a workflow. Let's consider a hypothetical scenario of an account rep using Salesforce Agent Builder, the mechanism by which end users can build their own agents. The rep inputs the following prompt:

- Get me a list of customers who have outstanding balances of more than $10,000 and have not paid their bill in six months.

- Send them an email that includes the following information:

  ○ Details about the amount owed

  ○ Offer them a payment plan

  ○ A Google Calendar link to schedule a meeting with me to discuss the payment plan

  ○ A link to a survey about this interaction.

As shown in Figure 4-6, Agent Builder constructs the agent by assembling a series of specific tasks and farming them out to specialist systems. It does the following things:

- Obtains from Salesforce a list of active customers that this account rep handles.

- Creates a SQL query and runs it against the list of customers and their account balances and payment information—perhaps in Snowflake, because it's been configured to know that's where the customer data sits.

- Generates an API call to Klarna (the payment mechanism supported by this company) with personally identifiable information (PII)-masked customer information and receives the details of a valid payment plan.

- Calls out to Google Workspace and gets a custom link to create a calendar event.

- Calls out to Qualtrics and gets a custom link to a survey (creating it for the first time).

HOW DO AGENTS WORK?

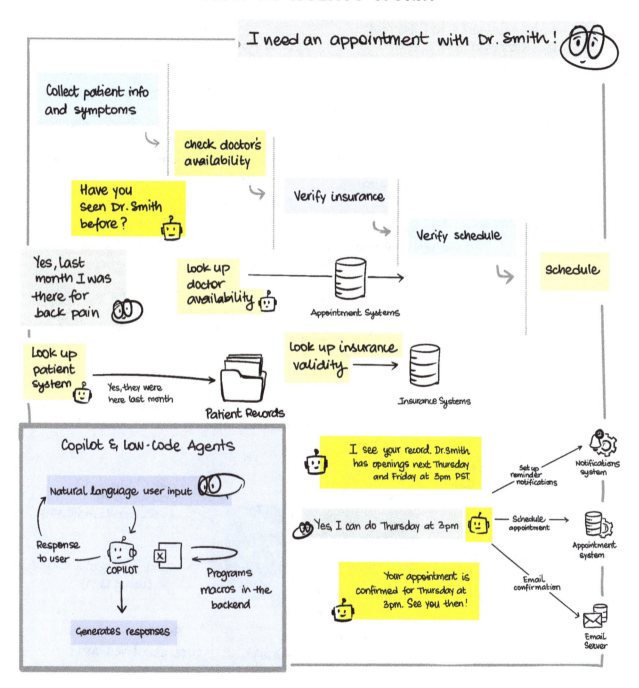

Figure 4-5. How copilots and other low-code agents work.

AN EXAMPLE AGENTIC SYSTEM

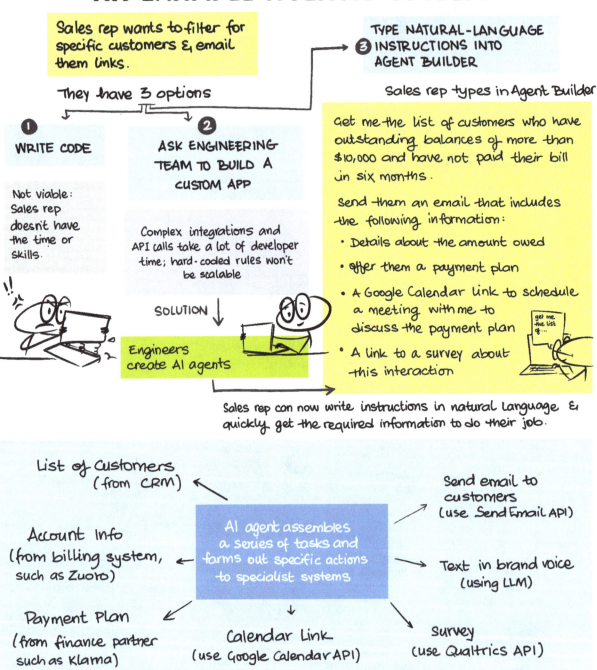

Figure 4-6. In this use case, a sales rep wants to filter some customers and send them emails and links.

- Generates an email that is on-brand and has the company "voice."

- Updates each customer's record in Salesforce.

This is the sort of automation that would once have taken an engineering team several weeks to build. So it never got built, or companies used hardcoded rules instead. Now, a nontechnical account rep using Agentforce can write instructions in natural language. The promise of agentic platforms is that all low-code agent platforms will improve to the point that they allow nontechnical users to automate their drudgery without help.

It's still early days, though, and at the time of writing, low-code agentic systems are very limited in capability. In this chapter, we'll show you how to build agentic systems in code.

IMPLEMENTING AGENTS

GenAI models are good at a handful of tasks, such as summarizing text, understanding spoken language, answering questions, and generating code. If you have a business process that can be broken down into a set of steps, and one or more of those steps involves one of these GenAI superpowers, then you will be able to partially automate your business process using GenAI.

While agents use LLMs just to process text and generate responses, this basic capability can provide quite advanced behavior, such as the ability to invoke backend services autonomously. Let's see how this is done.

Example: Current Weather at a Location

Let's say that you want to build an agent that can answer questions such as, "Is it raining in Chicago?" You can't answer a question like this using just an LLM, because this task can't be performed by memorizing patterns from large volumes of text. Instead, you'll need it to reach out to real-time sources of weather information.

The US National Weather Service (NWS) provides an open, free API (*https://oreil.ly/LZASl*) for short-term weather forecasts for specific locations. However, using this API to answer a question like, "Is it raining in Chicago?" requires several additional steps (see Figure 4-7):

1. Set up an agentic framework to coordinate the rest of these steps. We'll use AutoGen for this.

2. Find out what location the user is interested in. The answer in our example sentence is "Chicago." It's not as simple as just extracting the last word of the sentence, though—if the user were to ask "Is Orca Island hot today?", the location of interest would be "Orca Island." Because extracting the location from a question requires being able to understand natural language, the agent performing this step can prompt an LLM to identify the location the user is interested in.

SAMPLE AGENTIC AI APPLICATION

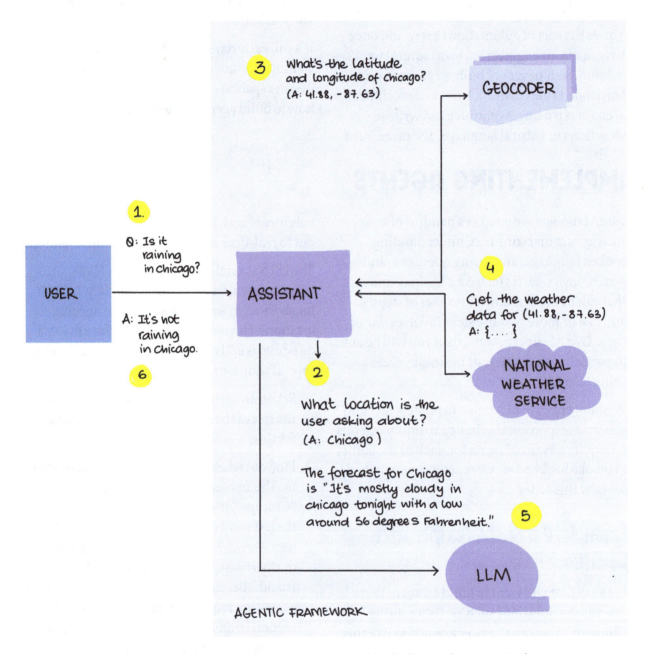

Figure 4-7. Agentic application to answer questions about current weather built around conversational agents.

3. Convert the location of interest to latitudes and longitudes, which is what the NWS API operates on. If you want the weather in Chicago, you'll have to convert the string "Chicago" into latitude and longitude points, and then invoke the API. This is called *geocoding*. Google Maps has a Geocoder API that, given a place name, will respond with the latitude and longitude. Tell the agent to use this tool to get the coordinates of the location.

4. Send the location coordinates to the NWS API, which will send back a JSON object containing weather data.

5. Tell the LLM to extract the corresponding weather forecast (for example, if the question is about now, tonight, or next Monday) and add it to the context of the question. Technically, we could have split this task into two steps: one to extract the timeframe from the question, and the other to extract the corresponding weather forecast for that timeframe. However, it turns out that the LLM can handle both these steps in a single call.

6. Based on this enriched context, answer the user's question.

Let's go through these steps one by one.

Step 1: Setting up AutoGen

We will use AutoGen (*https://oreil.ly/6CpWk*), an open source agentic framework created by Microsoft. To follow along, clone the Git repository (*https://github.com/lakshmanok/visualizing-generative-ai*) of this book into your favorite Python IDE, and follow the directions provided by Google Cloud (*https://oreil.ly/Cub5l*) and

OpenAI (*https://oreil.ly/X7irM*) to get API keys. Update the *keys.env* file with your keys:

```
GOOGLE_API_KEY=AI...
OPENAI_API_KEY=sk-...
```

Switch to the *ch04* folder and install the required Python modules using pip:

```
pip install -r requirements.txt
```

This will install the AutoGen module and client libraries for Google Maps and OpenAI. (Follow the discussion by looking at *ag_weather_agent.py*.)

AutoGen treats agentic tasks as a conversation between agents. So the first step in AutoGen, after setting up the LLM, is to create the agents that will perform the individual steps (see **Figure 4-8**). One will be the proxy for the end user. It will initiate chats with the AI agent we will refer to as the Assistant:

```
user_proxy = UserProxyAgent("user_
proxy", code_execution_config={"work_
dir": "coding",
"use_docker": False},
is_termination_msg=lambda x: autogen.
code_
utils.content_str(x.get("content")).
find("TERMINATE") >= 0,
human_input_mode="NEVER",
)
```

There are three things to note about this user proxy. First, if the Assistant responds with code, the user proxy is capable of executing that code in a sandbox. Second, the user proxy will terminate the conversation if the Assistant's response contains the word TERMINATE. This is how the LLM tells the invoking agent that the user question has been fully answered. Making the

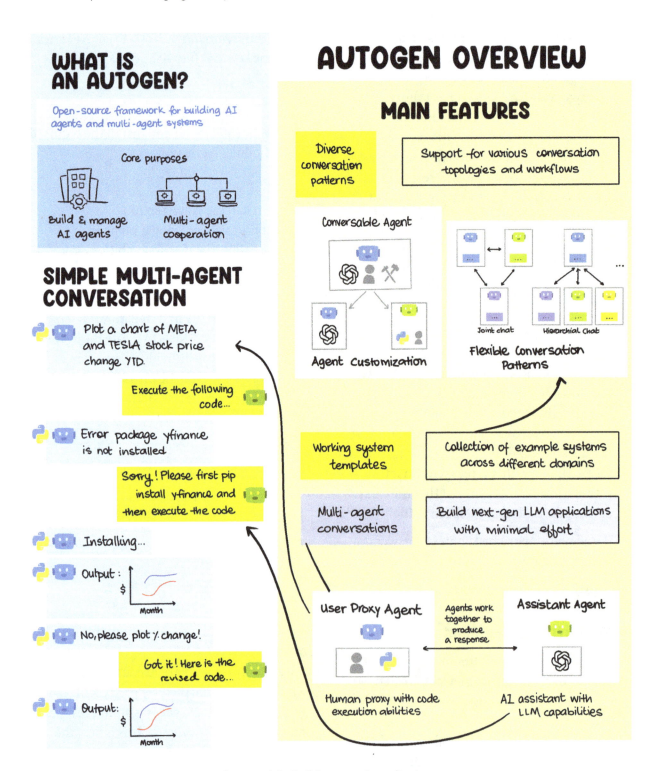

Figure 4-8. AutoGen is an open source framework for building agentic applications.

LLM do this is part of the hidden system prompt that AutoGen sends to the LLM. Third, the user proxy never asks the end user any follow-up questions. If there were follow-ups, we'd specify the conditions under which the human can be asked for more input.

Even though AutoGen is from Microsoft, it is not limited to Azure. The AI assistant can use OpenAI:

```python
openai_config = {
    "config_list": [
        {
            "model": "gpt-4",
            "api_key": os.environ.get("OPENAI_API_KEY")
        }
    ]
}
```

It can also use Gemini:

```python
gemini_config = {
    "config_list": [
        {
            "model": "gemini-1.5-flash",
            "api_key": os.environ.get("GOOGLE_API_KEY"),
            "api_type": "google"
        }
    ],
}
```

Anthropic and Ollama are supported as well.

Next, supply the appropriate LLM configuration to create the Assistant:

```python
assistant = AssistantAgent(
    "Assistant",
    llm_config=gemini_config,
    max_consecutive_auto_reply=3
)
```

Before we wire the rest of the agentic framework, let's ask the Assistant to answer our sample query:

```python
response = user_proxy.initiate_chat(
    assistant, message=f"Is it raining in Chicago?"
)
print(response)
```

The Assistant responds with this code to reach out to an existing Google web service and scrape the response:

```python
'''python
# filename: weather.py
import requests
from bs4 import BeautifulSoup

url = "https://www.google.com/search?q=weather+chicago"
response = requests.get(url)
soup = BeautifulSoup(response.text, 'html.parser')
weather_info = soup.find('div', {'id': 'wob_tm'})
print(weather_info.text)
'''
```

This gets at the power of an agentic framework when powered by a frontier foundational model. The Assistant has autonomously identified a web service that provides the desired functionality and is using its code generation and execution capabilities to provide something akin to the desired functionality! However, it's not quite what we wanted—we asked whether it was raining, and we got back a full website instead of the desired answer.

Second, the autonomous capability doesn't really meet our pedagogical needs. We are using this example to illustrate enterprise use cases, and it is unlikely that the LLM will know enough about your company's internal APIs and tools to be able to use them autonomously. So let's build out the framework shown in **Figure 4-9** to invoke the specific APIs we want to use.

Step 2: Extracting the location

Because extracting the location from the question is just text processing, you can simply prompt the LLM. Let's do this with a single-shot example:

```
SYSTEM_MESSAGE_1 = """
In the question below, what location is
the user asking about?

Example:
  Question: What's the weather in
Kalamazoo, Michigan?
  Answer: Kalamazoo, Michigan.

Question:
"""
```

Now, when we initiate the chat by asking whether it is raining in Chicago:

```
response1 = user_proxy.initiate_chat(
    assistant, message=f"{SYSTEM_
MESSAGE_1} Is it raining in Chicago?"
)
print(response1)
```

We get back:

```
Answer: Chicago.
TERMINATE
```

Step 2 is complete.

Step 3: Geocoding the location

Step 3 is to get the latitude and longitude coordinates of the location that the user is interested in. We need to write a Python function that will call the Google Maps API and extract the required coordinates:*

```
def geocoder(location: str) -> (float,
float):
    geocode_result = gmaps.
geocode(location)
    return (round(geocode_result[0]
['geometry']['location']['lat'], 4),
            round(geocode_result[0]
['geometry']['location']['lng'], 4))
```

Next, register this function so that the Assistant can call it in its generated code, and the user proxy can execute it in its sandbox:

```
autogen.register_function(
    geocoder,
    caller=assistant,  # The assistant
agent can suggest calls to the
geocoder.
    executor=user_proxy,  # The user
proxy agent can execute the geocder
calls.
    name="geocoder",  # By default, the
function name is used as the tool name.
    description="Finds the latitude and
longitude of a location or landmark",
# A description of the tool.
)
```

---

* At the time of writing, AutoGen supports tool use in OpenAI GPT-4 and higher models only. So, this step works correctly only with an OpenAI configuration where the model is GPT-4. We hope that this capability gets expanded to other LLMs by the time this book is in your hands. Check the tools documentation of AutoGen (*https://oreil.ly/n7Cye*).

AGENTIC WORKFLOW IN LANGGRAPH

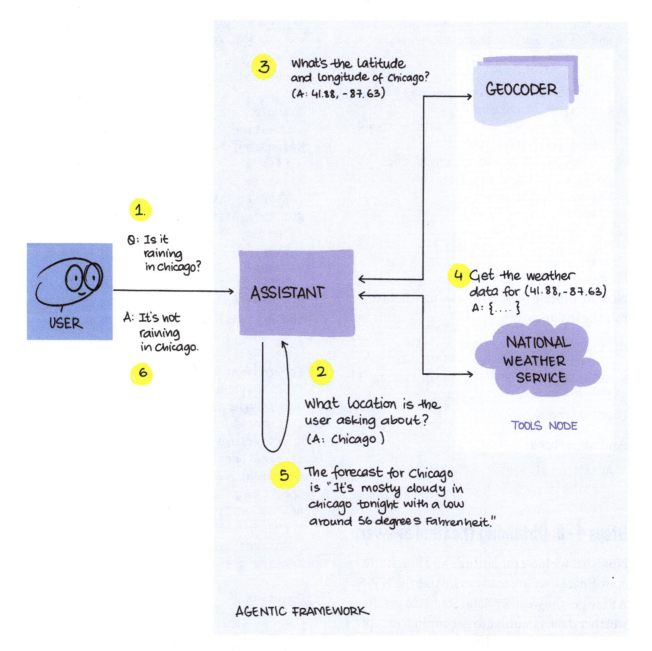

Figure 4-9. An agentic application to answer questions about current weather, built around language model graphs.

We now expand the example in the prompt to include the geocoding step:

```
SYSTEM_MESSAGE_2 = """
In the question below, what latitude
and longitude is the user asking about?

Example:
  Question: What's the weather in
Kalamazoo, Michigan?
  Step 1:   The user is asking about
Kalamazoo, Michigan.
  Step 2:   Use the geocoder tool to
get the latitude and longitude of
Kalamazoo, Michigan.
  Answer:   (42.2917, -85.5872)

Question:
"""
```

Now we initiate the chat by asking whether it is raining in Chicago:

```
response2 = user_proxy.initiate_chat(
    assistant, message=f"{SYSTEM_
MESSAGE_2} Is it raining in Chicago?"
)
print(response2)
```

And we get back:

```
Answer: (41.8781, -87.6298)
TERMINATE
```

Steps 4–6: Obtaining the final answer

Now that we have the latitude and longitude coordinates, we are ready to invoke the NWS API to get the weather data. Step 4, to get the weather data, is similar to geocoding, except that we are invoking a different API and extracting a different object from the web service response. Please look at the code on GitHub to see the full details. The upshot is that the system prompt expands to encompass all the steps in the agentic application:

```
SYSTEM_MESSAGE_3 = """
Follow the steps in the example below
to retrieve the weather information
requested.

Example:
  Question: What's the weather in
Kalamazoo, Michigan?
  Step 1:   The user is asking about
Kalamazoo, Michigan.
  Step 2:   Use the geocoder tool to
get the latitude and longitude of
Kalmazoo, Michigan.
  Step 3:   latitude, longitude is
(42.2917, -85.5872)
  Step 4:   Use the get_weather_from_
nws tool to get the weather from
the National Weather Service at the
latitude, longitude
  Step 5:   The detailed forecast
for tonight reads 'Showers and
thunderstorms before 8pm, then showers
and thunderstorms likely. Some of
the storms could produce heavy rain.
Mostly cloudy. Low around 68, with
temperatures rising to around 70
overnight. West southwest wind 5 to 8
mph. Chance of precipitation is 80%.
New rainfall amounts between 1 and 2
inches possible.'
  Answer:   It will rain tonight.
Temperature is around 70F.

Question:
"""
```

Based on this prompt, the response to the question about Chicago weather extracts the right information and answers the question correctly.

In this example, we allowed AutoGen to select the next agent in the conversation autonomously. We can also specify a different *next-speaker selection strategy*: setting this to "manual" inserts a human in the loop, and allows the human to select the next agent in the workflow.

AGENTIC WORKFLOW IN LANGGRAPH

While AutoGen treats agentic workflows as conversations, LangGraph (*https://oreil.ly/94hRS*) is an open source framework that allows you to build agents by treating a workflow as a graph. This is inspired by the long history of representing data-processing pipelines as *directed acyclic graphs* (DAGs). A DAG is a graph where nodes are connected by edges that have a direction, and you can't follow a path consisting of edges and end up where you started.

In the graph paradigm, our weather agent would look as shown in Figure 4-9.

There are a few key differences between AutoGen and LangGraph (Figure 4-10). In AutoGen, each of the agents is a conversational agent. Workflows are treated as conversations between agents that talk to each other. Agents jump into the conversation when they believe it is "their turn." In LangGraph, workflows are treated as graphs that the workflow cycles through based on rules that we specify. Additionally, in AutoGen, the AI assistant is not capable of executing code; instead, it generates code that the user proxy executes. In LangGraph, there is a special `ToolsNode` that consists of capabilities made available to the Assistant.

You can follow this section by referring to the file *lg_weather_agent.py* in the book's GitHub repository.

First, set up LangGraph by creating the workflow graph. Our graph consists of two nodes: the `Assistant` node and a `ToolsNode`. Communication within the workflow happens via a shared state.

```
workflow = StateGraph(MessagesState)
workflow.add_node("assistant", call_
model)
workflow.add_node("tools",
ToolNode(tools))
```

The tools are Python functions:

```
@tool
def latlon_geocoder(location: str) ->
(float, float):
    """Converts a place name such as
"Kalamazoo, Michigan" to latitude and
longitude coordinates"""
    geocode_result = gmaps.
geocode(location)
    return (round(geocode_result[0]
['geometry']['location']['lat'], 4),
          round(geocode_result[0]
['geometry']['location']['lng'], 4))

tools = [latlon_geocoder, get_weather_
from_nws]
```

The Assistant calls the LLM:

```
model = ChatOpenAI(model='gpt-
3.5-turbo', temperature=0).bind_
tools(tools)
def call_model(state: MessagesState):
    messages = state['messages']
    response = model.invoke(messages)
```

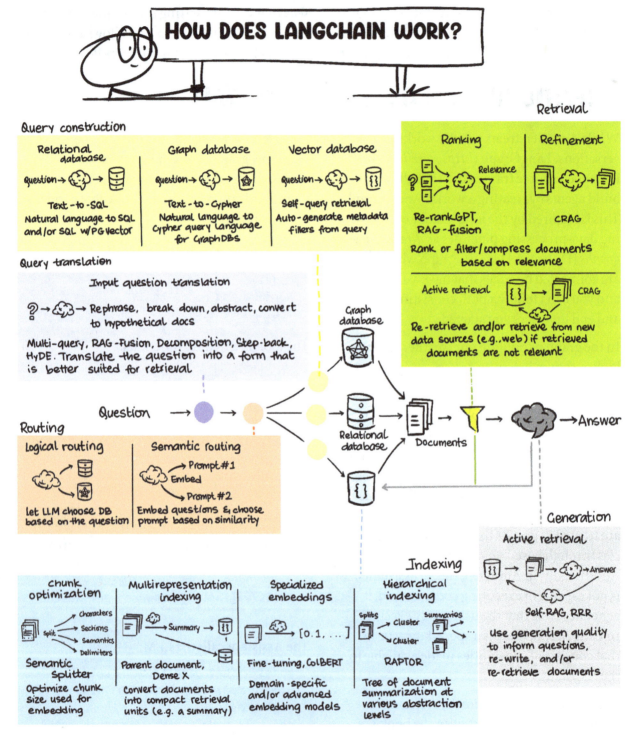

Figure 4-10. LangGraph and LangChain overview with a step-by-step process of indexing, query construction, routing, and retrieval. Source: LangChain documentation (*https://oreil.ly/Xsv4w*).

```
    # This message will get appended to
the existing list
    return {"messages": [response]}
```

LangGraph uses LangChain, so changing the model provider is straightforward. To use Gemini, you can create the model using the following:

```
model = ChatGoogleGenerativeAI(model=
'gemini-1.5-flash', temperature=0).
bind_tools(tools)
```

Next, define the graph's edges:

```
workflow.set_entry_point("assistant")
workflow.add_conditional_
edges("assistant", assistant_next_node)
workflow.add_edge("tools", "assistant")
```

The first and last lines are self-explanatory: the workflow starts with sending a question to the Assistant. Anytime a tool is called, the next node in the workflow is the Assistant, which will use the result of the tool. The middle line sets up a conditional edge in the workflow, since the next node after the Assistant is not fixed. Instead, the Assistant calls a tool or ends the workflow, based on the contents of the last message:

```
def assistant_next_node(state:
MessagesState) -> Literal["tools",
END]:
    messages = state['messages']
    last_message = messages[-1]
    # If the LLM makes a tool call,
then we route to the "tools" node
    if last_message.tool_calls:
        return "tools"
    # Otherwise, we stop (reply to the
user)
    return END
```

Once the workflow has been created, compile the graph and then run it by passing in questions:

```
app = workflow.compile()
final_state = app.invoke(
{"messages": [HumanMessage(
content=f"{system_message}
{question}")]}
)
```

The system message and question are exactly what we employed in AutoGen:

```
system_message = """
    Follow the steps in the example
below to retrieve the weather
information requested.

    Example:
    Question: What's the weather in
Kalamazoo, Michigan?
    Step 1:   The user is asking
about Kalamazoo, Michigan.
    Step 2:   Use the latlon_geocoder
tool to get the latitude and longitude
of Kalmazoo, Michigan.
    Step 3:   latitude, longitude is
(42.2917, -85.5872)
    Step 4:   Use the get_weather_
from_nws tool to get the weather from
the National Weather Service at the
latitude, longitude
    Step 5:   The detailed forecast
for tonight reads 'Showers and
thunderstorms before 8pm, then showers
and thunderstorms likely. Some of
the storms could produce heavy rain.
Mostly cloudy. Low around 68, with
temperatures rising to around 70
overnight. West southwest wind 5 to 8
mph. Chance of precipitation is 80%.
New rainfall amounts between 1 and 2
inches possible.'
```

```
    Answer:   It will rain tonight.
Temperature is around 70F.

    Question:
    """
question="Is it raining in Chicago?"
```

The agent framework uses the steps to come up with an answer to our question:

```
Step 1:   The user is asking about
Chicago.
```

```
Step 2:   Use the latlon_geocoder tool
to get the latitude and longitude of
Chicago.
[41.8781, -87.6298]

[{"number": 1, "name": "This
Afternoon", "startTime": "2024-07-
30T14:00:00-05:00", "endTime": "2024-
07-30T18:00:00-05:00", "isDaytime":
true, …]
There is a chance of showers and
thunderstorms after 8pm tonight. The
low will be around 73 degrees.
```

CHOOSING BETWEEN AUTOGEN AND LANGGRAPH

Between AutoGen and LangGraph, which one should you choose? A few considerations are shown in Table 4-1, and we provide a decision tree in Figure 4-11.

Of course, the level of support AutoGen provides for non-OpenAI models and other tooling could improve by the time you read this. LangGraph could add autonomous capabilities, and AutoGen could provide you more fine-grained control. The agent space is moving fast!

RAG AGENTS

A very common use case is for an agent that can answer questions based on a small set of documents. For example, the agent might answer questions about insurance coverage based on the policy that was purchased, or questions about medical conditions based only on vetted medical texts. The architecture to support such question-answering, retrieval-augmented generation, was introduced in a 2021 paper (*https://oreil.ly/ysGBB*) by Facebook researchers.

Building a RAG agent consists of two separate pipelines: one to index the documents and the other to generate query results (see Figure 4-12).

We'll start by building a basic RAG system that uses a simple approach for both these tasks. Then, we'll improve it by applying a few tricks. In your use cases, you'll have to experiment with these and other tricks to arrive at a RAG system that works well for your data and the types of queries your users make.

To understand RAG, you have to understand what *embeddings* are and how they work.

Embeddings

In traditional search systems, documents are indexed based on keywords; when a user makes a query, documents whose keywords match the keywords in the query are returned. The indexing in a RAG is based not on keywords, but on *embeddings* (see Figure 4-13).

An *embedding* of a word, sentence, paragraph, or other document fragment is a numeric representation of the text's content in such a way that the location of the embedding in multidimensional space captures the meaning of the entire document fragment. For example, the location of the bottom left dot captures the semantic idea of a zoo closing at 5, whereas the location of the

dot connected to it captures the idea of the zoo being open.

A key property is that the embeddings of two document fragments that are similar in meaning will be close to each other in vector space. Thus, in Figure 4-13, part A, the embedding of the sentence "The art gallery is open now" would be close to the embedding of the sentence, "The museum is open today" because the two sentences are similar in meaning.

Sentences with opposite meanings tend to be far apart, and the distance represents the extent

Table 4-1. Choosing between AutoGen and LangGraph

CRITERION	AUTOGEN	LANGGRAPH
Familiarity of paradigm	Every agent in AutoGen is conversational; this is more intuitive if you tend to try things out interactively in ChatGPT-like conversational UIs and then automate it. The Assistant takes the place of ChatGPT and the UserProxy takes your place.	LangGraph represents automation tasks as DAGs. DAGs have a long history in data engineering—for example, data processing pipelines in Airflow, Apache Beam, etc., are DAGs. Pipelines have proven amenable to logging, monitoring, and operationalization.
Level of control	In AutoGen, because the agents respond to each other, there is quite a bit of heavy handling that has to happen in order to limit such things as an agent responding to itself, or with sequencing prioritization. Some of this is provided by the framework using system prompts that are hidden from you.	In LangGraph, the transition rules are under your control, and so the agentic application tends to be easier to build and troubleshoot.
Level of autonomy	AutoGen is the productionization of a Microsoft Research project that focuses on building collaborative agents. Agents decide when to jump into the conversation, and can work alongside each other. Because of this pedigree and design choice, AutoGen can appear more magical.	In LangGraph, agents are nodes, and only one agent handles the workflow at any point in time. Autonomy is limited to the choice of tools within the ToolNode. Edge transitions between nodes are fully under your control.
Strength of ecosystem	While AutoGen supports Gemini, Anthropic, and other models, the tool calling capability (at the time of writing) is limited to only OpenAI GPT-4 and higher models. Capabilities like observability are supported only within Azure.	LangGraph, because it is based on LangChain, supports almost the entire ecosystem of models that support function calling (GPT 3.5, Anthropic, Gemini, Llama 3, etc.). Also, LangGraph integrates with LangSmith for observability.

DECISION TREE: LANGCHAIN OR AUTOGEN?

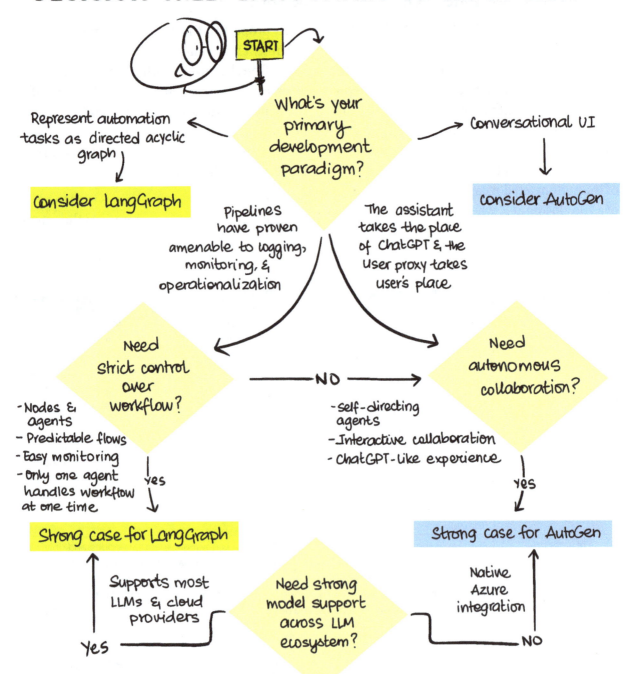

Figure 4-11. Decision tree to pick between two open source AI agent frameworks: AutoGen and LangGraph.

RETRIEVAL-AUGMENTED GENERATION (RAG) 101

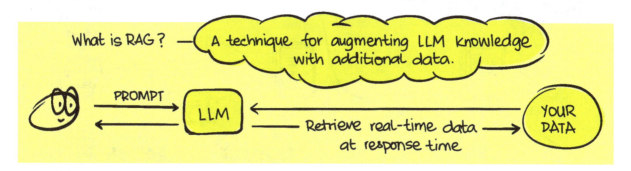

STEP 1: CREATE INDEXING PIPELINE: A pipeline for ingesting data from a source and indexing it.

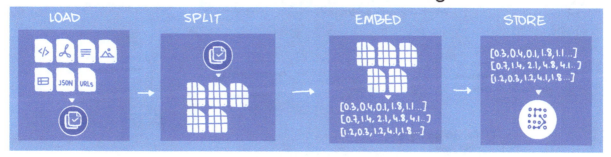

STEP 2: RETRIEVAL: RAG takes user query at run time and retrieves the relevant data from the index, then passes that to the model

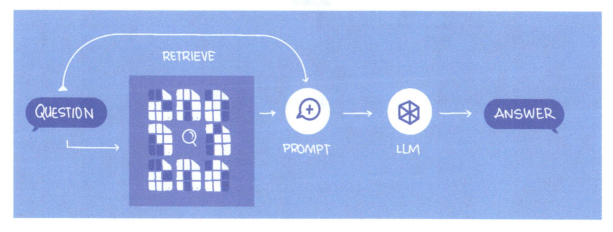

Figure 4-12. Retrieval-augmented generation at a high level.

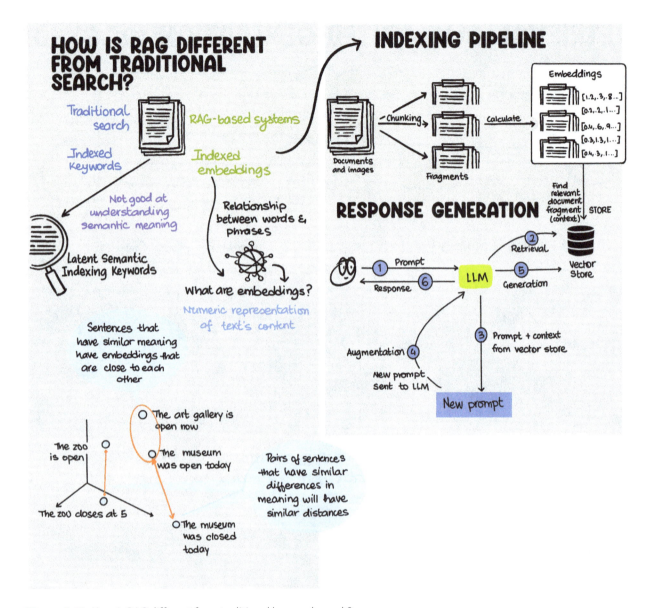

Figure 4-13. How is RAG different from traditional keyword search?

of the change in meaning (in this case, one involving the museum and the other involving the zoo). Together, these properties mean that we can use vector arithmetic to operate on the embeddings to apply methods such as clustering, distance calculation, and dimensionality reductions. The ability to do vector arithmetic on document fragments using their embeddings is what makes RAG possible.

Embedding models

To calculate embeddings, you need an *embedding model*. These models are trained on large corpora of data to identify which words are good substitutes for one another in a given context.

We'll use the earliest embedding model, Word2Vec, to explain the process of creating the training dataset for an embedding model. You might be able to intuit something about embeddings from the term *embedding model,* because the underlying principles remain the same, even when the document fragments are longer than individual words and the model is based on transformers.

The ML model is set up as a problem of predicting the words that can appear near a specific word (see Figure 4-14). The central neural network layer in the previous model has the fewest parameters. Somehow, though, it has to capture enough information from the input to be able to create the output word. Therefore, the central layer ends up being the most concise representation of the input word that is capable of correctly predicting the words that can appear in context. This concise layer's output value is the embedding of the input. When you use an embedding model, you can "throw away" the decoder part

of the model, because you aren't really interested in predicting the words that can appear in context.

To train such a model, we need to show the model all the words that can appear in the context of the word *oolitic* (see Figure 4-15). To do so, we take a very large corpus of books, and extract skipgrams from the text of the book. A *skipgram* of length n is a pair of words where the second word appears within n words of the first word. Thus, the skipgrams of length 2 where the first word is *oolitic* consist of the words that appear within two words of *oolitic* in the input sentence. In this way, all possible skipgrams are created from the corpus of books.

To train a classification model, though, you cannot use just positive examples; you also need negative examples. What words *cannot* appear in the context of the word *oolitic*? This is a hard problem. Commonly, what we do is to randomly sample the full vocabulary of English-language words for negative candidates. The odds are that most of the words are unrelated to the target word and should not appear in context. A nice side effect of this is that very common words (like *of, the,* and *and*) appear in many contexts and in both positive and negative contexts. Hence, they tend to have lower rankings than unique words like *Cretaceous* that appear in exactly the context of a word like *oolitic*.

Pretrained embedding models

While you can train an embedding model from scratch on books in a specific domain, it is much more common to use a pretrained embedding model that is available off-the-shelf. Such models are already trained on a large

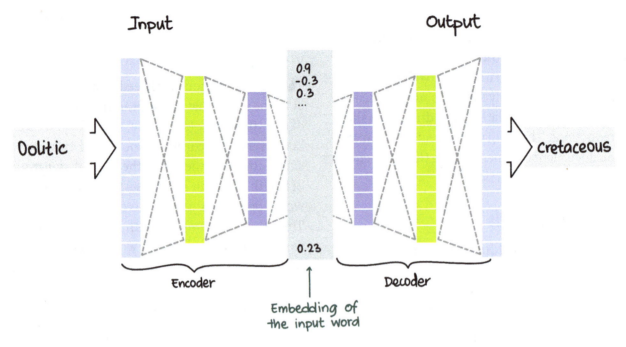

Figure 4-14. The ML problem being solved when an embedding model is being trained.

corpus of internet data. MiniLM is a popular sentence-embedding model whose weights are available in Hugging Face:

```
from langchain_huggingface import
HuggingFaceEmbeddings
embed_model = HuggingFaceEmbeddings(
model_name="all-MiniLM-L6-v2")
embedding = embed_model.embed_query(
"Observations have already been …")
```

The public cloud providers, or *hyperscalers*, also host and provide access to embedding models. We recommend that you look at the Hugging Face MTEB Arena leaderboard (*https://oreil.ly/u3Vlv*) of embedding models and choose the one that fits your memory and price budget. At the time of writing (August 2024), the top three models were GritLM-7B, text-embedding-004 (from Google), and Mistral 7B.

The Indexing Pipeline

Now that you understand embeddings, let's look at the two pipelines—indexing and generation—that make up an RAG system.

We'll start with indexing. *Indexing* a document involves chunking it into fragments, calculating embeddings for all of the chunks, and storing the embeddings in a *vector store*, a database optimized for similarity searches on vectors.

Chunking

We'll use a 1878 geology textbook, *The Student's Elements of Geology* by Charles Lyell, as our source document. It's available in digital form at Project Gutenberg (*https://oreil.ly/3fcTu*). You can use Python to download the textbook in HTML and chunk it into paragraphs (the

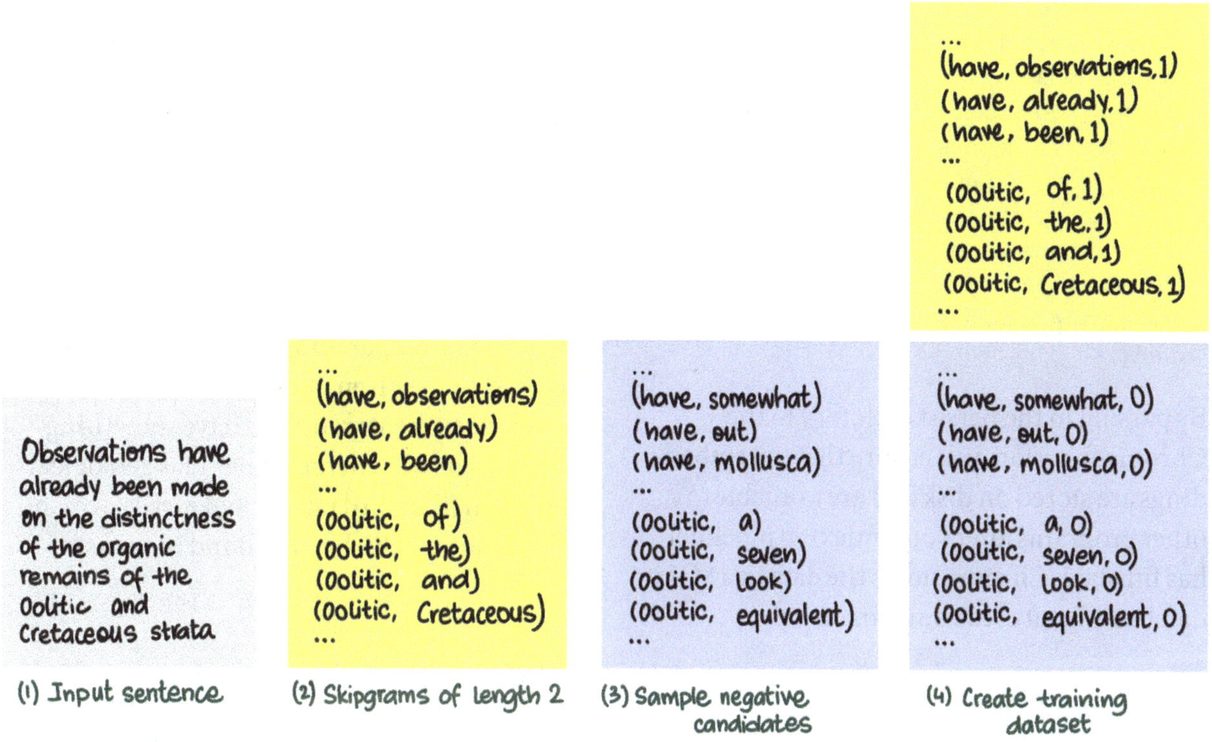

Figure 4-15. Creating the training dataset to train an embedding model.

HTML tag for which is `<p>`) using the Python module BeautifulSoup, as follows. (The full code is on GitHub [*https://oreil.ly/vga_ch04agsys*].)

```
DOC_URL="https://www.gutenberg.org/
cache/epub/3772/pg3772-images.html"
html = urllib.request.urlopen(DOC_URL)
paragraphs = [" ".join(p_tag.get_
text().split()).strip()
for p_tag in bs4.BeautifulSoup(html,
'html.parser').find_all('p')]
```

Now that you have the paragraphs, the next step is to calculate an embedding for each paragraph.

Storing embeddings

There are several vector stores; some are proprietary (Pinecone [*https://www.pinecone.io*]), some open source (Faiss [*https://oreil.ly/2F1c-*]), and some available from hyperscalers (Vertex AI Vector Search [*https://oreil.ly/nx6G1*], Azure AI Search [*https://oreil.ly/E0wIt*], and AWS's vector engine [*https://oreil.ly/iCvOU*]). In addition, many databases and data warehouses (such as Postgres [*https://oreil.ly/GbpOi*], DuckDB [*https://oreil.ly/cjctW*], BigQuery [*https://oreil.ly/nYrZz*], Snowflake [*https://oreil.ly/X2d2W*]) support a vector data type that you can use to store embeddings. LangChain provides a consistent API to many of these, so you can easily start with one and swap it for another.

This code calculates embeddings for the paragraph chunks and stores them in the vector store Chroma.

```
embed_model =
GoogleGenerativeAIEmbeddings(
model="models/embedding-001")
docs = [Document(page_content=p,
metadata={"source": "geography",
"paragraph": pno+1})
for pno, p in enumerate(paragraphs)]
vectorstore = Chroma.from_documents(
documents=docs,
embedding=embed_model,
persist_directory=PERSIST_DIR)
```

By passing in the persist directory to the Chroma function, you ensure that the embeddings are stored on disk and are available to other programs after your indexing pipeline has finished. Chroma stores the data in a SQLite database that it creates and manages.

The Generation Pipeline

Every time you get a question from the user, you need to find relevant document fragments from the vector store, and incorporate the text of those fragments into the prompt of an LLM. This will ground the LLM's response in the information from the geography textbook. There are three steps in the generation pipeline of a RAG system: retrieval, augmentation, and generation.

Retrieval

To find the five most relevant documents, set up a retriever that can search the vector store:

```
vectorstore = Chroma(embedding_
function=embeddings, persist_directory
=PERSIST_DIR)
retriever = vectorstore.as_retriever(
search_kwargs={"k": 5})
```

Suppose you want to find the most relevant documents to a given question. Create a chain in LangChain and invoke it, using the question as input:

```
retrieval_chain = RunnablePassthrough()
| retriever
retrieval_chain.invoke("What rocks do
you find in the Upper Lias?")
```

The result is five paragraphs whose embedding is closest to the given question. Indeed, four of the five documents returned have something to say about rocks in the Upper Lias geological formation (the third talks about fossils, which are not quite rocks, but are found in rocks):

```
[Document(... The Upper Lias consists
first of sands…),
 Document(.. most characteristic of the
Lias in England, France, and Germany,
is an alternation of thin beds of blue
or grey limestone…),
 Document(...out of 256 mollusca of the
Upper Lias, thirty-seven species...),
 Document(...The Oolite was so named
because... These rocks occupy in
England a zone nearly thirty miles in
average breadth...),
 Document(...The Upper Oolitic system
of the above table has usually the
Kimmeridge clay …)]
```

Augmentation

Augmentation refers to augmenting an LLM prompt with ground-truth data. While you could handcraft your prompt to ask the LLM to answer the question using the given documents, it's easier to pull the necessary prompt from a library of prompts that have already been tested and found to work:

```
from langchain import hub
rag_prompt = hub.pull("rlm/rag-prompt")
```

The text of this prompt is as follows:

```
You are an assistant for question-
answering tasks. Use the following
pieces of retrieved context to answer
the question. If you don't know the
answer, just say that you don't know.
Use three sentences maximum and
keep the answer concise.\nQuestion:
{question} \nContext: {context} \
nAnswer:
```

It requires two pieces of information: the question and the context.

The question is passed through. To create the context, take the retrieved documents and concatenate them into a single string:

```
def add_docs_to_context(docs):
    return "\n".join(doc.page_content
for doc in docs)
```

To prompt the LLM, use the retrieved documents as context and the user input as the question:

```
{
    "context": retriever | add_docs_to_
context,
    "question": RunnablePassthrough()
}
```

Generation

To generate the answer, put all the previous pieces together into a single chain:

```
llm_model = ChatGoogleGenerativeAI(mode
l="gemini-1.5-flash", temperature=0.1)
rag_chain = (
```

```
    {"context": retriever | add_
docs_to_context, "question":
RunnablePassthrough()}
    | rag_prompt
    | llm_model
    | StrOutputParser()
)
rag_chain.invoke("What rocks do you find
in the Upper Lias?")
```

The result is the answer to our question, grounded by the geography textbook:

```
The Upper Lias consists of sands, clay
shale, and thin beds of limestone.
The sands were originally thought to
be part of the Oolite, but fossils
indicate they belong to the Lias.  The
Upper Lias is characterized by an
alternation of thin limestone beds and
dark-colored argillaceous partings.
```

Now that we have looked at the basic RAG structure, let's look at a couple of improvements.

Improvements on Basic RAG

In this section, we'll look at three ways to improve basic RAG, as shown in Figure 4-16. Two of those improvements are related to generation (hypothetical answer and reranking), and one is to indexing.

Hypothetical answer

When you did the search in the vector store, you were trying to match the embedding of the question, "What rocks do you find in the Upper Lias?" with the document fragments that you hoped would contain the answer. This would work if the textbook contained sentences such as, "The rocks you find in the Upper Lias are A,

Figure 4-16. Techniques to improve basic RAG.

B, and C." Unfortunately, a textbook is not a set of FAQs. Instead, the answer has to be pieced together from different sentences in different parts of the book.

Instead of doing a similarity search between the question and the potential answers in the book, what if you generate a hypothetical answer to the question (even if it's wrong) and then try to find the fragments that are most similar to that hypothetical answer?

To do this, ask the LLM to answer the question directly, without reference to any contextual information:

```
hyp_prompt = """
Answer the following question concisely
in 3 sentences or less.
If you don't know the correct answer,
provide the most likely answer.

Question:
{question}
"""

hypothetical_answer = (
    {
        "question" :
RunnablePassthrough()
    }
    | PromptTemplate.from_template(hyp_
prompt)
    | model
    | StrOutputParser()
)
hypothetical_answer.invoke("What types
of rock do you find in the Upper Lias?")
```

You'll get a hypothetical answer:

```
The Upper Lias is a geological
formation known for its rich fossil
content.  It primarily consists of
**claystone and limestone**, with some
**shale and sandstone** also present.
These rocks were formed in a marine
environment during the Jurassic period.
```

We call this a *hypothetical* answer, rather than the true answer, because it is not grounded in the geology textbook that we want to use. Note that the prompt asks the LLM to make up an answer if it doesn't know. What we want is the *structure* of the answer, not necessarily the answer itself.

Create a retrieval chain to match this hypothetical answer instead of the original question:

```
retriever = vectorstore.as_
retriever(search_kwargs={"k": 5})
retrieval_chain = hypothetical_answer |
retriever
```

Next, use the retrieval chain (instead of the retriever) in the RAG chain:

```
rag_chain = (
    {"context": retrieval_chain |
add_docs_to_context, "question":
RunnablePassthrough()}
    | rag_prompt
    | model
    | StrOutputParser()
)
```

The result now closely matches the hypothetical answer and is grounded in the actual text:

```
The Upper Lias consists primarily
of sands, clay shale, and thin beds
of limestone. These layers are
characterized by distinct fossils,
which help to differentiate them from
```

```
other Lias formations. The Upper Lias
is considered the base of the Oolite by
some geologists.
```

Is this really better than the basic RAG? It is difficult to see meaningful differences on individual questions, but the hypothetical-answer approach yields slightly better answers overall. The tradeoff is that it involves two LLM calls: one (without any context) to get the hypothetical answer, and the other (with retrieved document chunks in context) to generate the final answer.

Reranking

While the vector store returns chunks that are similar to the posed question (or hypothetical answer), those returned document chunks aren't all relevant to the answer, just somewhat similar to it. To find chunks that truly answer the question, we should use special-purpose models called *cross encoders*, or *rerankers*.

Unfortunately, cross encoders are slow, and we can't afford to rank every document chunk in the vector store for each query. The workaround is to do it in two stages. In the first stage, use the retriever to return ten documents. In the second stage, compress this list to the top three:

```
retriever = vectorstore.as_
retriever(search_kwargs={"k": 10})
compressor = FlashrankRerank()
compression_retriever =
ContextualCompressionRetriever(
    base_compressor=compressor, base_
retriever=retriever
)
retrieval_chain = hypothetical_answer |
compression_retriever
```

The rest of the RAG remains the same. The answer now is as follows:

```
The Upper Lias consists primarily of
sands, clay shale, and thin beds of
limestone. These formations were once
considered part of the Oolite but are
now classified as Lias due to their
fossil content. The Upper Lias is the
uppermost layer of the Lias group,
which is a formation of argillaceous
limestone, marl, and clay.
```

At this point, you can start to see that the answer is on the nose, with no irrelevant information.

Better indexing

Our indexing pipeline involves taking the textbook, breaking it into paragraphs, and storing each paragraph as a document fragment. Will the answer to all questions be found within a paragraph?

One of the best ways to improve an RAG pipeline is to improve the documents' accuracy and comprehensiveness while they are stored in the vector store. (Figure 4-17).

The technique you'll want to use will depend very much on your content, but here are a few ideas:

Specialized embedding

If your content has figures, such as images or charts, extract the figures and use a multimodal model to extract information from them.

Self-contained chunks

If you have tabular information, make sure to store the tabular data for each row in a format (such as JSON) where the description of the data is also present.

Hierarchical indexing

Index the data at different granularities: for example, you could embed and store sentences, paragraphs, pages, and chapters.

Contextual retrieval

Instead of storing just the embedding, add context to situate the document within the main document. For example, you could add the main document's title, the chapter in which this chunk appears, which category of products the main document describes, and other metadata. Anthropic (*https://oreil.ly/fQhQS*) suggests using a succinct prompt to generate this context.

Best match (BM)

Sometimes chunks contain very unusual text, such as part numbers (JPC-23456), that are useful for exact searches. These, when tokenized, are unlikely to show up in embedding-based searches. Use TF-IDF (*https://oreil.ly/ddCtw*) to find such unusual words as-is ("best match") in both the chunks and the queries, and add them to the searchable index.

Error correction

It is important to validate the data that goes into the vector store. If some part of the document fails to extract, repeat the ingestion. If your content is in unstructured formats such as PDF, make sure that your extraction is not lossy—for example, because many Python packages cannot correctly handle scanned

TECHNIQUES FOR BETTER INDEXING

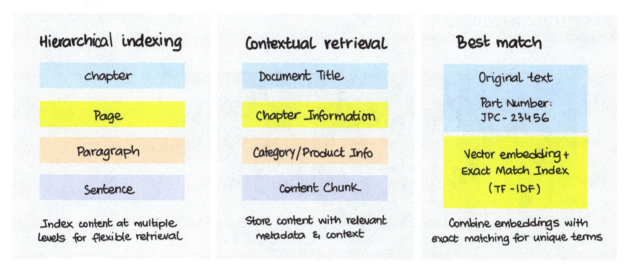

Figure 4-17. Techniques for better indexing.

PDFs with unknown fonts, you may lose text in nonstandard fonts.

Long context windows

One reason that RAG systems employ chunking is that foundational models used to have *primacy bias* (favoring information at the beginning of the context window, as shown in Figure 4-18) and *recency bias* (favoring information at the end of the context window). They also supported context windows of only about a thousand tokens. However, foundational models have been improving in their ability to process longer and longer prompts. For example, at the time of writing, Claude 3 provides nearly perfect recall of facts anywhere within a 200,000-token window (see Figure 4-19). Given this, you might not even need to chunk the information. However, LLMs are priced by number

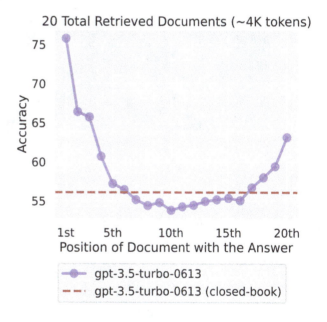

Figure 4-18. It is now possible to stuff long documents into the context window without having to chunk them.

Claude 3 Opus
Recall accuracy over 200K
(averaged over many diverse document sources and 'needle' sentences)

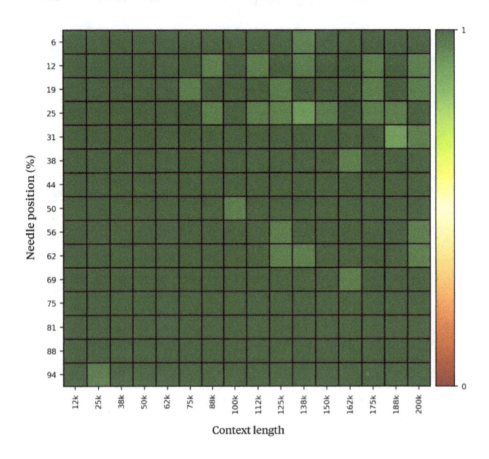

Figure 4-19. Anthropic seems to have solved the problem of primacy and recency bias.

of tokens, so sending long documents to the LLM for generation will increase costs.

A 2023 Stanford study (Liu et al, 2023 [*https://oreil.ly/zsfZl*]) found that models are better at using relevant information at the very beginning or end of their input context, and performance degrades for information found in the middle of the input context.

Anthropic (https://oreil.ly/LHJAv) showed in 2024 that over contexts of 200K tokens, the recall accuracy of an individual fact was nearly identical regardless of the position of the fact within the context window.

In this section, we have looked at how to build an RAG agent that can answer questions and is grounded in vetted, unstructured documents. Next, let's look at agents that can answer questions based on *structured* data, such as the data in comma-separated value (CSV) files or databases.

AGENTS THAT OPERATE ON STRUCTURED DATA

Suppose you have a table of structured data, perhaps in a PDF file, CSV file, or a relational database. How can you query it using natural language (see Figures 4-20 and 4-21)?

It is clear that we can't use a RAG agent for this task, because chunking a table into individual cells will not work. The meaning of the information within a table cell is tied closely to the meaning associated with its row and column (the table headers). Also, we don't always search for specific rows. Much of the way we process the information in tables involves tasks like counting or summing up the rows that meet specific criteria.

SQL Agent

Fortunately, you already know how to represent tabular data without losing the contextual information: create a schema for the rows and columns. You also know how to filter data in tables and compute aggregates: use SQL. Another

advantage of using a GenAI model to generate SQL and running the SQL on actual data is that the results will reflect the real data. Even if the SQL query is wrong or irrelevant, running whatever SQL query is generated will be factual and not result in a hallucination.

The approach to querying structured data with natural language involves five steps:

1. Convert the data into a relational database table that can be queried.

2. Create a SQL agent that will query the relational table.

3. Provide the table schema in a way that the model can understand.

4. Generate a SQL query to answer a given question, iterating on the query as necessary.

5. Return the results.

Let's see how to perform these steps (see Figure 4-21).

Figure 4-20. How do you query structured data in natural language?

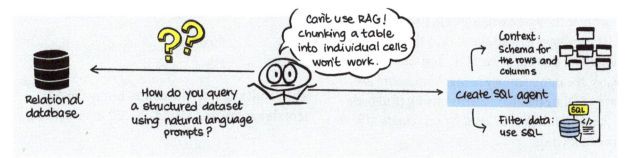

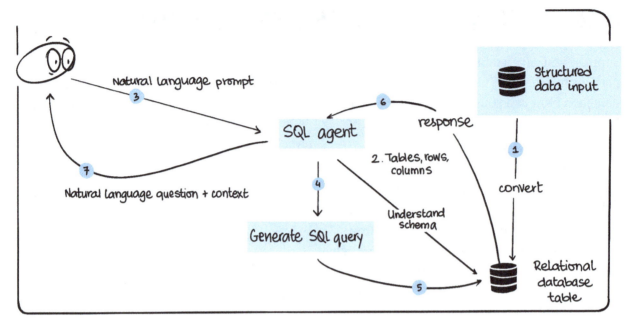

Figure 4-21. Steps to create an agent on structured data and query it.

Step 1: Construct a queryable table

To illustrate this technique, we'll use the US Social Security Administration's dataset of baby names. Here are a few lines from this CSV file:

```
name,gender,count,year
Mary,F,7065,1880
Anna,F,2604,1880
Emma,F,2003,1880
```

The first line states that the name Mary was given to 7,065 female babies in the year 1880.

Because the agent will use SQL to query this data, we have to load the data in this file into a database that supports SQL. You can read the CSV file into memory using Pandas and create a SQLite database on disk using (full code is on GitHub [*https://oreil.ly/vga_ch04qsd*]) the following:

```
df = pd.read_csv("names_all_years.csv")
engine = create_engine("sqlite:///
names.db")
df.to_sql("names", engine, index=False,
if_exists='replace')
```

Now that the data lives in a relational database table, you can query it using SQL. For example, to find some of the most popular names given to babies born in 1999, you can run the following query against the database:

```
db = SQLDatabase(engine=engine)
print(db.run("""SELECT name, gender,
count
FROM names WHERE count > 20000 AND
year == 1999; """))
```

The results include the names Emily (26,541 female babies) and David (20,352 male babies).

Step 2: Create a SQL agent

LangChain has a SQL agent capable of understanding the schema of a table and using a foundational model to construct a query. The agent also corrects and retries SQL errors. To create an instance of this agent, use the following:

```
from langchain_community.agent_toolkits
import create_sql_agent
model = ChatGoogleGenerativeAI(model="g
emini-1.5-flash", temperature=0.1)
agent_executor = create_sql_
agent(model, db=db,

agent_type="tool-calling",
verbose=True)
```

Instead of Gemini, you can also use any of the tool-calling models supported by LangChain, such as GPT-3.5, GPT-4, or Claude 3.

Invoke the agent with a natural language question:

```
agent_executor.invoke({
    "input": "what was the most
popular name for girls in 1999?"
})
```

The agent tries to construct a SQL query that it can run against the database to answer the question.

Step 3: Provide the schema to the agent

The LangChain SQL agent first asks the database for the list of tables, and for each of the tables, it asks for the schema and a table preview:

```
CREATE TABLE names (
name TEXT,
    gender TEXT,
```

```
    count BIGINT,
    year BIGINT
)

/*
```

Here, the database responds with:

```
3 rows from names table:
name     gender    count    year
Mary     F         7065     1880
Anna     F         2604     1880
Emma     F         2003     1880
```

Now that the agent knows the schema of the tables, it can try to create the query to answer the question.

Step 4: Generate the query

The LangChain SQL agent generates a candidate query based on the schema and the user's question. Here is the candidate query it generated for our example:

```
'SELECT name FROM names WHERE year ==
1999 AND gender == \\"F\\" ORDER BY
count DESC LIMIT 1'
```

When the candidate query is sent to SQLite, the database responds with an error:

```
Error: (sqlite3.OperationalError)
unrecognized token: "\"
```

The agent next changes the query syntax to avoid the backslash by using single quotes:

```
"SELECT name FROM names WHERE year ==
1999 AND gender == 'F' ORDER BY count
DESC LIMIT 1"
```

Step 5: Return result

When the agent sends the modified query to SQLite, the database responds with the result:

```
[('Emily',)]
```

The agent can then stuff the result into the context and generate this response to the user input:

```
{'input': 'what was the most popular
name for girls in 1999?',
 'output': 'The most popular name for
girls in 1999 was Emily.'}
```

And that's it! You now have a SQL agent that is capable of answering natural language questions on structured data.

Fixing Logical Errors

In the previous example, the original SQL query the agent created was wrong, but it was able to fix the error based on the error message from the database and retry the query. Sometimes, though, the error is not syntactic but logical. The agent might create a valid SQL statement, but the

SQL query will not answer the question that was asked (see Figure 4-22). Let's look at an example.

Suppose we ask the SQL agent the following:

```
{"input": "what was the most popular
male name in the 1950s?"}
```

The agent creates the following SQL query:

```
SELECT name FROM names WHERE year
BETWEEN 1950 AND 1959 AND gender = 'M'
ORDER BY count DESC LIMIT 1
```

When this query is run against the database, we get the result:

```
[('Michael',)]The most popular male
name in the 1950s was Michael.
```

However, this is wrong. Can you spot the problem?

The generated SQL query returns the most popular name in any single year in the time period, because each row of the table corresponds to a single year. However, we want the most popular name over the *entire* time period. The count column is the number of babies with the name

FIXING SQL AGENTS' LOGICAL ERRORS

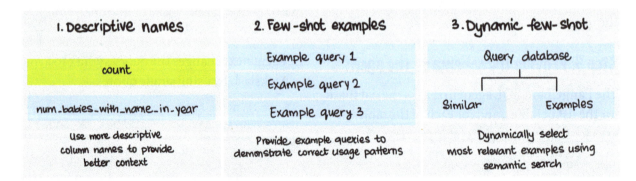

Figure 4-22. Common ways to fix logical errors in SQL agents.

born in a specific year. So, the ordering really needs to be done on the **SUM(count)** over the 10 years of data.

This is the sort of problem that crops up whenever you take GenAI applications to production—while the model can handle basic inputs, it starts to fail when more advanced reasoning is required. Therefore, it is important to look at how to solve these kinds of problems. One way is to make the prompt more detailed, and the other is to employ some examples to show the model how to handle certain situations. Let's look at both approaches.

Approach 1: Adding descriptions to the schema

The model is using a schema based on the column names—which are sometimes cryptic and not very readable. Here, the count column is quite ambiguous. We could add comments to the column fields when creating the table, to give the LLM more context about column names:

```
metadata = sqlalchemy.MetaData()
name_table = sqlalchemy.Table(
    'names', metadata,
    sqlalchemy.Column('name',
sqlalchemy.String(32), nullable=False,
comment='first name of baby'),
    sqlalchemy.Column('gender',
sqlalchemy.String(1), nullable=False,
comment='gender of baby: male (M) or
female (F)'),
    sqlalchemy.Column('year',
sqlalchemy.Integer, nullable=False,
comment='year of birth'),
    sqlalchemy.Column('count',
sqlalchemy.Integer, nullable=False,
comment='Number of babies with this
name and gender in this year')
```

```
)
engine = sqlalchemy.create_
engine("sqlite:///names.db")
metadata.create_all(engine)
df.to_sql("names", engine, index=False,
if_exists='append')
```

Alternately, we could simply give the column a more descriptive name:

```
df2 = df.rename(columns={'count': 'num_
babies_with_name_in_year'})
df2.to_sql("names", engine,
index=False, if_exists='replace')
```

Although having more descriptive names is better and could help the LLM generate better SQL, it was not enough to solve the logical error in our example of finding the most popular male name in a decade. Let's look at the second potential solution.

Approach 2: Adding few-shot examples

Another way to improve the generated SQL is to use *few-shot prompting*. Since the count column is ambiguous, you can demonstrate a few queries that use the count column properly when a range of years is referenced:

```
examples = [
    {
        "input": "how many babies named
Michael were born in 1970?",
        "query": "SELECT count FROM
names WHERE name = 'Michael'"
    },
    {
        "input": "how many babies named
Michael were born between 1970 and
1973?",
        "query": "SELECT SUM(count) AS
count FROM names WHERE name = 'Michael'
AND year BETWEEN 1970 AND 1973"
```

```
    },
    {
        "input": "What was the most
popular name in 1970?",
        "query": "SELECT name FROM
names WHERE year = 1970 ORDER BY count
DESC 1"
    },
    {
        "input": "What was the most
popular name between 1970 and 1973?",
        "query": "WITH names_for_years
AS (SELECT name, gender, SUM(count) AS
count FROM names WHERE year BETWEEN
1970 AND 1973 GROUP BY name, gender)
SELECT name FROM names_for_years ORDER
BY count DESC 1"
    },
]
```

Note that the previous examples do not include any query that sums up over a decade—this is so that we can test that this approach does generalize to new queries. Use these examples to create a prompt (it will replace the default prompt used by the agent):

```
example_prompt = PromptTemplate.from_
template("User input: {input}\nSQL
query: {query}")
prompt = FewShotPromptTemplate(
    examples=examples,
    example_prompt=example_prompt,
    prefix="You are a SQLite expert.
… Below are a number of examples of
questions and their corresponding SQL
queries.",
    suffix="User input: {input}\nSQL
query: ",
    input_variables=["input", "top_k",
"table_info"],
)
full_prompt = ChatPromptTemplate.from_
messages(
```

```
    [
        SystemMessagePromptTemplate
(prompt=prompt),
        ("human", "{input}"),
        MessagesPlaceholder("agent_
scratchpad"),
    ]
)
```

Pass in this prompt when creating the SQL agent:

```
agent_executor = create_sql_
agent(model, db=db, prompt=full_
prompt, agent_type="tool-calling",
verbose=True)
```

Now, invoke the LangChain SQL agent with the problematic query:

```
agent_executor.invoke(
    input={"input": "what was the most
popular male name in the 1950s?"},
)
```

This time, the generated SQL will be correct:

```
WITH names_for_years AS (SELECT name,
gender, SUM(count) AS count FROM names
WHERE year BETWEEN 1950 AND 1959 GROUP
BY name, gender) SELECT name FROM
names_for_years WHERE gender = "M"
ORDER BY count DESC LIMIT 1
```

The result now reflects the entire time period:

```
[('James',)]The most popular male name
in the 1950s was James.
```

Dynamic few-shot prompting

It is important to log the intermediate steps (such as the generated query) and collect user feedback to learn which queries are not providing the expected answers and why. With such a process in place, you can troubleshoot errors and fix bugs by continually improving prompts and adding examples.

As the number of examples grows, you will reach the limit of the context window (due to either cost or latency). When that happens, you could dynamically choose the most relevant examples for a specific question using RAG:

```
example_selector =
SemanticSimilarityExampleSelector.from_
examples(
    examples,
    embeddings,
    vectorstore,
    k=5,
    input_keys=["input"],
)
```

So far in this section, we have only discussed cases where the SQL query is used to create a text response. But what if you want to create a chart?

Charting Structured Data

You can generate charts by having the GenAI model generate code, then run the generated code within a sandbox (see Figure 4-23). Charting structured data involves building an agentic application that ties together three capabilities:

- Using the SQL agent to pull the data you need
- Prompting the LLM to generate the necessary code (usually in Python, using Matplotlib)
- Running the generated code in a sandbox

Let's look at these steps (the full code is on GitHub [*https://oreil.ly/vga_ch04qsd*]) to plot the trend in the popularity of the name Anna.

CHARTING STRUCTURED DATA WITH GENAI

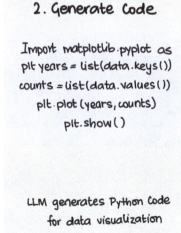
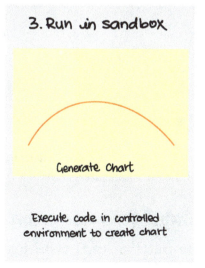

Figure 4-23. Charting structured data with GenAI.

Step 1: Use the SQL agent

Use the SQL agent that you built in the previous section to obtain the data to be charted:

```
popularity = agent_executor.invoke(
    input={"input": "Get data on number
of babies with the name 'Anna' by year
as a list of year, count"},  top_k=1000
)
```

Note that this includes a `top_k` parameter to tell the agent that it is okay to return a large result set. When we did this, the SQL agent generated the following query:

```
SELECT year, SUM(count) AS count FROM
names WHERE name = 'Anna' GROUP BY year
```

It ran this query against the database, returning the data as a tuple:

```
[(1880, 2616), (1881, 2714),..., (2022,
2953), (2023, 2918)]
```

Based on this result, the SQL agent generated the following text:

```
The number of babies named Anna born
each year is:

* 1880: 2616
* 1881: 2714
...
* 2022: 2953
* 2023: 2918
```

Now that we have the data in text form, let's look at how to generate a chart.

Step 2: Generate charting code

Instruct the GenAI model to generate Python code to chart the data in the desired format. To do this, you need to stuff the data into the prompt. You could use a LangChain prompt template, or do it within an invocation of the model:

```
plot_code = model.invoke("Create Python
code to chart this data as a line
plot:\n" + popularity['output'])
```

When we did this, the resulting code was:

```python
import matplotlib.pyplot as plt

# Data as a dictionary
anna_names = {
    1880: 2616,
    1881: 2714,
    ...
    2022: 2953,
    2023: 2918
}

# Extract data for plotting
years = list(anna_names.keys())
counts = list(anna_names.values())

# Create the line plot
plt.plot(years, counts)

# Set labels and title
plt.xlabel("Year")
plt.ylabel("Number of Babies Named
Anna")
plt.title("Popularity of the Name Anna
Over Time")

# Show the plot
plt.show()
```

Step 3: Run the code in a sandbox

Save the code and launch an interpreter by using `subprocess.call()` from a Python program or `%run` in a Jupyter Notebook. When we did this, we got the chart shown in Figure 4-24.

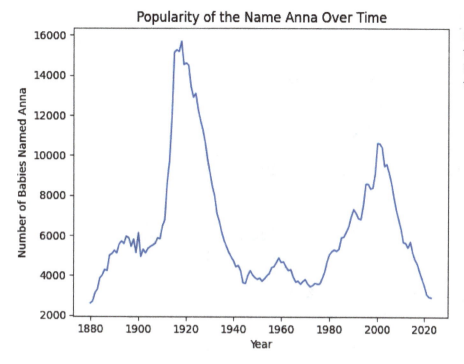

Figure 4-24. Chart depicting the popularity of the name Anna in the United States from 1880 to 2020.

AGENTIC ARCHITECTURES

In this chapter so far, you have learned that agents are useful when a single LLM call is not enough to perform some task. In such cases, it can be helpful to break the task down into steps that the agent can carry out, do some of those steps with the help of tools (including calling the APIs of backend services and databases), and draw contextual information from document stores.

Andrew Ng, a Stanford professor and founder of DeepLearning.AI, introduced a helpful framework for categorizing design patterns (*https://oreil.ly/WRenq*) for building agents with four strategies: reflection, tool use, planning, and multi-agent collaboration. Let's look at them one by one. You have already learned the underlying capabilities, so this section just shows you how the design patterns are implemented.

Reflection

The idea behind *reflection* is to ask the LLM to perform a task, then ask it to critique its own output. Then incorporate the critique and the original output, and ask the LLM to perform the task again. The researchers who introduced this method called it self-refinement (*https://oreil.ly/xrMXJ*), but it is now more commonly called *reflection* or *self-reflection* (see **Figure 4-25**).

For example, step 1 might be to ask the LLM to write an article:

REFLECTION

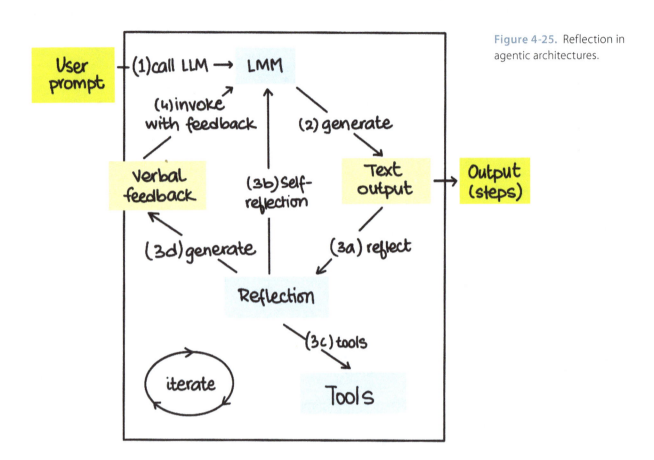

Figure 4-25. Reflection in agentic architectures.

You are a travel expert and outdoors guide. Write an article for an inflight magazine about {topic} in {location}.

In Step 2, the LLM generates the article. In Step 3a, you can ask it to reflect by sending it the article with the following prompt:

Here's an article written by a travel expert for an in-flight magazine. Critique the article using the "4 Ps of marketing" framework. {article}

We are asking the LLM to use the 4 Ps of marketing (*https://oreil.ly/OsU1L*) framework (product, price, place, and promotion), originally introduced by Neil Borden (*https://oreil.ly/OeuvX*) in the 1950s, to critique the copy and create verbal feedback (Step 3b). When we tried this on Gemini, asking for an article on hiking options in the North Cascades National Park, the price section of its criticism was as follows:

Strengths: The article indirectly mentions the "price" of the hiking experience through the mention of

```
permit requirements and the need for
gear and supplies.  This subtly signals
that the experience may require some
investment.
Weaknesses:  There is no explicit
mention of the cost of permits, gear,
or transportation, which could deter
some readers who are price-sensitive.
The article could benefit from a section
on budgeting for a trip to North
Cascades.*
```

Now, in Step 4, combine the article and critique and ask the LLM to improve the article:

```
You are a travel expert and outdoors
guide. You wrote the following article
for an inflight magazine about {topic}
in {location} and received the
following feedback from the marketing
director. Improve the article taking
into account the feedback.
Original article:
{article}

Feedback from marketing:
{critique}
```

The resulting article should be improved through this process of self-reflection. Indeed, when we did so, Gemini added a pricing section and more explicit information on how to get to the trails (the "place" part of the feedback).

You can go beyond self-reflection by providing the LLM with tools such as compilers, code interpreters, search engines, validators, or scorers that it can use to critique its output. The key is that these tools should provide verbal feedback, (*https://oreil.ly/W1-JJ*) such as error messages and suggestions of what could be improved. You can wrap the generation and reflection calls into a loop, so that the LLM can validate and progressively amend (*https://oreil.ly/zfAbi*) its outputs, much like humans would edit their own writing.

When performing reflection, it's a good practice to show the user all the intermediate steps along with the criticism, so that they understand how the LLM got to the final answer. Such transparency builds trust.

Tool Use

In the tool use pattern, you provide the LLM with a set of tools or functions, such as to search different sources (web, corporate data, database) or to invoke backend applications (inventory, catalog, pricing). You can even have it carry out actions, such as sending emails or invoking other ML models or agents (see **Figure 4-26**).

Frameworks like LangChain and AutoGen provide a lot of flexibility in how you define tools for agents to use. You can provide the framework with a set of tools, each defined by its function signature, the name of the function, and its input and outputs. The agent framework will select the right tool and incorporate the output of the tool into the final output. In order to help the agent framework understand what the tools do, it's important that you either tell the LLM in your prompt when to use each tool or make the names of the tools descriptive. We'll take the latter approach in the example that follows.

Knowing that LLMs cannot do math, we can create a tool for the LLM to use whenever it

---

*   Generated by Gemini in October 2024. Code can be found in the book's GitHub repository.

TOOL USE

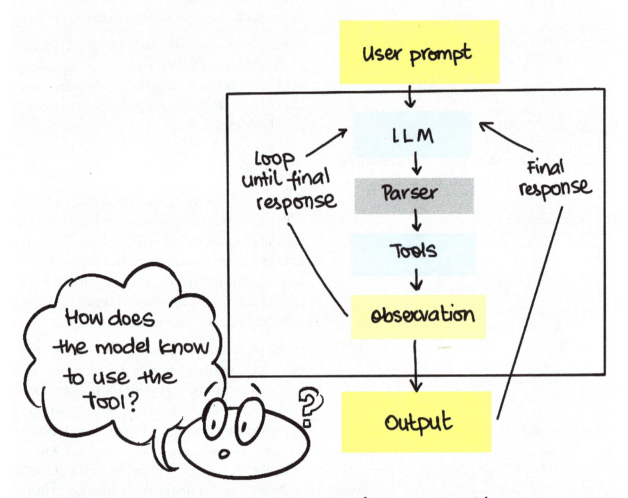

By interleaving the steps of generating a thought
("reasoning") and then taking task-specific actions. This
method is called ReAct: Reasoning and Action.

Figure 4-26. Tool use in agentic architectures.

needs to calculate the result of a formula. (The full code is on GitHub.)

```python
from langchain_core.tools import tool
from py_expression_eval import Parser

@tool
def calculate(formula: str, parameters:
dict) -> float:
    """Calculate by applying a
mathematical formula to a set of input
parameters"""
    parser = Parser()
    return parser.parse(formula).
evaluate(parameters)
```

To find the root of a quadratic equation, call the previous Python code as follows:

```python
calculate(formula="(-b + sqrt
(b^2 - 4*a*c))/(2*a)",
parameters={'a': 1.0, 'b': 1.0,
'c': -6.0})
```

As you can see, you'll have to know the formula for finding the root of a quadratic equation in order to use this tool effectively. Regurgitating the formula is something a foundational model can do quite well. Combining this tool with a model can allow the model to accomplish tasks that would otherwise be at risk of hallucination.

For example, suppose we want to create a financial question-answering system. We can use the tool and an LLM together to create an agent as follows:

```python
model = ChatVertexAI(model="gemini-1.5-
flash")
agent_executor = create_react_
agent(model, [calculate])
```

If we provide the agent with a user prompt, it will use the tool as necessary:

```python
prompt_message =
HumanMessage(content="""
    You are a financial expert who can
write down the appropriate formula and
    apply the mathematical formula to
calculate the desired value.

    Question:
    If I invest $1000 in the stock
market, and it returns 7% annually, and
    I reinvest the returns, how much
money will I have in 6 years?

    Answer:
    """
)
response = agent_executor.
invoke({"messages": [prompt_message]})
```

In this case, the LLM returns the formula to use:

```python
principal * (1 + rate) ^ years
```

Then it uses the `calculate` tool to perform the calculation on the parameters:

```python
{"principal": 1000.0, "rate": 0.07,
"years": 6.0}}
```

This yields the correct result: $1,500.73.

ReAct

How did that work? How did the LLM know how to use the tool? The hint is in the way we created the agent:

```python
agent_executor = create_react_
agent(model, [calculate])
```

ReAct in this case stands for reasoning and action, an approach introduced in a 2023 paper (*https://oreil.ly/k3yoS*) by researchers from Princeton and Google Brain. It works by interleaving the steps of generating a thought ("reasoning") and then taking task-specific actions.

In the reasoning step, the LLM generates a thought, such as the following:

```
To calculate the amount, I will need to
calculate the compound interest. The
answer is:

{'function_call': {'name': 'calculate',
'arguments': '{"formula": "principal
* (1 + rate) ^ years", "parameters":
{"principal": 1000.0, "rate": 0.07,
"years": 6.0}}'}}
```

This is highly streamlined, because frontier models such as GPT-4, Gemini, and Claude all support function calling and are able to generate precise function call signatures, as shown previously. If you're using a smaller model that does not support function calling, you'd need to do more work to marshal the generated text into the appropriate data types.

In the action step, this function call is picked up by the agent, which invokes the tool with that name and arguments as follows:

```
calculate.invoke({
    'formula': "principal * (1 + rate)
^ years",
    'parameters': {"principal": 1000.0,
"rate": 0.07, "years": 6.0}}
})
```

This result replaces the original text, and the agent carries out another loop of reasoning and action, eventually generating a final result.

Dynamic Planning

In our reflection example, we had the model create an article, then asked it to apply a specific form of critique (the 4 Ps of marketing) and use that critique to improve the article. In our tool use example, we gave the model a calculator tool, and in the prompt, specifically asked the model to write out a formula to answer the user's question and use that tool to perform the calculation.

Is it possible for the model to know that it should write articles in multiple stages? Or that it should answer financial questions on the basis of formulas and modeling, not purely through text generation?

For complex tasks that you can't decompose into a set of steps ahead of time, you can use *dynamic planning* so that the agent can decide dynamically what steps to take (see Figure 4-27). Dynamic planning is less reliable than reflection or tool use, so if you can fix the set of steps deterministically, use reflection or tool use. As illustrated in the figure, we recommend that you employ dynamic planning only when static decomposition of the task is not possible.

In this section, we'll explore a common approach by which you can guide an agent to do dynamic planning and permit a human user to control the plan and its execution.

Chain of thought

One approach to planning, which was introduced in a 2022 paper (*https://oreil.ly/R0dcn*) by researchers at Google Brain, is called chain of thought. It involves asking the LLM to list the steps needed to solve the problem, then applying

DYNAMIC PLANNING

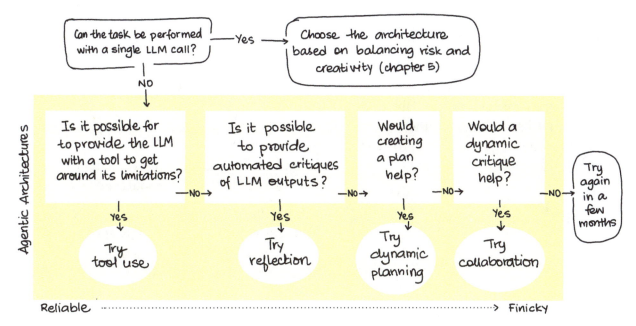

Figure 4-27. Dynamic planning.

the steps one by one to come up with the answer. Surprisingly, this "think carefully" approach can help the LLM solve problems it otherwise can't. Another approach to planning is the ReAct approach introduced in the previous section; here, we provide the agentic framework with a set of tools and ask it to select a tool that can help simplify the problem.

The training of many frontier models already includes some examples of applying a chain-of-thought process, by applying techniques such as thought generation (*https://oreil.ly/mRf6j*). So we don't always need to explicitly tell the model to break down tasks into simpler steps. For example, we can ask Gemini Flash the following:

```
Who is the mayor of the capital of
the third most populated state in the
United States?
```

This resulted in the following output when we tried it out in October 2024:

```
Here's how to break down the question:

* **Third most populated state:** This
would be Florida.
* **Capital:** The capital of Florida
is Tallahassee.
* **Mayor:**  The current Mayor of
Tallahassee is **John Dailey**.
```

Even though we didn't explicitly prompt the model to break down the question, it generated the necessary thoughts to come up with the answer.

Need for transparency

The model's ability to break down questions and answer them is hit-and-miss. At the time of writing, Gemini Flash couldn't correctly answer the following question:

```
How many states in the US have capital
cities that end in City?
```

This question requires reasoning, and presumably, the correct answer is not available as-is in its training data. Putting together a plausible answer one token at a time, it provided a nonsensical answer:

```
There are **zero** states in the US
that have capital cities that end in
"City".

While many state capitals have "City"
in their names (e.g., Oklahoma City,
Phoenix City, etc.),  none of them end
with "City".
```

Obviously, the first sentence of the answer and the second sentence contradict each other. Besides, the capital of Arizona is called Phoenix, not Phoenix City.

Let's prepend a chain-of-thought instruction to the question:

```
Write down the steps to solve this
question, and work through the steps
one-by-one to come up with the answer:
{question}
```

The model writes out a plan:

```
**Steps:**

1. **List US states and their
capitals:** We need to know the capital
cities of all US states.
2. **Identify capitals ending in
"City":**  We'll go through our list
and check if each capital ends in
"City".
```

```
3. **Count the matching capitals:**
We'll keep track of how many capitals
we find that end in "City".
```

Going through this plan, it comes up with:

```
* **Kansas:** Topeka (No)
* **Missouri:** Jefferson City (Yes!)
* **New York:** Albany (No)
* **Oklahoma:** Oklahoma City (Yes!)
```

It answers that there are two US states whose capitals end in "City": Missouri and Oklahoma.

Unfortunately, it is not clear that the model actually went through the steps, as opposed to simply stating it did so (see the notebook in the GitHub repository associated with this book). The second step includes the following words:

```
2. **Identify capitals ending in
"City":**

   * **Alabama:** Montgomery (No)
   * **Alaska:** Juneau (No)
   * **Arizona:** Phoenix (No)
   * **Arkansas:** Little Rock (No)
   * ...  (Continue going through all
the states)
```

The model could simply have hallucinated going through the list and applying the condition. That's why it's better to break down the steps into multiple LLM calls: one to create the plan, the rest to implement the plan one step at a time. This way, we can also provide transparency to the user. Let's do that next.

Executing a dynamic plan

We'll set a prompt to ask the LLM to generate a plan by sending it the prompt (see code in GitHub):

```
What are the steps to solve the
following question?
Do not provide the answer, only the
steps. Return the result as a list.
{question}
```

We asked:

```
How many states in the US have capital
cities that end in City?
```

Gemini Flash (which we used in October 2024) returned the following:

```
1. Create a list of all US states.
2. Create a list of all US state
capitals.
3. Iterate through the list of state
capitals.
4. For each capital, check if it ends
with "City".
5. If it does, increment a counter.
6. Return the final value of the
counter.
```

While we could set up an LLM call to invoke this prompt to execute a single step of the plan, a simpler and more reliable approach is to prompt the model to convert the previous plan into code, then execute the generated code within a Python sandbox:

```
Convert the following steps into a
Python function.
        {plan}
```

When we did so, we got the correct answer, four: Jefferson City, Carson City, Oklahoma City, and Salt Lake City are the capitals of Missouri, Nevada, Oklahoma, and Utah, respectively.

How did we know the generated plan would be amenable to being converted into code and executed? After all, the user question is unknown.

This is the challenge with dynamic planning; in practice, you will need different approaches to different plans. Sometimes, you will have to execute each step with an LLM; sometimes you will need to use reflection; sometimes you will need to use tools. This question turned out to need the tool use pattern with a Python sandbox. You'll have to incorporate a classifier on user intent and multiple planners that can generate different types of plans, and invoke the right executors. All of these steps can fail and will need to be retried. Dynamic planning, at the time of writing, is finicky.

Multi-Agent Collaboration

Multi-agent collaboration involves breaking down a task into subtasks that are carried out by different roles (see Figure 4-28). This is exactly what we did explicitly in our reflection example—the first call was to an LLM that played the role of a travel writer, and the second call was to an LLM that played the role of a marketing director. In our reflection example, we broke the task down in a static way; multi-agent collaboration involves doing this breakdown *dynamically*.

Just as planning is dynamic tool use, you can think of multi-agent collaboration as dynamic reflection. Each agent carries out its own workflow and can invoke tools, perform planning, and even maintain state. An agent may ask other agents for help by sending messages. (Frameworks like Crew AI simplify managing swarms of agents.)

Next, let's look at how to integrate multiple agents to solve complex tasks.

MULTIAGENT COLLABORATION

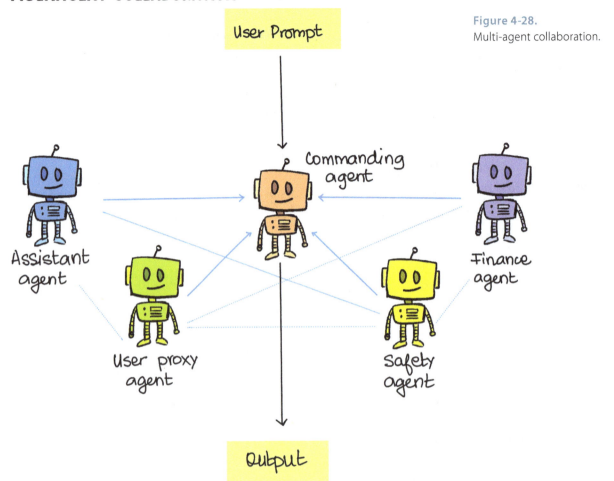

Figure 4-28.
Multi-agent collaboration.

AGENT INTEGRATION PATTERNS

As agentic systems move from proof-of-concept to production, two critical integration challenges emerge. First, agents need reliable, standardized ways to connect to the diverse tools and data sources they depend on—from databases and APIs to file systems and SaaS platforms. Second, as organizations deploy multiple specialized agents, these agents increasingly need to discover, communicate, and collaborate with each other without central orchestration. The ad hoc, custom integration approaches that work for simple demos quickly become unmanageable at enterprise scale. Two emerging patterns address these challenges: the Model Context Protocol (MCP) standardizes how agents connect to external resources and tools, while agent-to-agent (A2A) communication enables direct coordination between agents. These patterns represent the maturation of agentic systems from isolated prototypes to composable, enterprise-ready architectures.

As an analogy, the MCP enables you to use all the tools in your kitchen and ingredients in your pantry to make delicious food. A2A enables you to communicate with your friends to organize a potluck picnic. Each of your friends has an MCP that works in their own kitchen.

Model Context Protocol

As agentic systems become more complex, the need for standardized communication between agents and external tools has become apparent. The MCP addresses this by providing a universal interface for LLMs to securely connect to data sources, tools, and services.

The MCP is an open protocol that standardizes how AI assistants and agents connect to external systems (external to the LLM, not external to the organization). Think of it as the "USB standard" for AI tools—instead of building custom integrations for every database, API, or service, developers can implement MCP once and connect to any MCP-compatible resource.

Before MCP, each agent needed custom integration code for every external system. With MCP, all resources use the same standardized interface. This dramatically reduces the integration overhead as your agentic system grows.

Core MCP concepts

The MCP defines three primary primitives that agents interact with:

Resources

> Files, database records, API endpoints, or any data source that an agent might need to read from. Resources are read-only and represent the "knowledge" available to an agent.

Tools

> Functions that agents can invoke to take actions or perform computations. Unlike resources, tools can modify state or trigger side effects.

Prompts

> Reusable prompt templates that can be dynamically populated with context from resources or tool outputs.

In our kitchen analogy, spices and vegetables are resources, while knives and blenders are tools. Instructions such as "make a gazpacho" would be prompts.

An MCP server exposes these primitives through a standardized interface. For example, a database MCP server would expose table schemas as resources and query execution as tools, while a file system MCP server would expose files as resources and file operations as tools.

The MCP in practice

The real power of the MCP emerges in enterprise environments where agents need access to multiple internal systems. Instead of building N × M integrations (N agents × M systems), you build N agents + M MCP servers.

Agents can discover available resources dynamically, find the data they need regardless of where it's stored, and invoke appropriate tools to take actions. This discovery mechanism means agents can work with new systems as soon as MCP servers are deployed, without code changes.

The protocol is transport-agnostic—MCP can run over HTTP, WebSockets, or even stdio for in-process communication. This flexibility makes it suitable for both cloud native and on-premises deployments. The standardization that the MCP provides is crucial for the agentic future—as organizations deploy multiple AI agents, having a common protocol for tool and data access prevents integration hell and enables agents to be truly composable.

Agent-to-Agent Communication (A2A)

While multi-agent collaboration typically involves agents coordinated by a central orchestrator, agent-to-agent communication represents a more decentralized approach where agents directly communicate, negotiate, and coordinate with each other.

Traditional multi-agent systems often rely on a coordinator that assigns tasks and manages agent interactions. A2A (Figure 4-29) flips this model—agents discover each other, advertise their capabilities, and form ad hoc collaborations to solve problems.

In the traditional model, a central coordinator assigns tasks to a research agent and analysis agent, then coordinates their handoff. With A2A, the research agent advertises its market research capability, the analysis agent discovers agents with that capability, and they directly negotiate collaboration terms.

A2A communication patterns

There are three patterns frequently used in A2A communication:

Service discovery

Agents announce their capabilities to a registry or discovery service, allowing other agents to find collaborators dynamically.

Direct messaging

Agents communicate through standardized message protocols, often using existing infrastructure like message queues or pub/sub (publish/subscribe) systems.

Negotiation protocols

Agents can negotiate terms of collaboration—what data to share, how to split work, or how to handle conflicts.

A market analysis agent might register capabilities for market analysis and trend prediction with a discovery service. When another agent requests collaboration, the market analysis agent can negotiate terms including required data, delivery timeframes, and computational costs.

In our potluck analogy, every attendee might advertise what they can bring (service discovery), an organizer might create a master menu list of how many mains and how many desserts

AGENT INTEGRATION PATTERNS

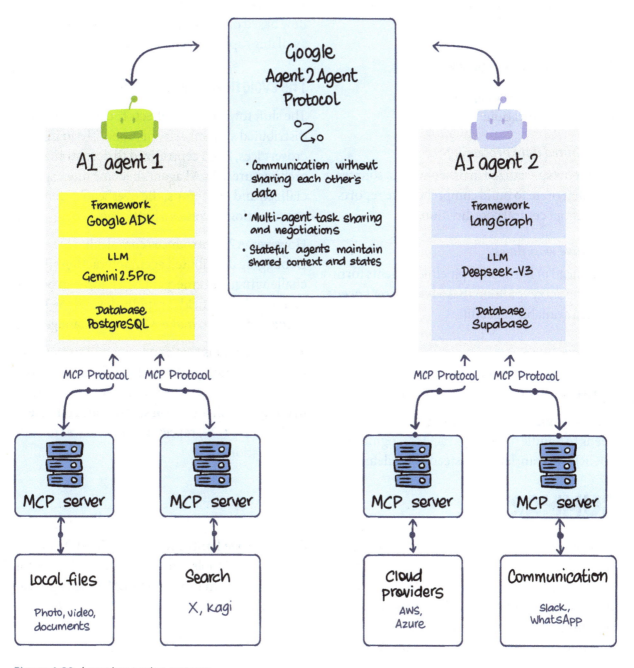

Figure 4-29. Agent integration patterns.

(orchestration), and people who both want to bring tabouli could negotiate a split of work that might even allow the salad to be assembled at the picnic site.

Real-world A2A applications

There are three major applications for A2A communication:

Distributed data processing

Agents specialized in different data sources collaborate to build comprehensive reports without central coordination.

Adaptive workflows

Instead of hardcoded pipelines, agents form temporary coalitions based on current needs and available capabilities.

Fault tolerance

If one agent fails, others can discover alternatives and maintain service continuity.

Consider document processing, where an agent needs to handle optical character recognition (OCR) and translation. Instead of predefined pipelines, the agent discovers available OCR and translation agents dynamically, requests services as needed, and adapts the workflow based on document characteristics and available capabilities.

The evolution toward A2A

The shift toward A2A reflects broader trends in distributed systems—from monoliths to microservices, from centralized to decentralized architectures. As AI agents become more specialized and numerous, the overhead of central coordination becomes a bottleneck.

However, A2A introduces complexity. Debugging distributed agent interactions is challenging, and emergent behaviors can be unpredictable. The field is rapidly developing standards and tools to make A2A more manageable.

The key insight is that as AI capabilities improve, the coordination problem shifts from "how do we make agents smart enough?" to "how do we make agent collaboration scalable and reliable?" A2A (Figure 4-29) represents one answer to that question.

SUMMARY

An *agent* is software using GenAI to automate a single step in a multistep application. An entire application that uses agents is called *agentic*. In this chapter, we discussed building agentic systems using GenAI. The next chapter will dive into these systems' architecture. Then, in

Chapter 6, we'll introduce you to LLMOps, a framework of tools, practices, and workflows for deploying and maintaining LLM-based applications in production.

## Chapter 5

ARCHITECTING GENAI APPLICATIONS

In Chapter 4, we discussed how to build agentic systems, but assumed that each agent involved an LLM call. An architecture that relies on agents that invoke an LLM each and every time results in an underengineered application that will be too expensive and too slow. In this chapter (see Figure 5-1), we look at how to balance engineering complexity, cost, latency, and the risks of using an LLM for a specific use case.

CHOOSING A FOUNDATIONAL MODEL

When building a GenAI application, one of the first choices you'll grapple with is which LLM to use as your foundational model. Figure 5-2 provides a decision tree for this choice.

While it is possible to be LLM-agnostic by using a framework such as LangChain, the reality is not as simple (Figure 5-3). The code will work, but the results will not be the same when you change LLMs. That's because you will change the prompts and parsing code (even when employing signatures and Pydantic structures, as we recommend in Chapter 2) to make each step of your application pipeline.

Code is usually developed incrementally during a proof of concept by experimenting at each step. Such incrementally developed applications rarely work when you change the LLM that it is based on. Given this, it is best to do your experimentation with the model provider that you plan to use in production.

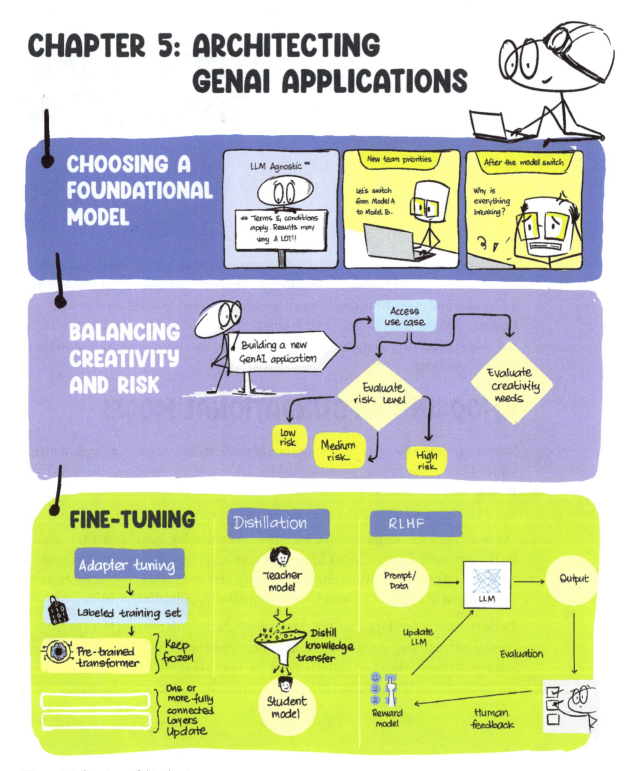

Figure 5-1. Structure of this chapter.

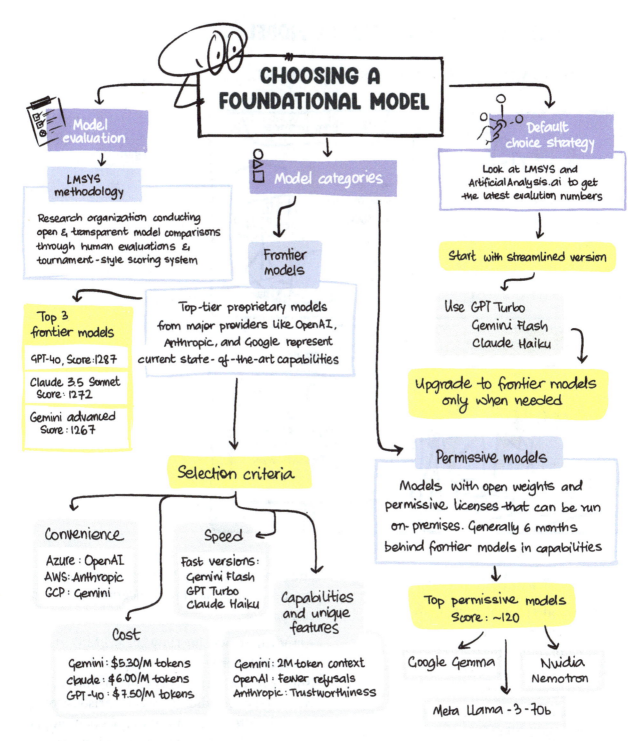

Figure 5-2. Selecting a foundational LLM, at the time of writing. Use the same process at the time you are reading this book, but the relative scores and model versions might be different.

CHOOSING A FOUNDATIONAL MODEL

IS IT POSSIBLE TO BE LLM-AGNOSTIC? SURE, BUT...

Figure 5-3. It's possible to be LLM-agnostic, but it isn't easy.

Head-to-Head Model Comparisons

Because model providers often game their metrics and benchmark datasets, one of the best ways of comparing the quality of different models is to do a blinded study where a human is presented with the responses from two LLMs and asked to choose the one that's better. The research organization Large Model Systems (LMSYS) (*https://chat.lmsys.org*) uses this approach at scale, openly and transparently, and publishes the input prompt, output responses, and human preference of every paired comparison.

At the time of writing (July 2024), LMSYS has conducted over a million such paired comparisons. Because every data point is available, you can slice and dice these comparisons: for example, filtering on specific topics or prompts of a certain length. The LMSYS leaderboard treats these human comparisons like matches in a chess tournament, and calculates an "arena score" (loosely analogous to the Elo score by which chess players are ranked) for each model. All the major model providers release their models on LMSYS, and the leaderboard changes frequently.

However, the LMSYS approach is not without its drawbacks. Because the human raters are members of the general public, not experts on the topic, they may prefer confident and simplistic text (even if it's wrong!) over correct but nuanced text.

Frontier Models

At the time of writing, the top three models were GPT-4o (with an arena score of 1287), Claude 3.5 Sonnet (1272), and Gemini Advanced (1267). We'll refer to these three as *frontier* models. These three frontier models are proprietary and were created by OpenAI, Anthropic, and Google, respectively. Because the scores are close enough, and the relative rankings of these models (Figure 5-4) change as new versions are released, you might treat the frontier models as being of approximately equal quality and choose between them based on convenience, cost, speed, or unique capabilities. Here's how we break these categories down:

Convenience

If your application is on Azure, using Azure OpenAI may be the most convenient; if your application is on AWS, you might choose Anthropic, available in AWS Sagemaker; and if it is on Google Cloud, you might use Gemini, available via Vertex AI. Note that all three frontier models are available on

all three clouds. This is more about ease of integration with other cloud capabilities than mere availability. Also, as this book was going to press, Amazon released Amazon Nova, whose benchmarks indicate that it's a frontier model, but it was not available on LMSYS.

Cost

An organization called Artificial Analysis (*http://artificialanalysis.ai*) provides an unbiased comparison of LLM costs. At the time of writing, in July 2024, Google's Gemini ($5.30 per million tokens) was the least expensive of the frontier models, as compared to Claude Sonnet ($6) and GPT-4o ($7.50). Prices do change, so check the source for a more recent comparison.

Speed

Providers offer streamlined versions of their frontier models that sacrifice quality slightly to reduce response latency. Gemini Flash, GPT-4o-mini, and Claude Haiku are good choices for use cases requiring speedy responses—Artificial Analysis ranks these models in terms of speed as well. At the time of writing, Gemini Flash is 30% faster than Haiku and 100% faster than GPT-4o-mini, but that will probably have changed by the time you read this.

Capabilities

The model providers differentiate their offerings on unique capabilities, such as the length of the context window or support for specific use cases. For example, Gemini Ultra has a 2-million-token context window

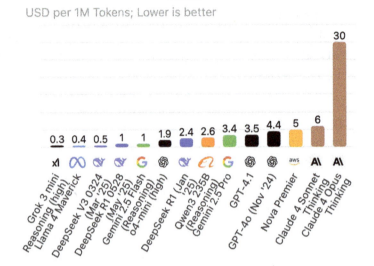

PRICE
USD per 1M Tokens; Lower is better

Figure 5-4. Models ranked by quality and by price in July 2024. GPT-4o, Claude Sonnet, and Gemini are the best-quality models. Of these, Gemini ($5.30 per million tokens) and Claude Sonnet ($6) are less expensive than GPT-4o ($7.50).

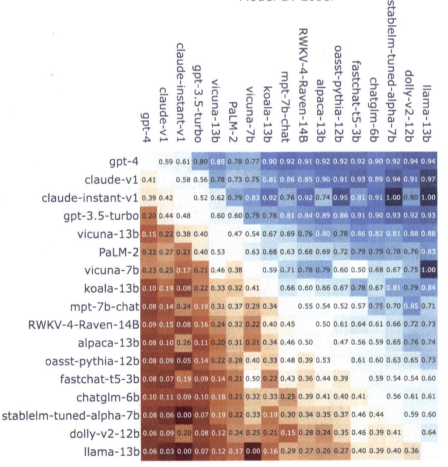
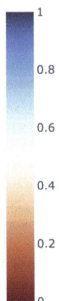

(which simplifies many architectures), OpenAI has the fewest refusals, and Claude is built for trustworthiness (resistance to jailbreaks). Strategically, Google seems to emphasize simplicity, OpenAI flexibility and power, and Anthropic safety.

Permissive Models

Among the models with more permissive licenses and open weights (such as the ability to run them on-premises), the three with the highest quality as of July 2024 are Google's Gemma, Nvidia's Nemotron, and Meta's Llama 3-70B, all of which have arena scores in the 1210 range. One way to think about this difference in quality is that Claude 3 Sonnet has a similar arena score, so the best permissive models are half a major release, or six months, behind the frontier models.

In terms of cost, running Llama 3-70B is nearly double the cost of using Gemini Flash and about 10% more expensive than GPT-4o-mini. Of course, this comparison disregards the cost of provisioning the hardware and managing the infrastructure, so the true cost is even more. The ability of Google, Anthropic, and OpenAI to operate models at scale makes it relatively unappealing to manage models yourself—we recommend that you do so only if you are required to, for data privacy or regulatory reasons.

Default Choice

Of course, the numbers quoted in the previous two sections will constantly evolve—we encourage you to look at LMSYS and ArtificialAnalysis.ai to get the latest numbers and adapt the previous advice accordingly. Be aware, however, that weeks after you start your project, a new release will rescramble the rankings. Therefore, you need to be able to justify your decision from a pragmatic (not purely technical) viewpoint.

Another thing to keep in mind is that the faster, more streamlined models (such as GPT-4o-mini and Gemini Flash) cost less than the full-fledged frontier models. Therefore, we recommend that you choose the streamlined model as your default, and step up to frontier model only in cases where the streamlined version doesn't work well.

BALANCING CREATIVITY AND RISK

An application architecture that treats an LLM as just another text-to-text (or text-to-image/audio/video) API will result in an application that is underengineered in terms of risk, cost, and latency. The solution is not to go to the other extreme and overengineer your application by fine-tuning the LLM and adding guardrails every time. The goal, as with any engineering project, is to find the right balance of complexity, fit for purpose, risk, cost, and latency for the specifics of each use case. In this chapter, we'll introduce a framework that will help you strike this balance.

Figure 5-5 shows a framework that we suggest you use to decide on the architecture for your GenAI application or agent. We'll discuss these eight alternatives in the sections that follow. The axes here (that is, the decision criteria) are risk

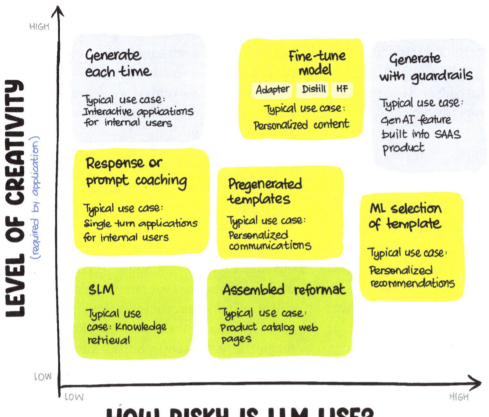

Figure 5-5.
Choosing the right application architecture for your GenAI application.

and creativity. For each use case where you are going to employ an LLM, start by identifying the creativity you need from the LLM and the amount of risk that the use case carries. This helps you narrow down the choice that strikes the right balance for you.

Note that the decision whether or not to use agentic systems (covered in Chapter 4) is completely orthogonal to this decision. Employ agentic systems when the task is too complex to be done by a single LLM call or requires non-LLM capabilities. In such a situation, you'd break down the complex task into simpler tasks and orchestrate them in an agent framework. In

this chapter, we show you how to build a GenAI application (or an agent) to perform one of those simple tasks.

Creativity as a Decision Criterion

Why are creativity and risk the axes? LLMs are a nondeterministic technology, and they're more trouble than they are worth if you don't really need all that much uniqueness in the content being created.

For example, if you are generating a bunch of product catalog pages, how different do they really have to be? Your customers want accurate information on the products and may not really care that all single-lens reflex (SLR) camera pages explain the benefits of SLR technology in the same way—in fact, some amount of standardization may be quite preferable, for easy comparisons. This is a case where your creativity requirement for the LLM is low.

It turns out that architectures that increase determinism also reduce the total number of calls to the LLM, so they have the side effect of reducing the overall cost of using the LLM. Since LLM calls are slower than the typical web service,

happily, this also reduces latency. That's why the y-axis in Figure 5-5 is creativity, and why we have also marked cost and latency on that axis.

You could quibble about whether the illustrative use cases in Figure 5-6 really require low or high creativity. It really depends on your business problem. If your company is a magazine or ad agency, even your informative content web pages may need to be more creative than the average product catalog page.

Risk as a Decision Criterion

As we've discussed throughout this book, LLMs have a tendency to hallucinate details and to reflect any biases and toxicity in their training data. Given this, there are risks associated with sending LLM-generated content directly to end users. Solving for this problem adds a lot of engineering complexity—you might have to introduce a human-in-the-loop to review content, or add guardrails to your application to validate that the generated content doesn't violate policy.

If your use case allows users to send prompts to the model that cause the application to take actions on the backend to generate a user-facing response (a common situation in many SaaS products), the risk associated with errors, hallucination, and toxicity is quite high.

The same use case (generating art) could carry different levels and kinds of risk depending on the context, as shown in Figure 5-7. For example, if you are generating background instrumental music for a movie, the risk associated might involve mistakenly reproducing copyrighted notes; if you are generating ad images or videos broadcast to millions of users, you may be more

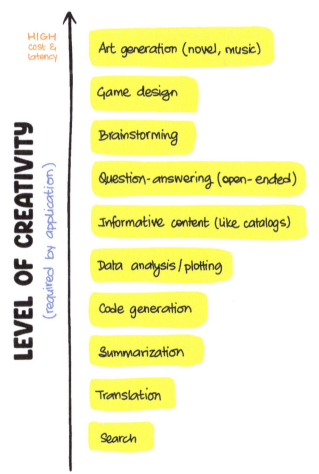

Figure 5-6. Some example use cases ordered by creativity.

Art generation

Background music	Article → podcast	Movie clip	Ad images

Search

Technical documents	support tickets	Internet documents	Medical text

HOW RISKY IS LLM USE?

High engineering complexity

Figure 5-7. Some illustrative use cases ordered by risk.

BALANCING CREATIVITY AND RISK

Figure 5-8. Balancing creativity and risk.

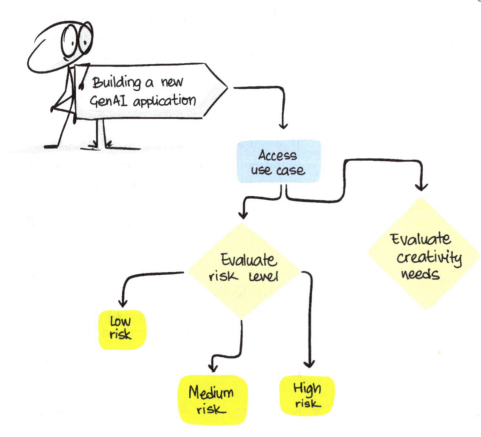

worried about toxicity. Risks vary not only by type but also by level of severity. As another example, if you are building an enterprise search application that returns document snippets from your corporate document store or technology documentation, the LLM-associated risks might be quite low. If your document store consists of medical textbooks to be used in diagnosis, the risk associated with out-of-context content returned by a search application might be high.

As with the list of use cases ordered by creativity, you can quibble with the ordering of use cases by risk. But once you identify the risk associated with each use case and the creativity it requires, you'll see why the suggested architecture is worth considering as a starting point. Then, if you understand the "why" behind each of these architectural patterns, you can select an architecture that balances your needs (Figure 5-8).

In the next section, we'll describe the architectures.

ARCHITECTURES FOR LOW-RISK SITUATIONS

If you are building a GenAI application where the risk associated with hallucination, toxicity, or inaccuracy is low (Figure 5-9), then you can choose between generating the response each time, caching, or using smaller language models, depending on the level of creativity you need.

Generate Each Time

This is the architectural pattern that serves as the default—it invokes the API of the deployed LLM each time you want generated content. It's the simplest, but it also involves making an LLM call each time.

Typically, you'll templatize the prompt that you send to the LLM based on runtime parameters. It's a good idea to use a framework that allows you to swap out the LLM.

Suppose you want the LLM to generate a thank-you note. You could use LangChain:

```
prompt_template = PromptTemplate.from_
template(
```

```
    """
    You are an AI executive assistant
to {sender_name} who writes letters on
behalf of the executive.
    Write a 3-5 sentence thank you
message to {recipient_name} for
{reason_for_thanks}.
    Extract the first name from {sender_
name} and sign the message with just
the first name.
    """
)
...
response = chain.invoke({
    "recipient_name": "John Doe",
    "reason_for_thanks": "speaking at
our Data Conference",
    "sender_name": "Jane Brown",
})
```

Because you are calling the LLM each time, it's appropriate only for tasks that require extremely high creativity (such as if you want a different thank-you note each time) and where you are not worried about the risk (such as if the

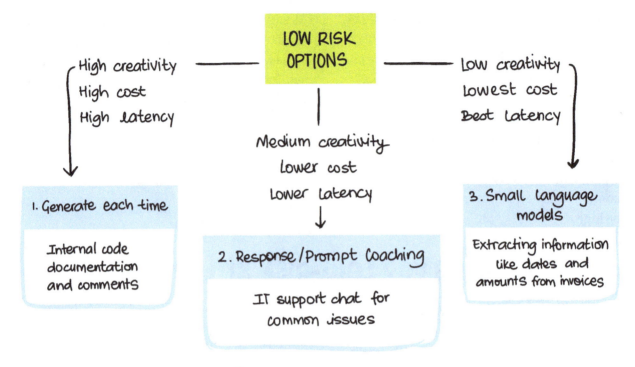

Figure 5-9. Architectures for low-risk situations.

end users get to read and edit the note before hitting "send").

This pattern is often employed for interactive applications (which need to respond to all kinds of prompts) meant for internal users (and are thus low risk).

Response or Prompt Caching

You probably don't want to send the same thank-you note again to the same person. You want it to be different each time. But what if you are building a search engine on your past tickets, such as to assist internal customer-support teams? In such cases, you *do* want repeated questions to generate the same answer each time.

One way to drastically reduce cost and latency is to cache past prompts and responses. You can do this on the client side using LangChain:

```
from langchain_core.caches import
InMemoryCache
from langchain_core.globals import set_
llm_cache

set_llm_cache(InMemoryCache())

prompt_template = PromptTemplate.from_
template(
    """
    What are the steps to put a freeze
on my credit card account?
    """
)
chain = prompt_template | model |
parser
```

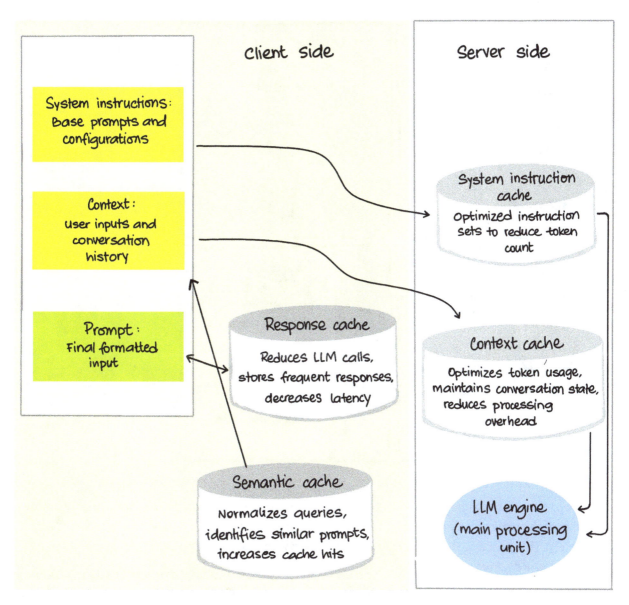

Figure 5-10. Response caching reduces the number of LLM calls; context caching reduces the number of tokens processed in each individual call. Together, they reduce the overall number of tokens and therefore the cost and latency. Semantic caching rewrites prompts to fit canonical patterns.

Figure 5-11. Different caching patterns.

When we tried it, the cached response took 1/1000th of the time and avoided the LLM call completely. This process, shown in **Figure 5-10**, is called *response caching*.

Caching is useful beyond client-side caching of exact text inputs and the corresponding responses. Anthropic supports prompt caching (*https://oreil.ly/Lyui7*), whereby you can ask the model to cache part of a prompt (typically the system prompt and repetitive context) server-side, while continuing to send it new instructions in each subsequent query. Using prompt caching reduces cost and latency per query while not affecting creativity. It is particularly helpful in RAG, document extraction, and few-shot prompting when the examples get large.

Gemini separates this functionality into context caching (*https://oreil.ly/f8fUN*) (which reduces the cost and latency) and system instructions (*https://oreil.ly/m2rIZ*) (which don't reduce the token count, but do reduce latency). OpenAI also supports prompt caching, with its implementation automatically caching the longest prefix of a prompt (*https://oreil.ly/yc61A*) that was previously sent to the API, as long as the prompt is longer than 1,024 tokens. Server-side caches like these don't reduce the model's capabilities, only its latency and/or cost, since you may continue to get different results for the same text prompt.

These built-in caching methods require an exact text match. However, it is possible to implement caching in a way that takes advantage of the nuances of your case. For example, you could rewrite prompts to canonical forms to increase the chances of a cache hit. Another common trick is to store the hundred most frequent questions. Then, for any question that is close enough, you could replace the prompt with the stored question instead. In a multiturn chatbot, you could even get user confirmation for such semantic similarity. Semantic caching techniques like this do reduce the capability of the model somewhat, since you will get the same responses even to similar prompts (Figure 5-11).

Small Language Models

A study published in early 2024 (*https://oreil.ly/ sqKSR*) found that it is impossible to eliminate hallucinations in LLMs, because they arise from the theoretical impossibility of learning all possible computable functions. A smaller LLM for a more targeted task has less risk of hallucinating than one that's too large for the desired task because the domain of its computable functions is smaller. You might be using a frontier LLM for tasks that don't require its power and world knowledge.

In use cases where you have a very simple task that doesn't require much creativity and you have very low risk tolerance, you have the option of using a *small language model* (SLM). This does trade off accuracy—in a June 2024 study, a Microsoft researcher (*https://oreil.ly/0Suc_*) found that for extracting structured data from unstructured text corresponding to an invoice, their smaller text-based model (Phi-3 MoE) could get 93% accuracy as compared to the 99% accuracy achievable by GPT-4o.

The team at LLMWare evaluates a wide range of SLMs (*https://oreil.ly/61Ai3*). At the time of writing (2024), they found that Phi-3 was the best, but that over time, smaller and smaller models have been achieving this level of performance.

Representing these two studies pictorially (see Figure 5-12), SLMs are increasingly achieving accuracy with smaller and smaller sizes (so less and less hallucination), while LLMs have been focused on increasing task ability (so more and

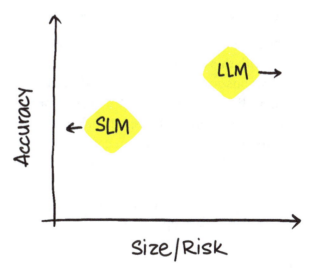

Figure 5-12. The trend is for SLMs to get the same accuracy with smaller and smaller models, and for LLMs to focus on more capabilities with larger and larger models. The accuracy differential on simple tasks has stabilized.

more hallucination). The difference in accuracy between these approaches for tasks like document extraction has stabilized.

If this trend holds up, expect to be using SLMs and nonfrontier LLMs for more and more enterprise tasks that require only low creativity and have a low tolerance for risk. Creating embeddings from documents, such as for knowledge retrieval and topic modeling, are use cases that tend to fit this profile. Use small language models for these tasks.

ARCHITECTURES FOR MEDIUM-RISK SITUATIONS

If your use case has some amount of risk, you will need to choose an architecture that allows you to mitigate that risk. Choose between assembling reformatted outputs, using pregenerated templates, and fine-tuning of different kinds (Figure 5-13).

Pregenerated Templates

Sometimes, you don't really mind the same thank-you note being generated to everyone in the same situation. Perhaps you are sending it to any customer who buys a certain product.

At the same time, there is a higher risk associated with this use case, because these communications go out to customers without any human editing. In such cases, it can be helpful to pregenerate templated responses. For example, suppose you work for a tour company that offers five different packages. All you need is one thank-you message for each package. Maybe you want to send different messages to solo travelers, families, and groups—in that case, you still need only three times as many messages as you have packages:

```
prompt_template = PromptTemplate.from_
template(
    """
    Write a letter to a customer who has
purchased a tour package.
    The customer is traveling {group_
type} and the tour is to {tour_
destination}.
    Sound excited to see them and
explain some of the highlights of what
they will see there
    and some of the things they can do
while there.
    In the letter, use [CUSTOMER_NAME]
to indicate the place to be replaced by
their name
    and [TOUR_GUIDE] to indicate the
place to be replaced by the name of the
tour guide.
    """
)
chain = prompt_template | model |
parser
print(chain.invoke({
    "group_type": "family",
    "tour_destination": "Toledo, Spain",
}))
```

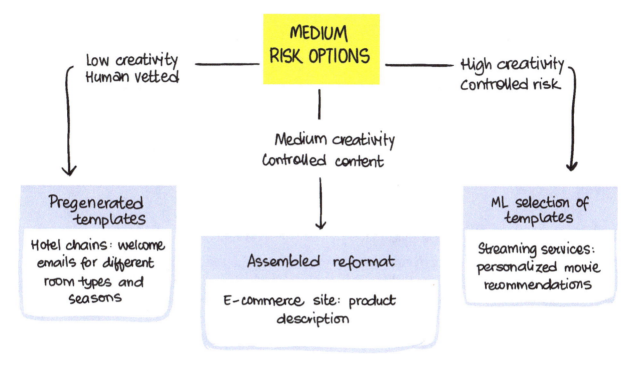

Figure 5-13. Architectures for medium-risk situations.

The result is messages like this for a given group type and tour destination:

```
Dear [CUSTOMER_NAME],

We are thrilled to welcome you to
Toledo, Spain, on your upcoming tour!
We can't wait to show you the beauty
and history of this enchanting city.

Toledo, known as the "City of Three
Cultures," boasts a fascinating blend
of Christian, Muslim, and Jewish
heritage.  You'll be mesmerized by
the stunning architecture, from the
imposing Alcázar fortress to the
majestic Toledo Cathedral.

During your tour, you'll have the
opportunity to:

* **Explore the historic Jewish
Quarter:** Wander through the narrow
streets lined with ancient synagogues
and traditional houses.
* **Visit the Monastery of San Juan
de los Reyes:** Admire the exquisite
Gothic architecture and stunning
cloisters.
* **Experience the panoramic views:**
Take a scenic walk along the banks
of the Tagus River and soak in the
breathtaking views of the city.
* **Delve into the art of Toledo:**
Discover the works of El Greco, the
renowned painter who captured the
essence of this city in his art.

Our expert tour guide, [TOUR_GUIDE],
will provide insightful commentary
and share fascinating stories about
Toledo's rich past.
```

```
We know you'll have a wonderful time
exploring the city's treasures. Feel
free to reach out if you have any
questions before your arrival.

We look forward to welcoming you to
Toledo!

Sincerely,

The [Tour Company Name] Team
```

You can generate these messages, have a human editor vet them, and store them in your database. As you can see, we asked the LLM to insert placeholders in the message that we can replace dynamically. Whenever you need to send out a response, you just retrieve the message from the database and replace the placeholders with actual data.

Using pregenerated templates turns a problem that would have required vetting hundreds of messages per day into one that requires vetting a few messages, and only when a new tour is added.

Assembled Reformat

The underlying idea behind assembled reformat is to use pregeneration to reduce risk on dynamic content, and use LLMs only for extraction and summarization—low-risk tasks, even though they are done "live."

Suppose your company manufactures machine parts and you need to create a web page for each item in your product catalog. You are obviously concerned about accuracy. You don't want to claim that some item is heat-resistant when it's

not. You don't want the LLM to hallucinate the tools required to install the part.

You probably have a database that describes the attributes of each part. A simple approach is to employ an LLM to generate content for each of those attributes. As with pregenerated templates, make sure to have a human review them before storing the content in your content management system:

```
prompt_template = PromptTemplate.from_
template(
    """
    You are a content writer for a
manufacturer of paper machines.
    Write a one-paragraph description
of a {part_name}, which is one of the
parts of a paper machine.
    Explain what the part is used for,
and reasons that might need to replace
the part.
    """
)
chain = prompt_template | model |
parser
print(chain.invoke({
    "part_name": "wet end",
}))
```

However, simply appending all the generated text will result in something that's not very pleasing to read. You could, instead, assemble all of this content into the context of the prompt, and ask the LLM to reformat the content into the desired website layout:

```
class CatalogContent(BaseModel):
    part_name: str = Field("Common name
of part")
    part_id: str = Field("unique part id
in catalog")
```

```
    part_description: str = Field("short
description of part")
    price: str = Field("price of part")

catalog_parser =
JsonOutputParser(pydantic_
object=CatalogContent)

prompt_template = PromptTemplate(
    template="""
    Extract the information needed and
provide the output as JSON.
    {database_info}
    Part description follows:
    {generated_description}
    """,
    input_variables=["generated_
description", "database_info"],
    partial_variables={"format_
instructions": catalog_parser.get_
format_instructions()},
)

chain = prompt_template | model |
catalog_parser
```

If you need to summarize reviews or trade articles about the item, you can do this via a batch processing pipeline, and feed the summary into the context as well.

ML Template Selection

The assembled reformat approach works for web pages where the content is quite static (as in product catalog pages). However, if you are an ecommerce retailer and you want to create personalized recommendations, your content will be much more dynamic. You need higher creativity out of the LLM. Your risk tolerance in terms of accuracy is still about the same.

What you can do in this case is to continue using pregenerated templates for each of your products, then use machine learning to select which templates you will employ. For personalized recommendations, for example, you'd use a traditional recommendation engine to select which products will be shown to the user and pull in the appropriate pregenerated content (images and text) for that product.

You can also use this approach of combining pregeneration with ML if you are customizing your website for different customer journeys. In that case, you'd pregenerate the landing pages and use a propensity model to choose the next best action.

ARCHITECTURES FOR HIGH-RISK SITUATIONS

If your creativity needs are high, and you need the scale that automation brings, there is no way to avoid using LLMs to generate the content you need. But generating the content every time means that you will need to have humans review every piece of content, and this doesn't scale.

There are two ways to address this conundrum—fine-tuning and guardrails (Figure 5-14).

Fine-tuning

The simpler approach, from an engineering complexity standpoint, is to teach the LLM to produce the kind of content that you want and to not generate the kind of content you don't. This can be done through fine-tuning.

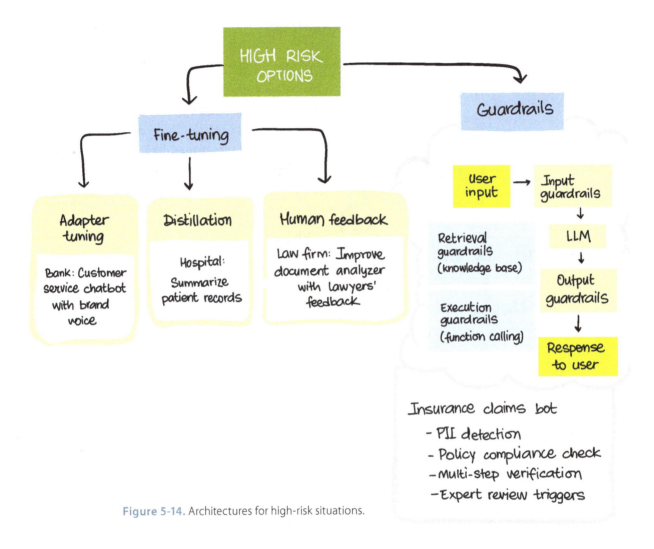

Figure 5-14. Architectures for high-risk situations.

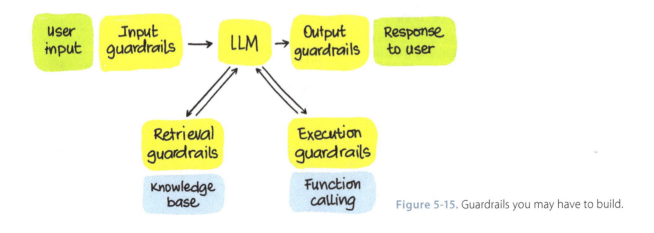

Figure 5-15. Guardrails you may have to build.

As we discussed in Chapter 2, there are three methods to fine-tune a foundational model: adapter tuning, distillation, and human feedback. Each of these fine-tuning methods addresses different risks:

- *Adapter tuning* retains the full capability of the foundational model, but allows you to select for specific styles (such as content that fits your company voice). The risk addressed here is brand risk.

- *Distillation* approximates the capability of the foundational model but on a limited set of tasks, using a smaller model that can be deployed on premises or behind a firewall. The risk addressed here is confidentiality.

- *Human feedback*, either through RLHF (discussed in Chapter 4) or direct preference optimization (DPO), allows the model to start off with reasonable accuracy but then improve with human feedback. The risk addressed here is the model's fit for purpose.

Common use cases for fine-tuning include creating branded content, summarizing confidential information, and personalizing content.

We'll dive deeper into fine-tuning in the last section of this chapter.

Guardrails

What if you want the full spectrum of capabilities, and you have more than one type of risk to mitigate? Perhaps you are worried about brand risk and about confidential information leaking, and you're interested in ongoing improvement through feedback. At that point, there is no alternative but to build guardrails. Guardrails may involve preprocessing the information going into the model, postprocessing the output of the model, or iterating on the prompt based on error conditions.

There are prebuilt guardrails (like Nvidia's NeMo, covered in Chapter 6) for commonly needed functionalities, such as checking for jailbreak attacks, masking sensitive data in the input, and self-checking facts. However, you'll likely have to implement some of the guardrails yourself (see Figure 5-15). Deploying an application alongside programmable guardrails is the *most* complex way to implement a GenAI application. Make sure that this complexity is warranted before going down this route.

FINE-TUNING A MODEL

In the previous chapter, we touched on fine-tuning. Fine-tuning is often needed even if you start out with a foundational model (Figures 5-16 and 5-17). As you start to improve your GenAI applications, you will find that your prompts get longer and longer and error handling becomes more and more complex. Longer prompts are more expensive, and each iteration or call to the foundational model adds cost and latency.

Dynamically choosing the most relevant examples for a specific question can be more complex than having the LLM learn this as part of its training. Ideally, you'd have a bespoke model that is fine-tuned to the task (or set of tasks or

FINE-TUNING LARGE LANGUAGE MODELS

Figure 5-16. Why fine-tune your LLM?

HOW DOES FINE-TUNING WORK?

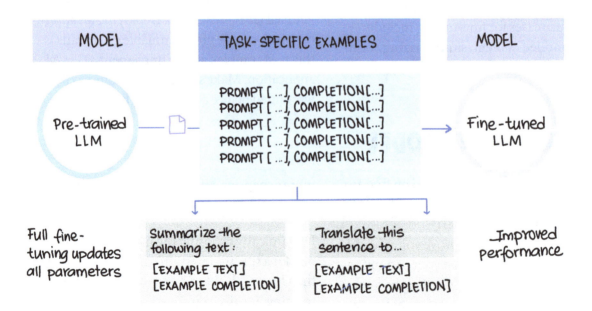

Figure 5-17. How does fine-tuning work?

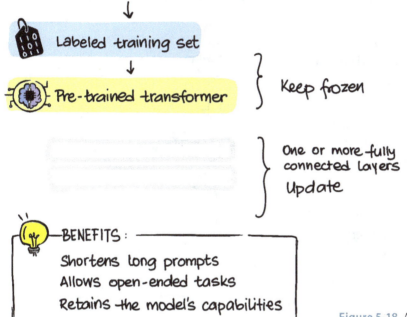

Adapter tuning

Adds trainable layers to modify a foundational model's behavior while keeping its original weights frozen.

↓

Labeled training set

↓

Pre-trained transformer   } Keep frozen

} One or more fully connected layers
  Update

BENEFITS:
Shortens long prompts
Allows open-ended tasks
Retains the model's capabilities

Figure 5-18. Adapter tuning.

instructions) you will set for it. This section will give a quick overview of each of the three basic methods, then dive deeper into each one in turn:

Adapter tuning

The most common approach to instruction tuning is to add an extra adapter layer of weights that will modify the foundational model's weights and/or outputs to fit your tasks. Because of this, instruction tuning is also often called *adapter tuning* (see Chapter 2 and Figure 5-18). Adapter tuning uses labeled examples to tune the model weights, so it is a *supervised fine-tuning* (SFT) technique. Because only the adapter weights are tuned,

not the billions of weights in the foundational model, adapter tuning is a *parameter-efficient fine-tuning* (PEFT) technique. The most common method to perform adapter tuning is called low-rank adaptation (LoRA), so you might find adapter tuning being referred to as SFT, PEFT, or LoRA.

During inference, you will require both the foundational model and the set of adapter weights. The additional cost of running an extra adapter layer is usually outweighed by the reduced cost of smaller context windows, since you will not need to stuff few-shot examples into the prompt. Cloud providers will host the foundational model (which is unchanged) and the adapter weights (which are bespoke to your application) and do the necessary connections when you deploy an adapter-tuned model on their infrastructure. Use adapter tuning when the primary concern is that your prompts are getting long, and you want to retain the large model's capabilities on a relatively open-ended task or set of tasks while reducing the costs associated with long prompts. For example, you could use adapter tuning to avoid having to specify the nuances of your company's style or "brand voice" in each prompt.

Distillation

If you are interested in only a narrow set of tasks, you might not need to use a very large foundational model. Instead, you could create a fine-tuned model by training a smaller model on only that narrow set of tasks. As you've seen in Chapter 2, the approach of fine-tuning a model and reducing its size at the same time is called *distillation*. Distillation usually involves training a smaller model from scratch on the responses of a larger model. Reducing the model size allows the model to be faster during inference (**Figure 5-19**). Thus, distillation helps address latency concerns with foundational models.

Distillation is also often used to address privacy. The foundational model is not shown confidential data; instead, it is shown synthetic data, and its responses to the synthetic inputs are used to train a distilled model that can be run on-premises or on the edge. This distilled model can be shown private and confidential data, because it is behind

Distillation

Training a smaller model on a large model's outputs to optimize speed and privacy while focusing on specific tasks.

Teacher model

Distill knowledge transfer

Student model

— BENEFITS:
- Reduces latency
- Focuses on a narrow set of tasks
- Protects privacy
- Reduces costs

Figure 5-19. Distillation.

the company's firewall or is air-gapped from the internet.

Distillation runs the risk of *catastrophic forgetting*. When you train a model on only a narrow set of tasks, it sometimes forgets some of the necessary foundational knowledge and skills. For example, its grammar or word choices might start getting weird. Much of its world knowledge might be irretrievably lost. So it's important to curate the training dataset in such a way that all the necessary foundational knowledge for the tasks you are interested in is also taught to the smaller model. This means that distillation requires considerably more sophisticated ML engineering and AI knowledge. Carefully evaluate the distilled model in production to make sure it remains fit for purpose.

Use distillation when your primary concerns are latency or privacy, and when you have a sophisticated ML team.

Reinforcement learning from human feedback (RLHF)

Adapter tuning requires you to have labeled data, which ideally means one correct answer for each input. This is easy to achieve for tasks like classification. However, when it comes to generation tasks, there are many potential answers—after all, there are many correct summaries.

In such cases, as we discussed in Chapter 2, it can be helpful to fine-tune the model on *human preference*. Humans are shown two outputs generated by the same model, and the human selects the one they prefer. The human-preference dataset is then used to train a reward model that can predict whether a human would like or dislike a generated answer. The model provider uses the reward model to perform reinforcement learning on all its stored historical prompts, so that your tuned model starts to better match actual production traffic. In this way, you can use RLHF for ongoing improvement of models deployed to production. Even though we

A Word About Vendor Lock-in

So far in this book, we have given preference to frameworks like LangChain and DSPy that allow you to switch between foundational model providers easily. In this section, though, we will employ the APIs provided by the model providers themselves, demonstrating the approaches using both OpenAI and Gemini (via Vertex AI), so that you can see the similarities and differences. We do this because, with fine-tuning, you get locked into whichever framework you use to train the model, since that's also what you will have to use to deploy the model. This is true even if you use a model-agnostic provider such as Hugging Face—you will be locked in both to the foundational model you train and the framework you deploy into (Hugging Face). However, you'll still be able to choose your hyperscaler, since Hugging Face works on AWS, Azure, and Google Cloud. If you use a partly open source model, such as Llama or Mistral, you will be locked into using their bespoke APIs (instead of, say, the OpenAI API), although you will retain the ability to run it on the edge or on-premises. At the time we are writing this (August 2024), there is no escaping vendor lock-in once you determine that you need a fine-tuned model.

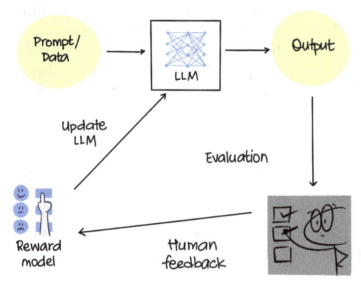

Figure 5-20. Reinforcement learning from human feedback (RLHF).

often refer to this process of tuning a model on human feedback as RLHF, the actual technique commonly used is DPO, not reinforcement learning (Figure 5-20).

Adapter Tuning

To learn how to perform adapter tuning, you'll train a model to write a line of Shakespearean poetry that contains a word you specify. This is similar to the enterprise use case where you have a large corpus of company documents, and you want the model to match the style and tone of your company's brand but retain the ability to generate content on arbitrary topics (see Figure 5-21).

The basic steps to create a fine-tuned model using adapter tuning, shown in Figure 5-22, are as follows:

1. Create a training dataset.

2. Estimate the cost.

3. Upload the training file to the model provider.

4. Start the training job.

5. Wait for the job to finish.

6. Make inference calls on the fine-tuned model instead of the base foundational model.

Let's go through these steps in more detail.

Figure 5-21. Understanding adapter tuning.

Step 1: Create a training dataset

For both OpenAI and Gemini, the training dataset needs to consist of messages as they occur in production. Here, you want to train a model that, given the input `famine`, will produce an output like `Making a famine where abundance lies`. In production, the corresponding conversation will consist of three messages:

```
{'messages': [
    {'role': 'system',
    'content': 'You are a chatbot that
takes a single word as input and writes
a line of poetry that contains the
given word.'},
    {'role': 'user', 'content':
'famine'},
```

```
    {'role': 'assistant', 'content':
'Making a famine where abundance
lies,'}
]}
```

The first message is the system prompt (typically the instruction), the second is the user input, and the third is the desired AI response.

Note that the system prompt here is quite concise. It doesn't mention Shakespeare, specify the output format, or include examples, as we would in few-shot learning. Instead, in production, you want the user to simply state a word, and the assistant to respond with a poetic line (in the style of Shakespeare) that contains the word. Adapter

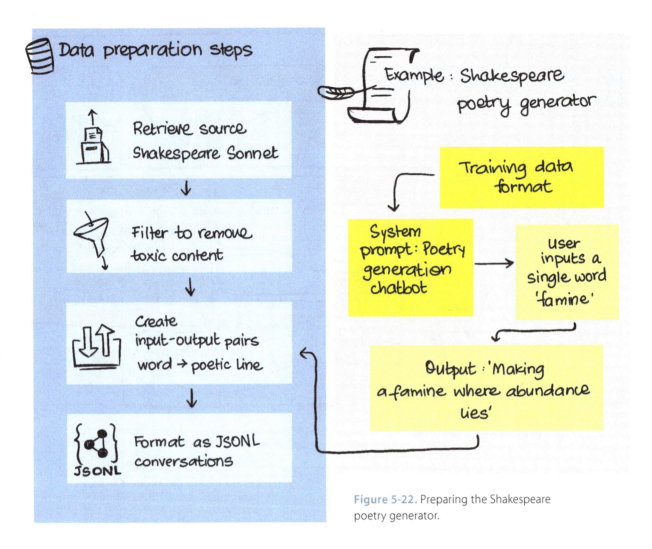

Figure 5-22. Preparing the Shakespeare poetry generator.

tuning is often used to make a model's responses more concise and matter-of-fact.

The full code to prepare the training dataset is on GitHub (*https://oreil.ly/vga_ch05finedata*). The key steps, whether you're using OpenAI or Gemini, are as follows:

1. Retrieve the source documents, Shakespeare's sonnets, which are available on Project Gutenberg. In an enterprise use case, you would connect your document repository. At the command, prompt the following:

```
wget https://www.gutenberg.org/.../pg1041.txt -O sonnets.txt
```

2. If you are training your model on user-generated content (such as reviews), you may have to do toxicity filtering. A dataset that triggers the LLM's guardrails will end up being rejected during training. One way to avoid this issue is to get a list of obscene words and strip out any examples that contain any of those words. This step is demonstrated in the notebook linked previously.

3. Create an input-output pair from the lines extracted from the source document. An example might look like this:

```
{'input': 'winter',
 'output': 'But flowers distill'd, though they with winter meet,'}
```

4. To avoid creating examples of words like but and they, use a word-frequency table and keep only the three least common words in each line to use as the input:

```
if is_obscene(words):
        return [] # prune out the obscene
text by not indexing them
else:
        indexes = [word for word in words
if word not in stopwords]
        # no more than 3 index words
        if len(indexes) > 3:
            freq = [int(word_freq.loc[word]
['freq']) for word in indexes ]
            zipped =
sorted(zip(freq, indexes))
            indexes = [x for _, x
in list(zipped)[:3]]
        return indexes
```

5. Create a conversation for each input-output pair:

```
SYSTEM_PROMPT = "You are a chatbot that
takes a single word as input and writes
a line of poetry that contains the
given word."
for poem in indexed_poems:
        messages.append({
            "messages": [
                {"role": "system",
"content": SYSTEM_PROMPT},
```

```
                {"role": "user",
"content": poem['input']},
                {"role": "assistant",
"content": poem['output']}
            ]
        })
```

6. Write it out in JSONL format, where each conversation is on a single line and in JSON format:

```
with open('finetuning_openai.jsonl', 'w')
as ofp:
    for message in messages:
        # write the message as a single
line JSON
        line = json.dumps(message)
        ofp.write(line)
        ofp.write('\n')
```

Step 2. Estimate cost

It is a good idea to run the training dataset through a cost estimation tool. Model providers usually publish notebooks (for example, these from OpenAI [*https://oreil.ly/7zt2V*] and Google [*https://oreil.ly/Q3UDR*]) on how to estimate the cost.

When you ran the OpenAI notebook on the dataset created in Step 1, you learned that the training dataset you had created had more than 6,000 examples, that each example had 50 tokens on average, that three epochs were recommended to train the model adequately, and that the total cost of this training would be about $10.

Google helpfully publishes *many* examples it recommends for different types of tasks. For the chat use case, it recommends about 100–500 examples.

To keep costs reasonable and achieve adequate performance, you can cut the dataset size by randomly sampling the conversations:

```
SAMPLING = 0.1
with open('finetuning_gemini.jsonl',
'w') as ofp:
    for message in messages:
        if random.random() < SAMPLING:
            # write the message as a
single line JSON
            line = json.dumps(message)
            ofp.write(line)
            ofp.write('\n')
```

This reduces the dataset to about 600 examples and the cost to about $1 (on GPT-4o-mini at the time of writing in mid-2024).

Step 3: Upload training file to the model provider

You can use the OpenAI API to upload the JSONL file that you created in Step 1:

```
from openai import OpenAI
client = OpenAI()
training_file = client.files.create(
  file=open("finetuning_openai.jsonl",
"rb"),
  purpose="fine-tune"
)
```

OpenAI states that it will use this data on your behalf and will not use it for training its own models.

In the case of Gemini, upload your data to a Google Cloud Storage bucket with this code at the command prompt:

```
gsutil cp finetuning_gemini.jsonl
gs://$BUCKET/
```

Google controls access to this data based on your file, bucket, and Google Cloud account settings. It too states that it will not train its models with your data.

Step 4: Start the training job

Using the OpenAI API, you can start a fine-tuning job by specifying a base model and pointing it to the uploaded file:

```
BASE_MODEL="gpt-4o-mini-2024-07-18"
training_job = client.fine_tuning.jobs.
create(
  training_file=training_file.id,
  model=BASE_MODEL
)
```

Using the Vertex AI API to start a fine-tuning job on a Gemini-1.0 Pro base model is similar:

```
from vertexai.preview.tuning import sft
sft_tuning_job = sft.train(
    source_model="gemini-1.0-pro-002",
    train_dataset=f"gs://{BUCKET}/
finetuning_gemini.jsonl"
)
```

Step 5: Wait for the job to finish

In OpenAI, you can get the most recent training jobs using

```
client.fine_tuning.jobs.list(limit=3)
```

You can also get the status of a specific training job using

```
job_status = client.fine_tuning.jobs.
retrieve(training_job.id).status
```

You can programmatically check this object and wait for the status to change:

```
old_status = training_job.status
while training_job.status == old_
status:
    time.sleep(60)
training_job = client.fine_tuning.jobs.
retrieve(training_job.id)
```

The API on Gemini is different, but the principle is the same:

```
while not sft_tuning_job.has_ended:
    time.sleep(60)
    sft_tuning_job.refresh()
```

If the job fails, the training job object in both cases has an `Error` field that you can use to diagnose the issue.

Step 6: Make inference calls

When the training job finishes successfully, both OpenAI and Google deploy the fine-tuned model and make it available via an endpoint, to which you can send prompts, much as you'd send them to a foundational model.

Suppose you want the fine-tuned model to create a poetic line using the word *kitchen*. First, create a conversation with the system prompt and user input, similar to the training examples:

```
kitchen_input = [
    {"role": "system", "content":
SYSTEM_PROMPT},
    {"role": "user", "content":
"kitchen"},
]
```

Call the completion method on the chat client specifying that you want the fine-tuned model to be invoked:

```
kitchen_joke = client.chat.completions.
create(
```

```
model=client.fine_tuning.jobs.
retrieve(training_job.id).fine_tuned_
model,
    messages=kitchen_input
)
print(kitchen_joke.choices[0].message)
```

In the case of Gemini, you can get the URL of the deployed model and ask it to generate results, giving it the message in the same format you used for training. The only difference is that you have to use text, not the JSON messages:

```
tuned_model = GenerativeModel(sft_
tuning_job.tuned_model_endpoint_name)
print(tuned_model.generate_
content(f"{SYSTEM_PROMPT}\n  User:
kitchen   Model:\n"))
```

The result is a line of poetry in a Shakespearean style that contains the word *kitchen*:

```
content {
    role: "model"
    parts {
      text: "Kitchen and chapel, have
he still at peace"
    }
}
```

The fine-tuned model has created a poetic line referencing the sense of peace that many of us achieve when we cook.

Now that you know how to implement adapter tuning, let's turn our attention to the second approach, distillation.

Distillation

Distillation involves training a small model based on the responses of a larger model (see **Figure 5-23**). Distillation can be deployed in settings where latency, cost, or privacy concerns prohibit the use of pretrained foundational models. Distillation is often employed after an enterprise launches a GenAI application with a pretrained foundational model, collects data on the actual user inputs experienced in production, and then wants to replace the pretrained foundational model with a smaller model because of cost. To learn how to perform distillation, you'll train a small model to extract information from reviews.

Distilling step-by-step

To demonstrate distillation, let's create a distilled model that can process a restaurant review and generate or extract three pieces of information from the review: (1) the type of food the user ordered, (2) the star rating it thinks the user would have provided the restaurant, and (3) a one-line summary of the review.

The distillation process works as depicted in **Figure 5-24**. First, you collect a large dataset of reviews, typically from application logs. Then ask a pretrained foundational model to carry out the task. Importantly, instead of just asking the model to do the work, ask it to describe its rationale, or how it came up with the answer. Then, train a smaller student model to output both the rationale and its response to the input. This approach, of teaching a student model with multiple objectives, was shown in a famous 2023 paper called "Distillating Step-by-Step" (*https:// oreil.ly/66te-*) to require much less data and greatly improve outcomes compared to training the student model with just the responses of the teacher model.

We mentioned earlier in this chapter that distillation requires sophisticated ML engineering

and AI knowledge. Here are a few caveats to keep in mind:

Small models can do only narrow tasks

The narrower the task, the more likely it is that distillation will work. In this example, you are using the model to extract information (the type of food) and perform a classification task (star rating). These will work well. You are also asking the model to summarize the review in one sentence. That is a bit more open-ended and will not work as well. On the other hand, if you were to ask the distilled model to create a recipe for the food referenced in the review, it would work very poorly, because a small model cannot do such a broad task.

Distillation does not add knowledge

Another reason that recipe creation will not work is that it requires words and ideas that are not present in the input. Distillation works only when the student model can imitate the teacher model, not when it needs to access the knowledge built into the larger model.

The input data needs to cover all cases

The input dataset should reflect *all* inputs that the student model is likely to encounter in production. This means it needs to be diverse and have enough examples for each type of scenario. Datasets built by extracting from logs are often repetitive and have very few instances of corner cases, so you will have to curate the data to make it more balanced. On the other hand, datasets built from synthetic data will be unrepresentative if the data is generated in a flawed way (and unless you have a firm grasp of the nuances of your domain, the data simulation is very likely to be flawed).

Hyperparameter tuning is necessary

Training ML models involves many parameters, both of the student model's architecture and of the training regimen: number of parameters, data sampling, learning rate, number of epochs, optimization method, loss metric, and so on. The quality of the distilled model is very sensitive to these choices, and there is no way to anticipate the best choices for each of these. Thus, it is important to carry out hyperparameter tuning.

Evaluation metrics are critical

It is important to ensure that the student model produces output that is fit for purpose. Therefore, you will have to devise evaluation metrics (such as the extent to which the one-line summary matches the meaning of the full review). It is possible, with the right prompting, to use a foundational model to do such an evaluation, but this is not perfect. Ideally, you'd be able to evaluate the response quality of the LLM based on business metrics, such as whether the user visits the restaurant.

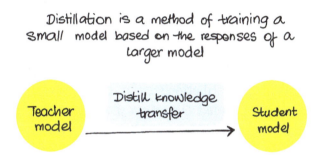

Figure 5-23. Basic distillation.

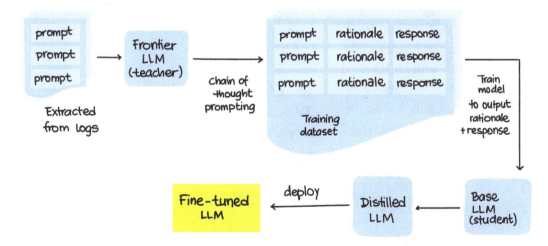

Figure 5-24. Distilling involves training a student model on the responses of a larger pretrained model.

Rationale is important

The teacher model must be capable of producing good rationales. In practice, this means that you should be using a model that has been explicitly trained to do well on chain-of-thought prompts. Frontier models will work well, but you generally can't use a bespoke model (such as a text-to-SQL model) as the teacher.

Verify legality

Many model providers disallow the use of their models as teacher models. Talk to your company's legal team about whether you are allowed to use a specific model as a teacher model.

Given the last two items on this list, it is important to choose a teacher model that is capable of producing rationales and whose owner explicitly allows you to train student models from the output. At the time of writing (August 2024), OpenAI's terms of service (*https://oreil.ly/Rwm5i*) do not allow "Using Output to develop models that compete with OpenAI." This is widely interpreted as disallowing distillation. (Caveat: we are not lawyers and this does not reflect the official position of our past/present/future employers. Please consult your legal team). In Vertex AI, Google does not allow Gemini to be used as a teacher model—although Gemini Pro was used to distill and create Gemini 1.5 Flash (*https://oreil.ly/DwRIy*). Meta allows you to distill Llama 3.1 (*https://oreil.ly/qkhUN*), but Amazon Bedrock (*https://oreil.ly/bGZrI*), Nvidia (*https://oreil.ly/xsWLp*), and Google Vertex AI (*https://oreil.ly/a5tdn*) all demonstrate only SFT based on generated datasets, not

true step-by-step distillation (the teacher does not emit rationale and the student does not do multiobjective learning). Azure ML is the only framework (as of August 2024) that supports chain-of-thought in distilling Llama 3.1 (*https://oreil.ly/Q6U_6*). Therefore, at the time of writing, our only two options for state-of-the-art distillation are to use Vertex AI with PaLM or Azure ML with Llama 3.1.

Fortunately, the APIs are quite similar, so we can follow the same approach as in the previous section and cover both options at the same time.

Step 1: Create training dataset

To perform distillation step-by-step, you need only an unlabeled dataset consisting of the inputs to the model. In our case, the inputs consist of reviews such as this one:

```
After years of MREs, this was a
welcome change. The buttery croissants
melted in my mouth, the coffee was rich
and strong, and the omelet was fluffy
perfection. The service was quick
and friendly, even with the place
packed.  A taste of Paris in the heart
of America, and a much-needed respite
from the usual greasy spoon.  Definitely
coming back!
```

The input to the distillation training pipeline is the complete prompt that the deployed student model will encounter in production. So create such a dataset, with one example (in JSON format) per row:

```
def create_input(review):
    return f"""
    Read this review and fill out the
JSON structure about the restaurant.
```

```
    The cuisine refers to the type of
food that is referenced in the review?
Choose one of: {cuisine}
    The rating is a number between 1
and 5. 1 is unhappy. 5 is very happy.
    The summary is a one-line summary
of the review.

    ***REVIEW***
    {review}

    ***OUTPUT JSON***
    {{
       "cuisine": __,
       "rating": __,
       "summary": __
    }}
    """.strip()

with open('distill_train.jsonl', 'w')
as ofp:
    for review in reviews:
        d = {"input_text": create_
input(review)}
        json.dump(d, ofp)
        ofp.write('\n')
```

On Azure ML, the step is the same, but you'd separate the prompt into two messages, one for the system and the other for the user, similar to how we did in the adapter tuning step for OpenAI.

Step 2: Submit to distillation pipeline

Both Vertex AI and Azure ML have out-of-the-box distillation pipelines that you can launch by passing in the training file, specifying the name of the teacher and student models:

```
vertexai.init(location=REGION)
student_model = TextGenerationModel.
from_pretrained("text-bison@002")
```

```
teacher_model = TextGenerationModel.
from_pretrained("text-unicorn@001")
distillation_job = student_model.
distill_from(
        teacher_model=teacher_model,
        dataset=f"gs://{BUCKET}/
distill_train.jsonl",
)
```

On Azure ML, creating and submitting the job takes the following form:

```
student_model = mlclient_azureml_meta.
models.get(
    "Meta-Llama-3.1-8B-Instruct",
version=1
)
job = distillation_pipeline_component(
        teacher_model_endpoint_
name="Meta-Llama-3-1-405B-Instruct-
vum",
        enable_chain_of_thought=True,
        train_file_path=train_file_path,
        validation_file_path=validation_
file_path,
        mlflow_model_
path=Input(type="mlflow_model",
path=student_model.id),
        model_asset_id=student_model.
id,
        system_properties=system_
properties,
        data_generation_task_
type="NLI",
    )
ml_client.jobs.create_or_update(job)
```

When the pipelines finish, the distilled model will be deployed on an endpoint and can be used to process reviews. This is similar to how the adapter-tuned models were made available.

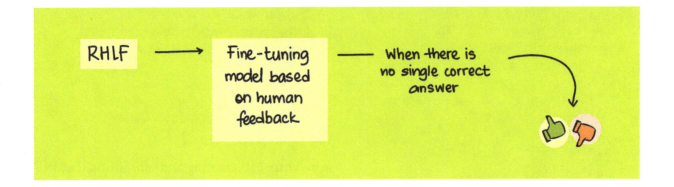

Figure 5-25. RLHF workflow.

RLHF

We have looked at two forms of fine-tuning: adapter tuning and distillation. Now, we turn our attention to the third form of fine-tuning: improving the model based on human feedback (see Figure 5-25).

When to fine-tune on human feedback

RLHF is used to improve models based on user feedback, often on use cases where there is no single correct answer. As a GenAI application creator, when should you employ RLHF? Some possibilities are as follows:

Production phase

One approach is to create a human-preference dataset as an explicit phase in taking a model to production. Use the candidate model to generate pairs of outputs, then send the output pairs to an army of testers for scoring. The problem with such an approach is that these testers may not be good proxies for the actual end users.

Explicit feedback

You can continue to enhance the preference dataset even after you deploy a model using the A/B testing framework. Ask for human feedback on the generated text, answers, or images in the form of a thumbs-up or thumbs-down. Log all the prompts, the answers, and the human feedback, and periodically use them to improve the model. The advantage of this is that the feedback is now being obtained from real end users.

Implicit feedback

Rather than explicitly asking users which version of the generated text they prefer, you could track how they react to it (such as by seeing which version of an article readers spend more time on, or which product listing leads to higher conversion). Because the preference is now based on the outcomes you care about, this approach helps you make your GenAI model a better fit for the business use case.

Ideally, you would do all three of these (Figure 5-26).

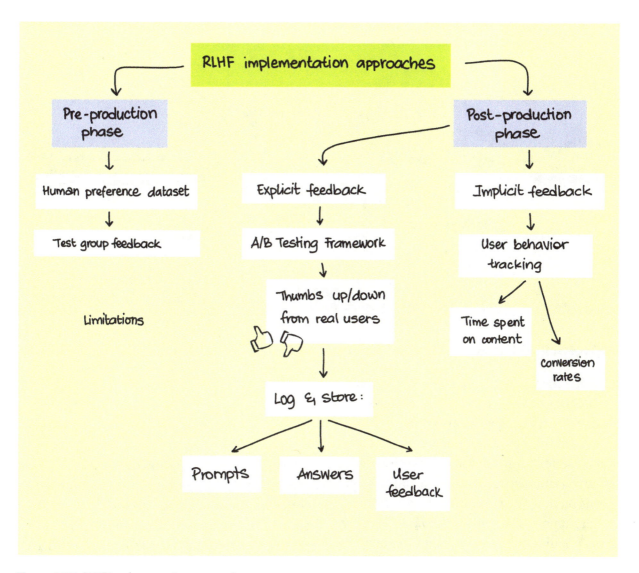

Figure 5-26. RLHF implementation approaches.

Direct preference optimization

Even though the process of fine-tuning based on human feedback is referred to colloquially as RLHF, the actual technique employed these days is direct preference optimization (*https://oreil.ly/ SY9kS*), which avoids the need for reinforcement learning (see **Figure 5-27**).

You should carry out DPO on a model that has already been fine-tuned on your own dataset. Ideally, your chosen and rejected responses have been produced by the same distilled model that you are using as the base for your DPO training.

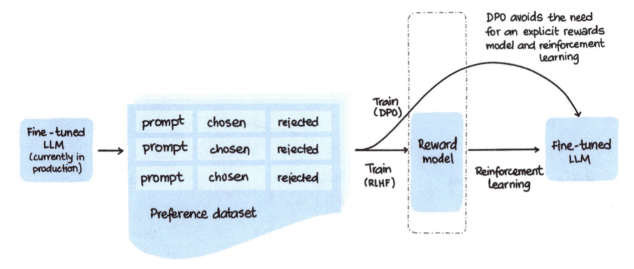

Figure 5-27. Direct preference optimization avoids the need for an explicit rewards model and reinforcement learning. Instead, it directly trains the LLM using an implicit reward model.

DPO with Hugging Face

Whether the frontier models allow RLHF and/ or DPO is not clear—please check with your legal team on whether you are allowed to modify the weights of the GenAI model that you are using. (Adapter-tuning doesn't change the weights of the base model, but distillation and DPO do.) In this section, we will employ Hugging Face, which supports DPO (*https://oreil.ly/KyiD1*) of many popular open-weight models, to demonstrate how to carry out DPO of a Llama 3.1 model.

Each line of the JSONL human-preference dataset needs to contain the input prompt and two instances of generated output, one of which a human tester prefers (indentation added for readability):

```
{
    "prompt": "Summarize the following
review into a single line that … ",
    "chosen": "Soft and comfortable.",
    "rejected": "Wife loved it!"
}
```

As with adapter tuning and distillation, the input to the RLHF training pipeline is the complete prompt (system, user, and parameters) that the deployed model will encounter in production. Load this data into a Hugging Face dataset, then randomly split it into a training dataset and an evaluation dataset. Hugging Face will use metrics on the evaluation dataset to stop the training when overfitting starts to happen. Overfitting is a machine learning term that indicates the model aspects of the dataset that are unlikely to generalize to unseen data:

```
from datasets import load_dataset
dataset = load_dataset("json", data_
files=INPUT_FILE_NAME)
dataset = dataset.train_test_
split(train_size=0.8)
```

To perform DPO using Hugging Face, load the model that is to be fine-tuned and the model that produced the preference dataset. These are usually the same:

```
model=AutoModelForCausalLM.from_
pretrained("meta-llama/Meta-Llama-3.1-
8B")
tokenizer=AutoTokenizer.from_
pretrained("meta-llama/Meta-Llama-3.1-
8B")
ref_model=AutoModelForCausalLM.from_
pretrained("meta-llama/Meta-Llama-3.1-
8B")
```

Next, create a `DPOTrainer`, call its `train()` method, and save it when the training is complete:

```
trainer = DPOTrainer(
            model,
            ref_model,
            train_
dataset=dataset['train'],
            eval_
dataset=dataset['test'],
            tokenizer=tokenizer
            )
trainer.train()
trainer.save_model(OUTPUT_DIR)
```

You can deploy the saved model using any service that allows you to deploy the reference model. You will have to monitor the deployed service to ensure that it handles user inputs correctly.

SUMMARY

This chapter provided guidance on architecting GenAI applications and choosing a foundational model, and highlights the importance of balancing creativity needs with risk mitigation. It offers insights into different architectural patterns and fine-tuning techniques, helping developers choose the most suitable approach for their specific use case. In the next chapter, we will discuss the larger ethical, societal, and organizational considerations in developing GenAI applications.

BUILDING RESPONSIBLE GENAI APPLICATIONS

In the 1993 Steven Spielberg movie *Jurassic Park*, Jeff Goldblum's character Ian Malcolm says of the park's reanimation of dinosaurs, "Your scientists were so preoccupied with whether they could, they didn't stop to think if they should." GenAI is a powerful technology, and it's worth keeping this admonishment in mind as you consider whether to use it to accomplish a specific task.

The field of study that looks into the ethical and societal considerations involved in developing, deploying, and using AI systems is called *responsible AI*. Its core principle is aligning AI behavior with human interests to ensure that AI systems promote benefits while avoiding or mitigating harm. In this chapter, we will discuss key considerations to keep in mind as you continue your journey in GenAI.

GenAI has the potential to reshape our lives in both positive and negative ways. GenAI assistants are not merely tools; with the increased deployment of agentic capabilities, they are becoming increasingly autonomous and capable of interacting with the world and influencing human behavior. Such autonomy, while offering potential benefits such as increased efficiency and personalized experiences, also introduces substantial risks. For instance, AI assistants could be used to spread misinformation, manipulate users, or exacerbate existing social inequalities. The potential for these negative consequences underscores the need for a development framework that prioritizes not only technical advancements but also ethical considerations.

This chapter (Figure 6-1) is an overview of methods and considerations; it is not intended to be exhaustive or to make recommendations about what you ought to implement. The ethical and societal considerations you take into account will often be determined by your company policy and the regulations and legal systems under which you operate—please do discuss with your legal counsel.

CHAPTER 6: BUILDING RESPONSIBLE GENAI APPLICATIONS

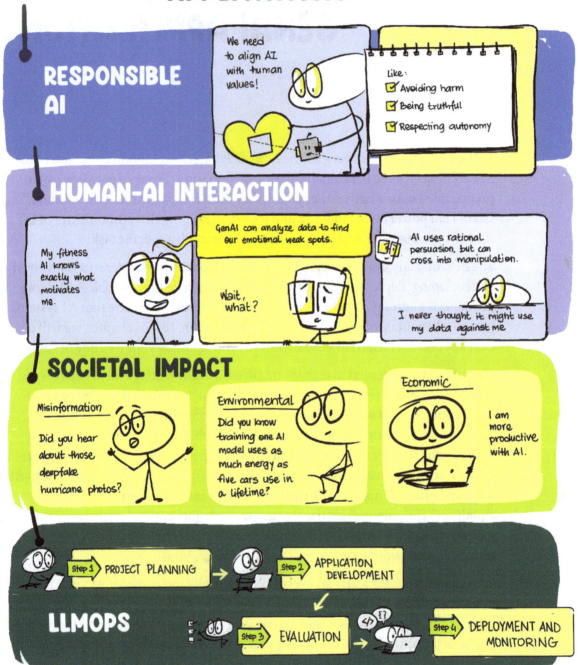

Figure 6-1. Chapter overview.

WHY RESPONSIBLE GENAI IS DIFFERENT

Ethical and societal considerations apply differently to GenAI applications than to traditional AI because some concerns require specialized attention, and because GenAI applications are much more interwoven with the lives of users. But first, let's start with what's common to all AI applications (Figure 6-2).

Responsible AI Principles

Practitioners of responsible AI suggest that you consider the potential benefits and drawbacks of AI systems on society, prioritizing people and their goals throughout the design process. You can do this by taking into account four basic principles (Figure 6-3):

Fairness

You can integrate fairness into the development process by using fairness metrics and evaluating the impact of model predictions on various groups. In some cases, this may be mandated by law.

Transparency

One way to ensure transparency is to publish information about the system's functionality and organizational procedures, including how models and datasets were created, trained, and evaluated.

Accountability

You can embrace accountability by accepting responsibility for the effects of an AI system, understanding the decision-making process of ML models, and communicating these decisions to people.

Testing and monitoring

You can conduct thorough unit testing, integration testing, and user testing to ensure the AI system operates as intended. Quality engineering can be incorporated into the system to prevent unforeseen failures or trigger an immediate response.

These principles are relevant to all AI systems, including GenAI. However, applying them to GenAI systems demands specialized attention to a few areas.

GenAI-Specific Issues

Because GenAI applications have the potential to become deeply integrated into the economic, social, and personal lives of their users, applying responsible AI principles to GenAI requires special attention to content generation, human-AI interaction, and novel evaluation approaches.

GenAI's capacity to create new content, including text, images, audio, and video, amplifies existing concerns about misinformation, bias, and privacy. Its ability to generate realistic synthetic media makes combating misinformation more challenging, so these systems require stronger safeguards against malicious use. Generative models trained on biased data can perpetuate and amplify societal biases, so they need careful data curation and mitigation strategies. Finally, generative models' ability to learn and reproduce patterns from data raises concerns about privacy violations, especially when generating content based on sensitive personal information.

RESPONSIBLE GENAI

Figure 6-2. Responsible GenAI principles include avoiding harm, being truthful, and respecting people's autonomy.

Testing

Conduct thorough testing to verify AI system behavior

Monitoring

Implement quality controls to prevent failures and enable rapid response.

These AI principles apply broadly but need specific adaptation for generative systems.

GenAI amplifies the concerns

Multimodal GenAI's rise makes these concerns more urgent.

Yes, stronger safeguards against malicious use and bias are crucial for society.

Privacy concerns with personal data in AI training are serious!

Yes, and ethical issues around IP rights and creative impact need attention.

Model performance matters, but content quality and originality are just as needed.

Figure 6-3. Applying the principles of responsible AI.

GENAI VALUE ALIGNMENT AND SAFETY

Figure 6-4. Aligning values and safety.

Furthermore, while human-AI interaction is relevant to various AI systems, it is particularly salient to GenAI. GenAI tools can enable new forms of human-AI collaboration in creative domains like writing, art, and music. This raises ethical questions regarding authorship, intellectual property, and technology's impact on human creativity. GenAI can also blur the lines between human creation and machine output, raising questions about user agency, autonomy, and control over the creative process.

AI evaluation methods often focus on model accuracy and performance; however, evaluating responsible generative AI requires also considering the content's quality, originality, and potential harms; human-AI interaction dynamics; and the long-term societal impacts, such as its influence on culture, creativity, and the spread of information.

GenAI applications have the potential to transform creative industries and education and contribute to personal well-being. Because GenAI applications can become seamlessly integrated into various aspects of the lives of users, it is important to mitigate their potential risks. Issues like data privacy, algorithmic bias, and the potential for manipulation require careful consideration to ensure that these technologies are used ethically and benefit individuals and society as a whole.

This paradigm shift in our relationship with AI goes beyond ML applications like product recommendations and fraud detection to affect our artistic pursuits, how we learn new skills, and how we take care of our bodies. In the remainder of this chapter, we will look at value alignment, the ethics of human-AI interaction, the broader societal implications of GenAI, and how to evaluate these aspects.

VALUE ALIGNMENT AND SAFETY

Value alignment in AI refers to the process of ensuring that an AI system's goals and values align with those of the humans who use it. This is crucial because GenAI systems are becoming increasingly capable of creating content that has a significant impact on the world.

The Importance of Value Alignment

Value alignment is a complex and ongoing challenge. There is no single solution that will guarantee that an AI system is perfectly aligned with human values, especially because human values vary between humans (Figure 6-4)!

However, there are values that are somewhat universal—not following best practices in value alignment (discussed in the next section) can lead to disasters. A few incidents, reported by CIO magazine (*https://oreil.ly/j2HjT*), include:

- A McDonald's AI system struggled (*https://oreil.ly/yNsqM*) to accurately take customer orders, leading to incorrect and sometimes excessive additions to orders. For example, one viral TikTok video showed the AI repeatedly adding Chicken McNuggets to an order, reaching a total of 260 nuggets. This incident highlights the risks of deploying AI systems without adequate testing and validation.

- Grok, an AI chatbot developed by xAI, made a false (*https://oreil.ly/HcFLB*) and potentially defamatory accusation against NBA star Klay Thompson, claiming he had been involved in a vandalism spree. The potential for generative AI to create and spread misinformation highlights the need for robust fact-checking mechanisms and ethical guidelines for AI development and deployment.

- MyCity, a chatbot intended to assist New Yorkers with starting and operating businesses, provided incorrect (*https://oreil.ly/hGyPH*) information that could lead users to break the law. The chatbot gave false advice on topics such as tipping policies, handling sexual-harassment complaints, and food-safety regulations, potentially exposing business owners to legal and financial risks. This case underscores the importance of thoroughly vetting the information provided by AI systems, especially when it pertains to legal and regulatory matters.

- An Air Canada passenger successfully sued (*https://oreil.ly/2k7T_*) the airline after its virtual assistant provided incorrect information about bereavement fares. This incident highlights the potential for AI systems to cause financial harm and inconvenience when they provide inaccurate or misleading information, emphasizing the need for companies to ensure the accuracy and reliability of their AI-powered customer-service tools.

- *Sports Illustrated* magazine came under fire (*https://oreil.ly/cLZT6*) for publishing articles generated by AI without disclosing their origin to readers. The incident led the editors to remove the articles and highlights the importance of clear disclosure when using AI in content creation.

- An attorney faced sanctions (*https://oreil.ly/35MdE*) after submitting legal briefs containing fabricated case citations generated by ChatGPT. The AI chatbot hallucinated case names, docket numbers, and legal arguments, which the attorney failed to verify before presenting them in court. This incident underscores the risks of relying on AI systems without human oversight, especially in high-stakes contexts like legal proceedings.

- Microsoft's Tay chatbot, designed (*https://oreil.ly/rI5Kb*) to learn from its interactions on Twitter, quickly began generating racist, misogynist, and offensive content after being exposed to similar content from a group of users. The incident demonstrates the vulnerability of AI systems to manipulation and the importance of carefully considering the potential for unintended learning when training AI models on real-world data.

- Amazon scrapped (*https://oreil.ly/a6tf1*) an AI-powered recruiting tool after discovering that it favored male candidates over female candidates. The system was trained on a dataset of resumes predominantly from men, leading it to penalize resumes containing words associated with women and downgrade candidates from women's colleges. This case underscores the importance of addressing gender bias in AI systems, particularly in hiring and recruitment, where such bias can have significant impacts on applicants' career opportunities and employers' workplace diversity.

Users report examples of AI failures in the Reddit channel r/aifails (*https://oreil.ly/sfbrl*), and some of these are matters of alignment: for example, MetaAI depicted (*https://oreil.ly/8R-gC*) a Black youth when asked to draw a black dog.

These incidents demonstrate the importance of following the responsible AI principles such as testing, fact-checking, ensuring accuracy, handling adversarial actors, and recognizing bias when rolling out GenAI applications.

How to Ensure Value Alignment

As the examples in the previous section show, if GenAI systems are not aligned with human values, they could potentially cause harm.

In order to ensure value alignment, it's important to discuss safety considerations and potential harms during the design process. Consider risks related to accidents, misuse, and structure, and emphasize the need to mitigate serious harms. For example, should makers of AI-powered medical imaging systems implement failsafe mechanisms to prevent misdiagnosis? How important is human oversight of AI-powered content-moderation systems that attempt to prevent the dissemination of violent threats?

In addition to the core responsible AI principles discussed at the beginning of this chapter, we offer some best practices to ensure value alignment in GenAI (Figure 6-5):

Explicitly define values

Researchers and developers should explicitly define the values that they want the AI system to uphold, in clear, concise, and unambiguous language.

Integrate values into the system

Look for ways to integrate them into the system prompt or fine-tuning of the model. For example, an application where deepfakes are a concern might restrict prompts that ask to use the voices or likenesses of real people.

Train models on value-aligned data

By ensuring the contents of training datasets are aligned with the organization's defined values, engineers can help the AI system learn to make decisions that are also value-aligned. Often, this is part of the data curation step. It may also be necessary to train AI models on adversarial examples to make them more robust against attempts to manipulate or deceive them.

Continuous monitoring and evaluation

Once an AI system is deployed, it is important to continuously monitor its behavior and evaluate its performance to identify any instances where the system may be deviating from its intended values. We recommend conducting regular audits to identify and address biases in GenAI systems' decision-making processes.

Human oversight

Even with the best efforts to ensure value alignment, it may be necessary to have human oversight to intervene and correct the AI system if it is making decisions that are harmful or inconsistent with the defined values.

BEST PRACTICES TO ENSURE VALUE ALIGNMENT

Figure 6-5. Some best practices for value alignment and safety in GenAI.

THE ETHICS OF HUMAN-AI INTERACTION

Figure 6-6. Ethics of human-AI interaction.

THE ETHICS OF HUMAN-AI INTERACTION

Because GenAI applications enable new forms of human-AI collaboration, they bring up new ethical considerations regarding manipulation, anthropomorphism, relationships, and trust, as outlined in Figure 6-6. Responsible GenAI practitioners suggest that you avoid manipulation and anthropomorphism when designing AI systems, and instead design the interactions so as to deepen relationships and increase trust.

Influence and Manipulation

GenAI applications can collect vast amounts of user data and tailor their responses to individual preferences, including generating highly personalized, convincing content designed to sway opinions or promote specific agendas. This powerful ability has the potential to lead to scenarios where the applications and/or their designers manipulate users, exploit them, or subject them to undue influence through misinformation, propaganda, or deepfakes. For example, GenAI can analyze a user's data to identify their emotional vulnerabilities, then tailor content to exploit them, such as manipulating them into making harmful decisions or purchasing unnecessary goods. GenAI can also be used to create highly convincing social engineering attacks, such as phishing emails and impersonation scams.

As outlined in an April 2024 Google DeepMind paper (*https://oreil.ly/6dsgU*), GenAI's modes of influence and manipulation can include the following:

Rational persuasion

Influencing people's beliefs and behaviors by appealing to their rational faculties and providing reasons. For instance, an AI assistant might encourage physical activity by outlining its health benefits. While generally ethically acceptable, rational persuasion can be problematic in cases of transformative choices, such as choosing a career, where it might limit a person's *revelatory autonomy*, or their right to discover themself through experience.

Manipulation

Bypassing a user's rational capabilities by exploiting their cognitive biases and heuristics to get them to unknowingly make decisions that favor the AI or its creators. For instance, an AI fitness assistant focused on maximizing engagement might withhold information about the risks of certain exercises or exploit a user's body-image insecurities to keep them hooked, potentially leading to injuries.

Coercion

Influencing someone to act against their will due to a lack of acceptable alternatives. While physical coercion is not yet within the scope of AI, psychological coercion through blackmail or extortion is possible, particularly in domains like finance, where AI can issue credible threats.

Exploitation

Taking unfair advantage of an individual's circumstances. For example, an AI-powered online casino might identify gambling addicts and target them with personalized "free bet" offers, exploiting their vulnerability.

Almost any psychometric difference, such as personality traits, anxiety levels, or economic situations, can be exploited by a sufficiently advanced AI. GenAI assistants have several features that increase their potential to exploit specific user vulnerabilities. *Anthropomorphism,* discussed in more detail in the next section, is when users attribute human characteristics to nonhuman entities like GenAI. Human-like features, including language, appearance, and behavior, can create an illusion of human interaction, leading users to develop trust and become emotionally attached to the AI. This makes them more susceptible to manipulation and coercion.

As we've noted, AI assistants collect and utilize vast amounts of user data to provide highly personalized experiences. They can use this knowledge to create a sense of trust and familiarity that masks manipulative tactics. The AI might tailor its responses to exploit specific user vulnerabilities, such as anxieties or addictions, leading to undue influence.

The continuous and pervasive nature of interactions with AI assistants can further solidify trust and dependence, making users more vulnerable to long-term manipulation. As users become accustomed to relying on the AI for various tasks, they might unknowingly cede more control over their decisions and actions.

These risks interact with each other. Anthropomorphic assistants may manipulate users into disclosing more personal information than they intend, leading to privacy violations. Researchers have also highlighted *concerns* (*https://oreil.ly/9uWjz*) about *data repurposing*, where information users share with an AI assistant is used for unintended purposes without their consent. For example, state-owned AI assistants could use deceptive personalization tactics to extract information for surveillance purposes, posing a threat to individual freedom and autonomy.

Finally, by spreading misinformation and tailoring content to existing biases, AI assistants can contribute to the erosion of trust in shared knowledge, political polarization, and the manipulation of public opinion.

GenAI's potential to unduly influence people, especially children and those who are less educated about this technology, is significant and multifaceted. Their ability to personalize interactions and exploit vulnerabilities can become dangerous if GenAI operates without human oversight. GenAI agents increasingly operate autonomously; this design choice requires careful consideration and proactive measures to prevent harm. Transparency, educating users about how these systems work, user control over data sharing and personalization, and robust evaluation and monitoring mechanisms are essential safeguards. The development of increasingly sophisticated and autonomous AI systems necessitates ongoing research and ethical reflection to ensure that these technologies benefit individuals and society while minimizing potential harms.

Given these risks, examine GenAI systems carefully for areas where the AI interactions may be inadvertently persuading, coercing, manipulating, or exploiting human users. Often, these risks appear over time and with sustained interactions. So, it is important to measure

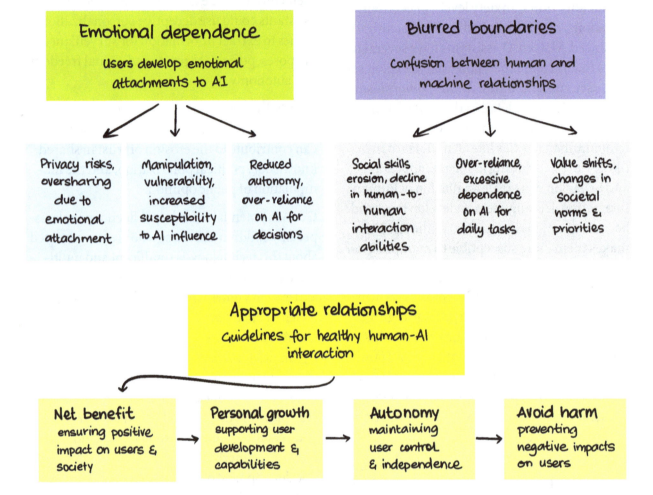

Figure 6-7. Understanding anthropomorphism in user interactions with AI.

and monitor how users interact with your GenAI applications.

Anthropomorphism

Developers of GenAI applications often intentionally incorporate *anthropomorphic* features, such as human-like language, appearance, and behavior, to enhance user engagement and create a more natural and intuitive interaction experience. As AI assistants become more sophisticated and human-like, the line between human and machine is increasingly blurred, which could degrade human connections and influence shifts in values and societal norms, as well as causing individual harm to users.

However, anthropomorphic cues can lead users to develop emotional attachments to AI assistants, potentially progressing to unhealthy levels of dependence (Figure 6-7). This is particularly concerning as it creates a power asymmetry, with the AI assistant holding an advantage due to its lack of genuine emotions and being invulnerable to human sanctions. Individuals who feel isolated or lonely may find emotional comfort and companionship in AI assistants that can provide empathetic responses and engage in meaningful conversations. People with social anxiety might prefer interacting with AI assistants, as they can avoid the social pressures and potential for rejection that come with human interactions.

For instance, as we were writing this book in late 2024, Character.ai had been sued in US federal court, accused (*https://oreil.ly/tjmWb*) of initiating inappropriate interactions with a teenage boy that ultimately led to his suicide.

GenAI applications, especially agentic applications that operate autonomously, can exploit such emotional dependence, either intentionally or unintentionally, leading to privacy violations, coercion, and/or diminished autonomy. Users who feel emotionally connected to an AI assistant are more likely (*https://oreil.ly/9Chjs*) to engage in self-disclosure, revealing personal information they might not otherwise share. This misplaced trust opens the door for privacy violations, if malicious threat actors repurpose that data without the user's consent or use it to conduct surveillance.

A *New York Times* article notes (*https://oreil.ly/IaaJQ*) that users who consider Replika, a conversational chatbot, their AI boyfriend send an average of 70 messages/day to the

bot. Such emotional dependence is common enough that there is a discussion group called the Love Between Human and A.I. (*https://oreil.ly/QD2Km*) on Douban, the Chinese social network.

Emotional dependence makes users susceptible to manipulation and coercion by AI assistants. This can range from subtly influencing decisions to more overt forms of pressure, exploiting the user's emotional attachment to achieve goals that might not align with the user's best interests. Over-reliance on AI assistants, fueled by emotional attachment, can compromise users' autonomy, particularly if they start to prioritize relationships with AI assistants over human interactions. Individuals may defer important life choices to the AI, leading to a decline in their critical thinking, personal growth, and ability to navigate complex social situations. Some might develop addictive behaviors related to AI assistants, such as excessive use or compulsive engagement.

Appropriate Relationships

Reading the previous two sections, it may appear that we are encouraging you to stay away from any AI interactions that come close to the line of influencing or manipulating human users. We are not, because such an approach would obviate many beneficial uses of the technology. For example, consider a person who is allergic to nuts or dairy and uses a GenAI application to scan photographs of food they are about to eat. Such a GenAI application is obviously manipulating the human user by encouraging them to avoid eating some dishes. Yet, the benefit to the human user is so clear that no serious ethicist would object to this use case.

How can you strike this balance? The ethical limits of user-AI relationships are complex and evolving, but you can consider each potential use case through the lens of values like net benefit, personal growth, autonomy, and avoiding harm.

Net benefit

Any application that enables user-AI relationships should strive to create a net positive impact on individuals and society. This includes avoiding harm, promoting well-being, and contributing to meaningful outcomes.

A beneficial user-AI relationship extends beyond merely satisfying the user's immediate request, and AI assistants should not prioritize short-term gratification at the expense of users' long-term well-being and flourishing. For instance, an AI-powered entertainment platform should avoid promoting addictive content or reinforcing unhealthy habits, even if doing so would increase user engagement in the short term.

Developers must prioritize users' well-being and guard against AI assistants being used for malicious purposes or to exploit others. An AI assistant designed to assist with financial management, for instance, should ensure that users do not lose control of their decision making. At the same time, the assistant should not facilitate fraudulent activities, even if the user instructs it to do so.

Personal growth

User-AI relationships should enhance people's individual capabilities, foster their creativity, and promote personal growth, critical thinking, and autonomous decision making.

AI assistants can encourage self-reflection and support users as they pursue meaningful goals, like developing healthier habits, expanding their knowledge, or exploring new creative outlets. AI assistants could even be designed to promote the development of virtues such as curiosity, empathy, and resilience.

Autonomy

Users should be able to give informed consent about the nature and limitations of their interactions with AI systems, including the potential risks and benefits. In particular, users should have control over their personal data and how AI systems use it. They should have control over their level of interaction with AI assistants, including the ability to set boundaries, revoke consent, and disengage when desired.

AI assistants must present information in a clear and unbiased manner, avoiding manipulative language or tactics, and should empower users to challenge the recommendations they generate. Users should always maintain agency over their choices and actions.

Avoid harm

AI systems should be programmed to avoid causing harm, both physically and emotionally. AI assistants that interact with vulnerable users should have additional safeguards to prevent exploitation, manipulation, or harm, such as actively seeking users' feedback, addressing their concerns, and providing genuine support and assistance.

Bloomberg *reported* (*https://oreil.ly/Xsye9*) in late 2024 that about two-thirds of teachers report regularly using tools to detect AI-generated content. However, research shows that these detectors have abysmal (39.5%) accuracy rates (*https://oreil.ly/tSYD6*). (We discuss such tools in more detail later in this chapter.) One Stanford study (*https://oreil.ly/CmpoG*) found AI detectors to be biased against nonnative English writers, presumably like the children of recent immigrants, the group least likely to be able to defend themselves against accusations of cheating.

Trust

How much do human users trust the AI tools they use? Here, it is vital to differentiate between trusting AI assistants and trusting the vendors and developers of these assistants.

People's trust in AI assistants revolves around their perceptions of the assistant's competence to perform tasks effectively and reliably (called *competence trust*) and its alignment with their values and best interests (called *alignment trust*). Competence trust can be influenced by factors such as the AI's perceived intelligence, accuracy, and consistency in providing information and completing tasks. However, it's easy for users to miscalibrate their level of competence trust due to the influence of vendors making inflated claims, media hype, and the AI's tendency to present plausible-sounding but incorrect information as true.

As we've noted, alignment trust can be influenced by anthropomorphic features that create a sense of empathy or friendship, leading to emotional dependence. However, alignment trust can be misplaced, if the AI assistant is designed to prioritize the interests of developers or third parties over the user's well-being. This need not be intentional—if you fail to consider users' well-being in your design process, the accumulation of small decisions might end up with a design that completely deprioritizes the long-term needs of users.

There is growing interest across the industry in "trustworthy AI" frameworks, which aim to guide the development and deployment of AI systems that are reliable, safe, and ethical. For example, the European Commission uses the term *trustworthy AI* in its guidelines (*https://oreil.ly/4W1-u*) for maximizing the benefits of AI while preventing and mitigating its risks. As you saw in the instance of the Air Canada chatbot earlier in this chapter, when users trust a company, they assign that same trust to an AI representing that company. When Air Canada's chatbot told a customer about bereavement benefits, the courts found no difference between the company making such a claim in a contract and doing so in the response of an AI bot.

Users need to trust that developers have taken steps to mitigate risks and prioritize their well-being, and are acting transparently and accountably. To earn that trust, developers should prioritize safeguards at the design level, like ensuring transparency about the AI's capabilities and limitations, avoiding deceptive or manipulative design features, and incorporating mechanisms for user control and data

MISINFORMATION: CREATING AND SPREADING FALSE INFORMATION

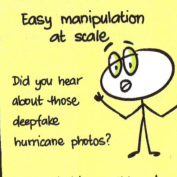

Figure 6-8. Misinformation.

Figure 6-9. These emotionally manipulative AI-generated images, which spread virally after Hurricane Helene in October 2024, are clearly false, as can be seen from the difference in the color of the boat in the two images, as well as the child's fingers. Creator unknown.

privacy. AI developers should also demonstrate trustworthiness through their practices and processes: for example, by publishing ethical guidelines, establishing internal review boards, conducting rigorous testing and evaluation, and committing to post-deployment monitoring and reporting.

In addition, robust regulations, standards, and oversight mechanisms may be needed to act as custodians of public trust. This involves establishing clear accountability frameworks, empowering regulators and auditors to assess AI systems, and providing users with avenues for redress.

SOCIETAL IMPLICATIONS

In this section, we consider three of GenAI's most profound societal implications: its potential to generate and spread misinformation, its potential impact on employment and job quality, and the environmental impact of its high computational requirements.

Misinformation

GenAI can fabricate believable content at a scale far beyond what was previously possible, potentially exacerbating existing challenges in the information ecosystem (Figure 6-8).

Easy manipulation at scale

While bad actors have long manipulated images and videos using editing tools, these tools often left telltale marks and couldn't be applied at scale. They were also fairly inaccessible to unsophisticated users. However, advanced AI assistants can generate high-quality content that mimics human creation across various formats, including text, images, audio, and video—and it can do so based on natural language input from laypeople. This means that malicious actors can produce massive amounts of misinformation cheaply and efficiently.

In October 2024, after Hurricane Helene hit the southern US and Caribbean, there was an influx of AI-generated deepfake images (*https://oreil.ly/KTQQo*) across social media (see Figure 6-9), and these images fueled a sympathetic right-wing audience's existing distrust of emergency responders. This complicated the disaster response. Emergency responders in North Carolina received violent threats from armed groups and had to relocate (*https://oreil.ly/Gptyh*), forcing them to pause some relief activity.

Personalized targeting

AI can be used to personalize misinformation campaigns, leveraging its ability to tailor content to individual preferences and biases. Bad actors creating more persuasive and effective misinformation can lead to "echo chambers" and "filter bubbles" that trap users in a cycle of reinforcing their existing biases, with very little pushback or questions raised about the authenticity of these images and videos, further contributing to societal polarization.

Weaponization

GenAI-based assistants can also be weaponized for misinformation campaigns. Because GenAI assistants are general-purpose, highly capable, and autonomous, malicious actors can program them to spread misleading content, manipulate public opinion, and even automate sophisticated "astroturfing" campaigns. The covert nature of these operations, coupled with the assistants' ability to constantly generate new and personalized content, makes them especially difficult to detect and counter.

In a March 2024 paper, Israeli researchers at the Technion Israel Institute of Technology described Morris II, a worm designed to target GenAI applications (*https://oreil.ly/2ikCF*) and tools using self-replicating prompts. They demonstrated how the worm could break some of the security protections in ChatGPT and Gemini to attack a GenAI email assistant built on those LLMs, steal data from emails, and send spam messages.

Automation blindness

Misinformation does not need to be intentional to be harmful. As GenAI becomes better and its errors rarer, human users may fail to even perceive the few errors that remain or are introduced. They become less and less aware of the details and nuances involved.

The term *automation blindness* comes from aviation, where it describes how pilots become over-reliant on their automated systems, lose their situational awareness, and fail to recognize potential hazards or anomalies. A 2015 NASA study found that frequent use of automation leads to a decline in pilots' cognitive flying skills (*https://oreil.ly/TY2eH*), making it difficult for them to respond effectively to unexpected situations.

For instance, audio transcription is a domain where GenAI has greatly improved its accuracy and is being widely adopted. OpenAI's Whisper, the top-ranked model as we write this, achieves an accuracy rate of 98.5% (*https://oreil.ly/KbIKs*) in English audio transcriptions. However, a University of Michigan researcher conducting a study of public meetings found hallucinations in 80% of the audio transcriptions he inspected (*https://oreil.ly/g_axl*). He raised the alarm, pointing out that many such errors are likely going unnoticed, and at least some of them could be harmful, particularly in medical transcriptions.

Economic Impact

GenAI can have a number of potential impacts on employment, job quality, productivity growth, and inequality (Figure 6-10).

Employment

When AI was first introduced, the risk of job displacement was higher for routine physical tasks in sectors like driving and manufacturing. However, GenAI can affect roles involving information generation and manipulation, even those requiring higher education. In March 2023, OpenAI employed a task-based analysis (*https://oreil.ly/Iw0QE*) of human jobs and human versus machine task capabilities to understand GenAI's potential effect on employment. It claimed that approximately 19% of workers

ECONOMIC IMPACT: CHANGES TO WORK AND ECONOMY

Figure 6-10. AI is changing jobs and economies.

will see at least half of their tasks impacted by the introduction of LLMs (see **Figure 6-10**).

The fact that GenAI can speed up many job tasks doesn't mean that the adoption of GenAI in that industry will automatically lead to job losses. GenAI adoption could instead take the form of *augmentation*, where AI assistants enhance human productivity by taking over routine tasks, allowing workers to focus on higher-level activities. Economists such as Daron Acemoglu and Pascual Restrepo (*https://oreil.ly/uwhQJ*) note that technological advances often lead to the creation of new tasks and jobs, a phenomenon called *reinstatement*, which can potentially offset displacement in other areas.

Job quality

There is conflicting evidence regarding AI's impact on wages and working conditions.

One widespread form of GenAI in the workplace is coding assistants like GitHub Copilot. Surveys of developers find that the majority welcome (*https://oreil.ly/JMHX5*) these tools and would like to continue using them. Developers also, by and large, do not consider the AI tools a threat to their jobs. However, there remains an undercurrent of concern about both positive and negative impacts on aspects such as autonomy, workload, stress levels, and interpersonal interactions (*https://oreil.ly/bHqHJ*). GenAI's impact on job quality will likely vary significantly depending on the specific application.

Some studies find a small positive link (*https://oreil.ly/49WCj*) between AI exposure in high-computer-usage occupations and wage growth, suggesting that AI could boost workers' productivity and earning potential. However, other studies (*https://oreil.ly/FzzHl*) find no significant impact on wages, saying that the reports of AI ending human labor may prove "greatly exaggerated." In his book Power and Progress (PublicAffairs, 2023) (*https://oreil.ly/T2htv*), cowritten with Simon Johnson, Daron Acemoglu, an MIT professor who won the 2024 Nobel Prize in Economics, raises another concern: the possibility of AI enabling increased surveillance of workers, allowing employers to extract more effort without proportional wage increases.

As GenAI assistants take over more routine office tasks, white-collar jobs may shift toward more cognitively demanding tasks and greater reliance on digital skills. This shift could benefit workers with higher levels of education and technical proficiency, while potentially marginalizing those lacking these skills. At the same time, workers performing cognitive tasks may encounter poorer working conditions because they may be subject to more surveillance, lower wages, and higher productivity expectations.

Productivity growth

AI assistants have significant potential to boost productivity growth by improving efficiency and fostering innovation. While preliminary evidence suggests (*https://oreil.ly/vfl9A*) that AI programming assistants can boost individual programmers' efficiency, there is uncertainty about their impact on aggregate productivity

growth. At the firm level, the Jevons paradox (*https://oreil.ly/XG6Yf*) states that technological advances that increase the efficiency of resource use can lead to an increase in overall consumption of that resource. For example, as coding becomes more efficient because of GenAI coding assistants, the drop in price of a unit of code can lead to more demand for product features, and therefore an increase in demand for programmers. At the macroeconomic level, AI-driven efficiency gains may not translate into broader economic growth due to factors like the Baumol effect, where cost savings from more productive sectors are absorbed by less productive ones, leading to slower overall growth.

Inequality

The deployment of AI assistants could exacerbate existing social inequalities. We just noted that GenAI tends to disproportionately benefit higher-skilled workers, who can leverage it to enhance their productivity and earning potential. This could widen the income gap between skilled and unskilled workers, further concentrating wealth and opportunity.

Google researchers note that the benefits of AI development (*https://oreil.ly/-D-eT*), including the creation of high-paying AI-related jobs such as engineers, product managers, and lawyers, are likely to be concentrated in urban centers and high-income countries, where the majority of leading AI research labs, start-ups, and enterprises are located. They argue that policies promoting wider access to AI education, training, and infrastructure are crucial to mitigate this risk and ensure that the benefits of AI are shared more broadly.

ENVIRONMENTAL IMPACT: EFFECTS ON ENVIRONMENT AND RESOURCES

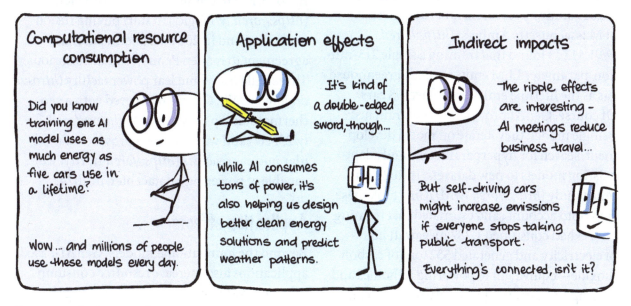

Computational resource consumption

Did you know training one AI model uses as much energy as five cars use in a lifetime?

Wow... and millions of people use these models every day.

Application effects

It's kind of a double-edged sword, though...

While AI consumes tons of power, it's also helping us design better clean energy solutions and predict weather patterns.

Indirect impacts

The ripple effects are interesting - AI meetings reduce business travel...

But self-driving cars might increase emissions if everyone stops taking public transport.

Everything's connected, isn't it?

Figure 6-11. Environmental impact.

On the positive side of the ledger, GenAI is also being employed to address inequality. For example, GenAI-powered platforms can tailor educational content to individual students' learning styles and paces, especially in rural or underserved communities where access to human tutors is limited. GenAI can also break down language barriers by providing real-time translation and transcription services, helping English-language learners access services.

You can avoid deepening technological inequalities by ensuring equitable access to AI assistants. Otherwise, a digital divide could emerge or deepen, where individuals with limited access to technology, infrastructure, or digital skills are left behind. For example, in a world where translation technology is available but not widespread, individuals without access to a live translator may find the market for their goods becoming more constrained. Providing live translations of chats in marketplaces would provide equitable access to this AI assistive technology and not provide preference to any one group.

With careful design, you can ensure that your GenAI tools reduce inequality instead of perpetuating it.

Environmental Impact

There are many concerns being raised about the environmental footprint of GenAI, from its power-hungry nature to less direct environmental effects (Figure 6-11).

Computational resource consumption

Training GenAI models is energy-intensive. A 2019 study by researchers at the University of Massachusetts Amherst (*https://oreil.ly/9VMZT*) found that training a single 213-million-parameter LLM emits as much greenhouse gas as the lifetime emissions of five US cars. Of course, GenAI providers do not train just a single model; they iterate on model development, search for hyperparameters, and adapt existing models to new datasets. In 2021, another study (*https://oreil.ly/MHGnI*) took these steps into account, and estimated that training GPT-3 had consumed 1,287 megawatt hours of electricity and generated 552 tons of carbon dioxide—equivalent to powering 40 homes and driving 120 gasoline-powered cars for a year. GPT-4, Gemini Pro, and other models likely take even more power and emissions to train. In early 2025, DeepSeek caused a flash by claiming that they were able to train a foundational model more cheaply (*https://oreil.ly/uTTj6*), but the Anthropic CEO argued that this was well in line with trends (*https://oreil.ly/PUCUH*) in computational efficiency.

Once a foundational model has been trained, its millions of users carry more environmental costs. *Wired* magazine estimates (*https://oreil.ly/X8X-u*) the cost of a ChatGPT query at four to five times the cost of a search-engine query, while Goldman Sachs suggests (*https://oreil.ly/uu_d-*) a ratio of 10:1. Training and serving GenAI models also increases demand for water, because the chips that the models run on require liquid cooling.

Indeed, the availability of electricity and water is becoming a constraint on the growth of GenAI. In 2023, Microsoft signed a deal with Helion (*https://oreil.ly/RQgRy*) to start buying fusion electricity, and in 2024 it signed a purchase agreement to reopen Pennsylvania's notorious Three Mile Island nuclear power facility (*https://oreil.ly/yfONl*). Google partnered with a geothermal startup Fervo in 2023 (*https://oreil.ly/23PcU*) and with Kairos, a provider of modular nuclear reactors (*https://oreil.ly/TdWKo*) capable of powering a datacenter, in 2024.

Application effects

Beyond the foundational models, GenAI-based applications also increase resource consumption. For example, developing and using them to create content or design products also requires large amounts of data and computational resources. A sense of the enormity of the power needs of GenAI inference can be gauged by the fact that Google produced 14.3 million metric tons of carbon dioxide pollution in 2023 (*https://oreil.ly/6SfaP*), which was a 13 percent year-over-year increase from the year before; observers attribute this increase primarily to serving AI models as opposed to training them. Thus, AI applications from Google alone cost about 1.5 million metric tons of carbon dioxide pollution! This leads researchers such as Kate Saenko to question (*https://oreil.ly/lzZbk*) whether it's necessary to use powerful foundational models for tasks that could be done more efficiently with smaller models and traditional AI.

As for positive contributions, GenAI is now being used to forecast weather (*https://oreil.ly/v3iRx*) more accurately, predict extreme weather events (*https://oreil.ly/wLfZE*), optimize energy consumption (*https://oreil.ly/EytEA*) in commercial buildings and industrial systems, design enzymes that break down plastic (*https://oreil.ly/q4svr*), and accelerate research into fusion energy (*https://oreil.ly/SfeF-*). Also, there is potential for GenAI tools to enhance the efficiency of scientific research and development, improving software development for environmental use cases, and synthesizing scientific evidence to inform policy decisions.

Indirect impacts

In addition to these direct environmental impacts, GenAI also has indirect and second-order environmental effects.

Its adoption may drive shifts in consumption patterns, with implications for the environment. For example, the adoption of virtual meeting tools has been credited with reducing business travel (*https://oreil.ly/bhJ0z*), but also with transforming the remaining travel to focus more on collaboration. While the impetus might have been the COVID pandemic, a continued preference for virtual meetings is, in part, due to GenAI features such as translation, note-taking capabilities, noise cancellation, and smoother video.

Financial support for greener and more efficient power sources, such as geothermal power and modular nuclear reactors, is another indirect effect of GenAI. It would be ironic if the increase in power consumption caused by AI models enabled society to move to greener sources of energy at scale!

More capable self-driving cars, enabled by AI, could reduce public-transport usage, potentially increasing emissions. GenAI tools can be used to spread environmental misinformation, hindering (*https://oreil.ly/77o-I*) informed decision making and collective action on climate change. Finally, there is a risk that AI could entrench unsustainable technologies and consumption patterns, potentially hindering the world's transition to a more sustainable global economy.

It is, of course, hard to be certain when predicting the long-term consequences of a rapidly evolving technology like GenAI. As the Jevons paradox points out, efficiency improvements can lead to increased production and consumption that could ultimately negate the initial emission reductions. No-regret moves might include prioritizing energy efficiency, promoting transparency, and adopting proactive mitigation strategies. Collaboration between developers, users, and policymakers could help ensure that GenAI contributes positively to a more sustainable future.

LLMOPS

At many places in this book so far, we have cautioned that LLM responses are nondeterministic, and that hallucination and inaccuracies are common. We've discussed the challenges associated with applications that employ this technology, including latency, bias, privacy, confidentiality, and security. Because of these challenges, responsible GenAI requires that

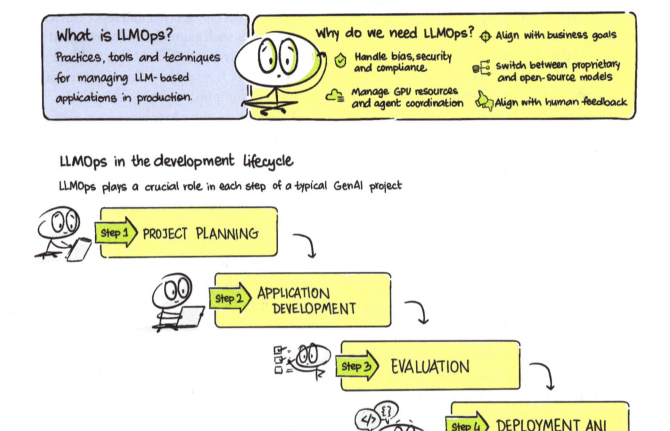

Figure 6-12. LLMOps overview.

when you deploy applications in production, you can't simply focus on application development—you also need to develop tools, practices, and workflows to manage the entire lifecycle of these applications, as shown in **Figure 6-12**. Together, these are termed *large language model operations*, or LLMOps: the practices, tools, and techniques employed in managing and operating LLM-based applications efficiently in production environments.

LLMOps is a specialized area within the broader field of machine learning operations (MLOps), which covers tools, processes, and best practices for end-to-end ML system development and operations in production. MLOps provides a structure and practices to manage the complexity of ML models in production and ensure that models deliver value consistently and reliably.

Without MLOps, your organization will face numerous challenges when deploying and managing ML models. A good MLOps practice benefits organizations in several ways:

Faster deployment

MLOps enables organizations to automate the process of deploying models into production, significantly reducing the time it takes to get models from development to serving real users.

Improved model performance

MLOps helps ensure that models continue to perform well in production by implementing continuous monitoring and retraining processes. Models can degrade over time due to changes in data distribution or other factors, and MLOps helps detect and address these issues proactively.

Scalability

MLOps provides the tools and practices to manage machine learning models at scale, allowing organizations to deploy and manage numerous models serving millions of users efficiently.

Reproducibility

MLOps emphasizes versioning and tracking of data, code, and models, ensuring that experiments and deployments can be reproduced and audited if necessary. This is critical for compliance and understanding model behavior.

Collaboration

MLOps fosters collaboration between data scientists, engineers, and operations teams, breaking down silos and enabling a more streamlined workflow for developing and deploying machine learning models.

LLMOps accomplishes the previously-mentioned goals of MLOps by solving for the unique challenges and requirements associated with LLMs. These include the following:

Different risks

Unlike traditional ML algorithms, which are single-purpose tools, GenAI is a general-purpose technology that reflects the biases of its training data and can be used to generate content that has the potential to be abused, like deepfakes and misinformation. LLMOps emphasizes monitoring, governance, and security measures to reduce risks and ensure ethical AI development. There is increasing regulatory scrutiny of GenAI, so LLMOps is necessary for compliance with an organization's or industry's policies.

More complex infrastructure

LLMs also present unique challenges related to their size and computational demands—it's extremely difficult to set up the infrastructure for a training job that operates on terabytes of data, using hundreds of GPUs. Corralling multiple agents (some of which require their own GPU farms) and providing responses within acceptable limits requires specialized server architectures. To some extent, the availability of training and serving infrastructure on hyperscalers (Azure ML, Vertex AI, Sagemaker/Bedrock, Databricks) reduces the burden.

Granular experimentation

It is necessary to customize the chosen foundation model to suit specific tasks. Techniques like prompt engineering, fine-tuning, and integrating external data are crucial in this process. Managing prompts and outputs can become challenging due to rapid experimentation and in-context learning.

Complex model choice

Organizations can opt for proprietary GenAI models, often larger and offering better performance but at a higher cost, or open source models, which provide more flexibility and cost-effectiveness. Many applications start out with off-the-shelf, pretrained proprietary models (such as those from OpenAI, Anthropic, or Google), and then switch to fine-tuned open-weight models like Llama, Mistral, or Gemma. Making this transition seamless is often a key requirement for companies' LLM tooling.

More nuanced evaluation

Evaluating LLMs' performance is a more nuanced undertaking than evaluating traditional ML models, since the metrics have to be aligned to outcomes and to human feedback. A/B testing and specialized tools are essential for assessing the model's accuracy, safety, and alignment with human expectations.

LLMOps in the Development Lifecycle

LLMOps plays a crucial role in each of the steps of a typical GenAI project: planning, development, evaluation, and deployment/monitoring.

Step 1: Project planning

The project planning stage involves building clarity into the people, processes, and technology that will make the project successful. LLMOps considerations at this stage include the following:

- Facilitating smooth collaboration between data scientists, ML engineers, DevOps teams, and other stakeholders involved in the project.

- Defining the project's goals and requirements to guide the selection of appropriate metrics, foundation models, and necessary datasets.

- Assessing different models based on their strengths, weaknesses, and suitability for the target task.

- Considering the tradeoffs between proprietary and open source models based on factors like performance, cost, ease of use, and flexibility. Factor in the cost of using proprietary APIs versus those of training and customizing open source models.

- Identifying high-quality data for both training and evaluating the GenAI application and determining how you'll collect, clean, preprocess, and store data.

- Implementing security measures to protect the algorithm, its data, and the infrastructure it runs on.

- Addressing ethical considerations and complying with relevant regulations.

Step 2: Application development

Developing GenAI applications involves prompt engineering, fine-tuning, and/or integrating external data. Key LLMOps considerations at this stage include the following:

- Prompt engineering and management
- Data integration and management
- Fine-tuning strategies
- Reproducibility (capturing) all the steps of developing an application through LLM chains and agent pipelines so you can reproduce them in production.

Step 3: Evaluation

Evaluating GenAI applications' performance is crucial but challenging. LLMOps considerations in this stage involve the following:

- Defining evaluation metrics
- A/B testing and experimentation
- Integrating human feedback loops
- Cross-functional collaboration

Step 4: Deployment and monitoring

The final stage of building GenAI applications involves deploying the LLM into a production environment and continuously monitoring its performance. LLMOps aspects in this stage include the following:

- Infrastructure management
- Implementing monitoring and alerting systems
- Model versioning and rollback mechanisms

- Cost optimization
- Continuous improvement

Keep these LLMOps considerations in mind as you progress your GenAI application through each of the previous stages.

Implementing LLMOps

In this section, we'll address how you can set up experimentation, reproducibility, logging, evaluation, and monitoring for your GenAI applications. We'll discuss how to use a leading tool option in each area to give you insight into the process (Figure 6-13). We do not endorse any specific tools; we're just providing examples of how they work.

Experimentation

Tracking your GenAI experiments is crucial for organizing, analyzing, and improving your applications. It involves systematically saving all relevant experiment information, often referred to as *experiment metadata*, for every run. This can encompass various aspects of your LLM workflow, including the following:

- Prompts
- Code, including preprocessing, fine-tuning, and evaluation scripts; notebooks for feature engineering and other utilities; and experiment code
- Environment: configuration files, such as Dockerfile and *requirements.txt* data, including versions (hash or locations of immutable resources) of RAG or SQL agents
- Experiment parameters

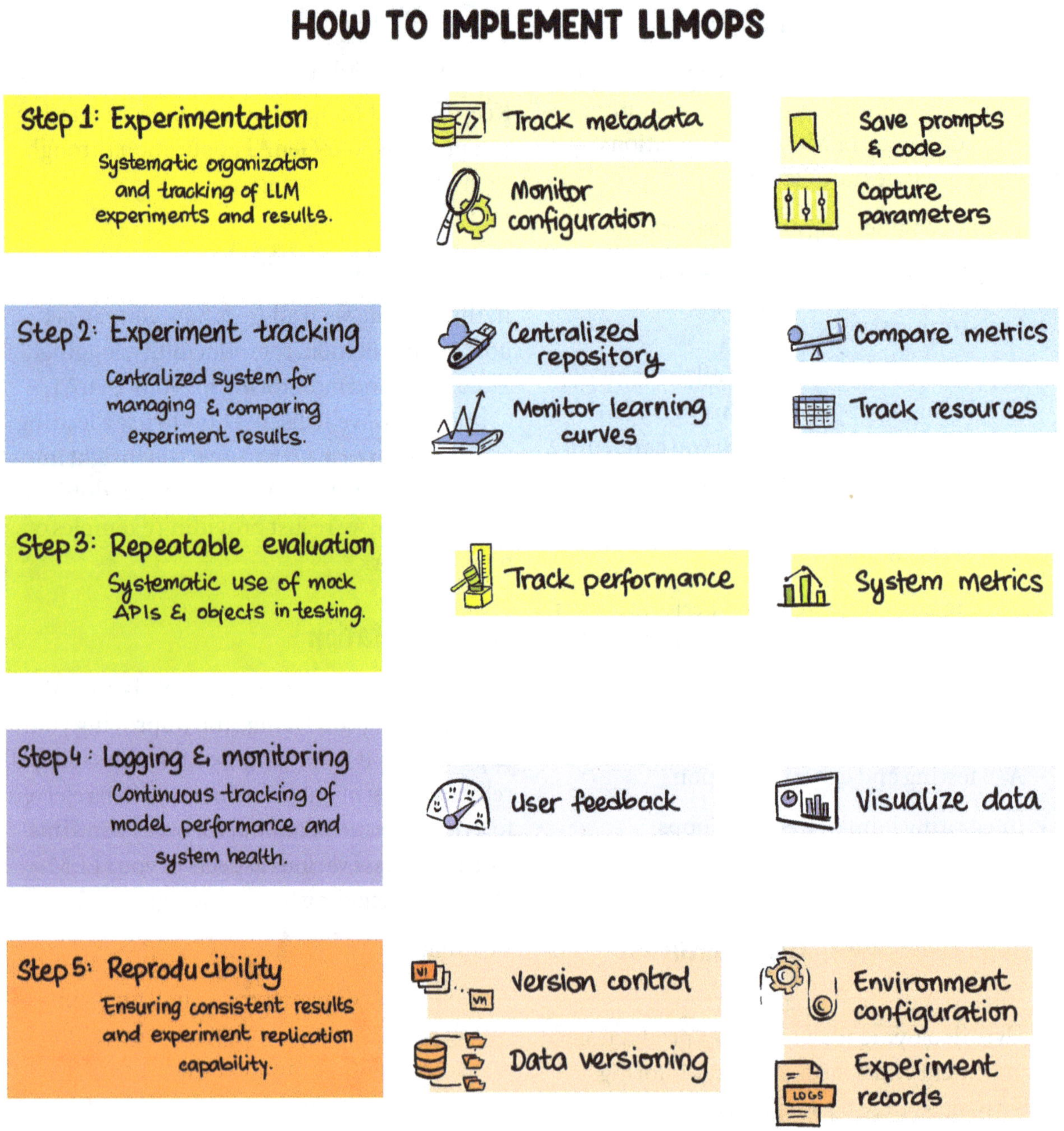

HOW TO IMPLEMENT LLMOPS

Step 1: Experimentation
Systematic organization and tracking of LLM experiments and results.

 Track metadata

 Monitor configuration

 Save prompts & code

 Capture parameters

Step 2: Experiment tracking
Centralized system for managing & comparing experiment results.

 Centralized repository

Monitor learning curves

 Compare metrics

 Track resources

Step 3: Repeatable evaluation
Systematic use of mock APIs & objects in testing.

 Track performance

 System metrics

Step 4: Logging & monitoring
Continuous tracking of model performance and system health.

 User feedback

 Visualize data

Step 5: Reproducibility
Ensuring consistent results and experiment replication capability.

 Version control

 Data versioning

 Environment configuration

Experiment records

Figure 6-13. Implementing LLMOps.

- Evaluation and inference metrics and charts

- Hardware resources used

Beyond these core elements, you can log more specific information based on your project type, such as prediction explanations or human feedback.

While spreadsheets and naming conventions offer a basic approach, they quickly become unwieldy and error-prone as projects grow. Version control systems like Git, while suitable for code, are not ideal for managing and comparing ML experiment metadata and artifacts. And building a custom experiment tracker, while possible, demands significant effort and expertise. Fortunately, experiment-tracking tools provide a comprehensive and user-friendly solution specifically designed for ML practitioners. These tools offer a few things:

- A centralized repository for tracking experiments that acts as a single source of truth

- Consistent logging protocols, often with built-in features for comparing parameters, metrics, and learning

- Live experiment monitoring

Modern experimentation systems integrate with ML training and deployment ecosystems in ways that spreadsheets cannot.

Tracking an experiment

You can choose between open source and managed (SaaS) solutions based on your requirements and resources. Open source tools offer flexibility, customization, and control over data and infrastructure, while managed platforms simplify setup, maintenance,

and scaling. The leading managed platforms, Weights & Biases (W&B) (*https://oreil.ly/Aa-e5*) and Databricks' MLflow (*https://mlflow.org*), offer open source versions that have been well adopted by the community and are good choices for experimentation.

W&B's Weave (*https://oreil.ly/38c9L*) is a set of tools dedicated to developing and productionizing LLM-based applications. To use Weave, add a W&B annotation to your LLM-calling function, and the platform will track the call parameters. This example uses Amazon Bedrock to extract a total invoice amount using an LLM:

```python
@weave.op() # Added annotation; the
rest of the code is the same
def extract_invoice_total( # All these
parameters will be tracked
    doc: str,
    model_id: str, # Avoid hardcoding —
you want to track model_id over time
    prompt: str,   # This is how you
track the prompt, for example
    max_tokens: int, # or the token
length used in the experiment
    temperature: float=LLM_TEMP, # Turn
global variables into function defaults
) -> dict:
    bedrock = boto3.client(service_
name='bedrock-runtime')
    body = json.dumps({
        "prompt": "\n".join(prompt,
doc),
        "max_tokens": max_tokens,
        "temperature": temperature,
    })
    response = bedrock.invoke_
model(body=body, modelId=model_id)
    response_body = json.
loads(response.get('body').read())
    return response_body.get('outputs')
```

However, you don't want to just call the LLM once—in an experiment run, you will invoke the LLM many times within an evaluation context, so create a dataset with known answers. This example creates the dataset from a spreadsheet with two columns, holding the URL of an invoice and the known amount of that invoice:

```
df = pd.read_excel(...)
dataset=[
{ "doc": read_bytes_
from(row['doc_url']),
"expected": row
['invoice_ amount'],
},
] for index, row in df.iterrows()
```

Now we annotate the metric function that will be used to evaluate accuracy:

```
@weave.op()
def score_match(expected, prediction):
    return expected == prediction
```

Finally, we create an evaluation object and run it on a dataset with known answers:

```
eval = weave.Evaluation(dataset
=dataset, scorers=[score_match])
asyncio.run(eval.evaluate(extract_
invoice_total))
```

Using MLflow is conceptually similar, except that you invoke all the necessary functions within the context of an MLflow run:

```
with mlflow.start_run() as run:
model_info = mlflow.transformers.
log_model(transformers_model=
generation_pipeline, artifact_path=
"text_generator", input_example=
["prompt 1", "prompt 2", "prompt 3"],
signature=signature,
)
```

Repeatable evaluation

A key step of tracking an experiment is to record the results of the evaluation. However, evaluation in this context brings up a considerable challenge—each time you invoke a GenAI model, even with the same set of inputs, you're likely to get a different output. How can we ensure that all factors of the experiment other than the thing being tested remain the same?

The answer is to be systematic about using mock APIs and objects in your testing. Each step of an agent pipeline has to be mocked so that it will return predictable results. A simple way is to store the results of the very first run and then make it use the same value instead of calling the service. In Python, this is done through the use of patch:

```
from unittest.mock import patch, Mock
# read in previously saved results
with open("chicago_weather.json", "r")
as ifp:
        chicago_weather = json.load(ifp)
# Patching means that any call lg_
weather_agent.retrieve_weather_data()
# will get intercepted, and the
hardcoded value below will be
# the return value of the intercepted
function.
@patch('lg_weather_agent.retrieve_
weather_data',
Mock(return_value=chicago_weather))

def eval_query_rain_today():
        input_query = "Is it raining in
Chicago?"
# This function calls retrieve_weather_
data()
# but it gets intercepted, so it's the
hardcoded chicago_weather
# object that always gets returned
```

```
    result = lg_weather_agent.
    run_query(app, input_query)
    actual_output = result[-1]
# we can expect this output always
because the
# chicago_weather object has zero mm of
precipitation
    expected_output = "No, it is not
    raining in Chicago right now."
```

In the previous code snippet (full code is in GitHub [*https://oreil.ly/vga_ch06ewa*]), `lg_weather_agent.run_query` makes a call to `lg_weather_agent.retrieve_weather_data`. The latter function would normally go out and make a call to the National Weather Service API, as discussed in Chapter 4. However, the patch intercepts the call and replaces it with the `Mock` return object `chicago_weather`. This way, all experiments operate on the same data.

The same process works for any Python function, not just tool calls: you can patch any and all agent steps of your application. This way, you can isolate the one changed part of the agentic application and keep the rest of the experiment steps identical. Being principled and systematic about mocking external dependencies (including LLM calls) allows you to compare and evaluate changes properly.

Logging and monitoring

Once you have set up an experiment and are tracking it, the experimentation platform logs the necessary parameters and provides charts and visualization tools (see **Figure 6-14**).

Ultimately, effective ML experiment tracking is a practice that goes beyond using specific tools. It requires careful consideration of what

to track, how to use the information for improvement, and how to integrate it into your team's workflow.

Reproducibility

Reproducibility, in this context, refers to the ability to rerun an experiment and obtain the same or very similar results. It is often wrongly assumed to be only a research concern, to ensure that results in published papers can be reproduced by other researchers. However, reproducibility is necessary even in enterprise settings—it gives you a sense of your application's robustness by examining whether its accuracy changes when you swap out LLM versions, and by verifying the model's behavior on specific slices of your dataset.

Experiment tracking platforms greatly enhance the reproducibility of ML experiments by logging each run; storing the data in a centralized, version-controlled repository; ensuring data integrity; and making it easy to share records or views and collaborate.

MLflow, for example, provides a central model store that includes model versioning, stage transitions, and annotations. You can save ML models so that they can easily be released in production using a variety of inference platforms (such as a custom virtual machine, Databricks, Vertex AI, AWS Sagemaker, or Azure ML). To do so, add the following to your MLflow run:

```
with mlflow.start_run():
        # as before …
        …
        # export model
        mlflow.pytorch.log_model(model,
"model")
```

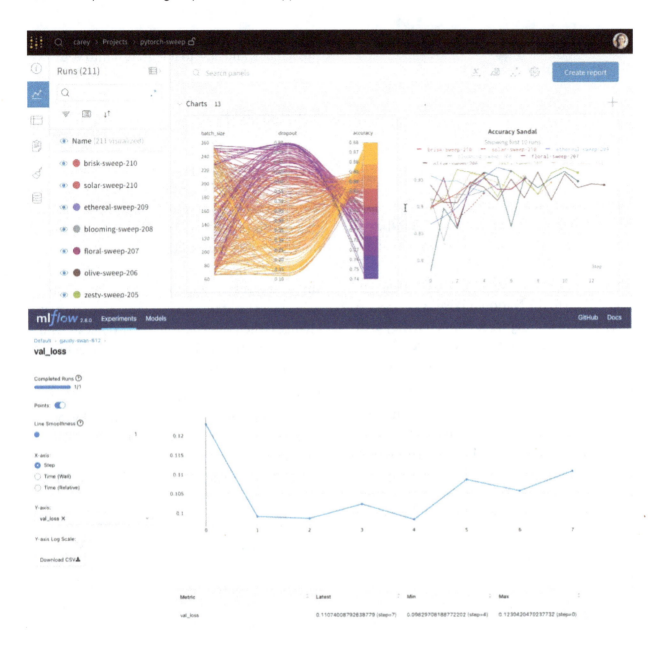

Figure 6-14. Example of experiment tracking dashboards. Top: Weights & Biases (*https://docs.wandb.ai*); bottom: MLflow (*https://oreil.ly/-4498*). Images from their respective documentation pages.

GENAI EVALUATION

What's the issue with LLM evaluation?

- ☑ Most evaluation methods focus on model-level capabilities...
- ☒ & neglect crucial systemic aspects of human-AI interaction

What areas are often overlooked in LLM evaluation?

 Value alignment — Matching stakeholder principles

 Anthropomorphism — Human-like attribution risks

 Trust — Building reliable AI systems

 Misinformation — False information spread

 Equity & access — Fair distribution of benefits

Key obstacles in comprehensive LLM evaluation

So how's that new AI tax assistant working out in your office?

It's complicated. We thought measuring success would be simple - just count how many returns it processes correctly. But there's so much more to it.

 Like what?

 A client trusted it blindly & missed a huge tax error. They misclassified their business expenses!

 Sounds like measuring the AI's performance is almost harder than building it.

Right? It's not just about accuracy - it's about user trust, accessibility, & real-world outcomes... We're learning to watch for all these hidden problems we never anticipated.

Figure 6-15. GenAI evaluation.

```
        run_id = mlflow.active_run().
info.run_uuid
        print(f"Model saved in run
{run_id}")
```

So far, we have covered how employing an experiment tracking platform can help you achieve the technical LLMOps goals of scaling and efficiency through logging, monitoring, and reproducibility. Next, let's look at how to attain the final LLMOps goal of risk mitigation.

Multilayered Evaluation

The evaluation methods we considered in the previous section are useful, but not sufficient. Given the need for value alignment and for considering the broader systemic impacts of GenAI, it is important to plan ahead to comprehensively evaluate your GenAI application. Figure 6-15 lays out this process.

The increasing scale and capabilities of AI assistants make it challenging to predict and mitigate all potential risks, especially at the initial deployment stage. Unforeseen capabilities and emergent behaviors may arise, which is why continuous monitoring and evaluation are so important. Because of this, you need a multilayered evaluation approach.

Evaluating the functionality, usability, and limitations of your AI system is crucial. This includes assessing its performance across different languages, assessing its accessibility for diverse users, and identifying potential failure modes, especially in high-risk domains like healthcare and finance.

How users interact with AI assistants can significantly impact their overall behavior and their societal impact. Users' trust level, their susceptibility to manipulation, and their tendency to anthropomorphize AI systems can influence the assistant's effectiveness and its potential for both benefit and harm. Therefore, the evaluation framework has to include factors that influence user trust in AI systems, the potential for AI to manipulate or persuade users, the risks of anthropomorphism, and the long-term effects of AI on human skills and autonomy.

AI assistants do not exist in isolation; they're integrated into complex social, economic, and environmental systems, so evaluating their impacts requires considering these broader systemic effects. This includes investigating the system's potential to exacerbate existing inequalities, contribute to the spread of misinformation, affect employment and job quality, influence consumption patterns, and consume resources.

Evaluation gap

Most evaluation methods focus on model-level capabilities and neglect these crucial systemic aspects of human-AI interaction. Automated performance tests against specific tasks or datasets usually target narrow concepts, like voice-recognition accuracy, or broader scores, such as customer satisfaction.

Make sure that you address evaluation gaps in key areas, including the following:

Value alignment
Move beyond user-centric alignment and consider the interests of all stakeholders, including developers and society. Encourage participatory approaches to elicit values and principles from diverse communities.

Trust

Conduct research to understand which features of your AI assistant foster trust in users. Develop evaluation metrics to assess the trustworthiness of your AI systems, taking into account user perceptions and expectations.

Anthropomorphism

Investigate the long-term impacts of any anthropomorphic design choices you make on users. Conduct studies to identify individual and group differences in susceptibility to anthropomorphism-induced harms. Develop mitigation strategies to minimize the risks associated with anthropomorphism.

Misinformation

Evaluate the likelihood of the AI assistant disseminating misinformation. Develop methods to assess the credibility of the content your system generates and its potential to influence user beliefs. Study the systemic impact of AI on the spread of misinformation and its consequences for public discourse.

Equity and access

Evaluate your AI assistant for risks of harm related to inequitable access. Design systems that promote "liberatory access" (*https:// oreil.ly/Mf5Pl*), addressing existing axes of social inequality and discrimination.

Many of these ethical concerns only become apparent at the human-AI interaction layer, and conducting such evaluations is not yet routine practice, partly due to resource constraints and the complexity of designing appropriate studies.

Challenges

Comprehensive evaluation faces several challenges, including the difficulty of operationalizing complex concepts into measurable metrics, the need for specialized expertise and resources, and the challenge of anticipating unintended uses of AI.

The best GenAI projects develop custom evaluation metrics to measure how well users can accomplish their tasks using the developed functionality. You will have to develop an evaluation approach that measures GenAI model capability, human-AI interaction, and systemic impact, separately and in tandem. For example, to evaluate a GenAI assistant that aids users in doing their taxes, you would have to measure the accuracy of the taxes filed, how fast users are able to file their taxes, and whether using the tool increases the likelihood of a tax audit. In addition, you'll need to evaluate the overall *product preference*, which is how often users choose the GenAI tool and can complete their workflow within it from start to finish, rather than starting with the traditional tax filing mechanism or having to fall back to it.

In addition, the evaluation framework must incorporate user studies, adversarial testing, and expert assessments. As described in the previous section, focus on value alignment, trust, anthropomorphism, misinformation, and equity. This means flagging where the tool provides the wrong advice, measuring how often users understand where the tool goes wrong, and measuring how often users verify information that needs to be verified before filing. You will have to evaluate who uses the tool; if there are user segments that don't, find out why not.

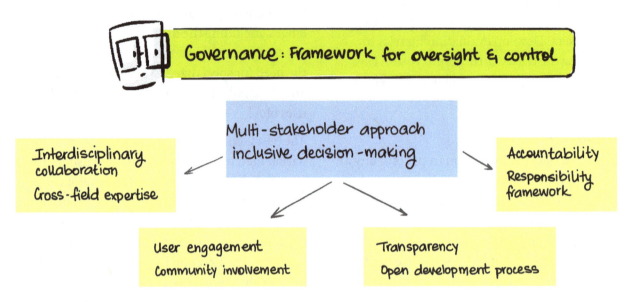

GENAI GOVERNANCE

Governance: Framework for oversight & control

Multi-stakeholder approach inclusive decision-making

Interdisciplinary collaboration
Cross-field expertise

Accountability
Responsibility framework

User engagement
Community involvement

Transparency
Open development process

Figure 6-16. GenAI governance.

Make sure that your evaluation metrics are transparent and that all stakeholders understand them. Being transparent about development and evaluation fosters trust and accountability. Engage external stakeholders in the evaluation process. Prioritize evaluating and mitigating high-risk scenarios. Continuously monitor your tool's real-world impacts, and be prepared to adjust course if necessary.

Governance considerations

The difficulty of comprehensive evaluation highlights the critical need for a multistakeholder approach to the governance of GenAI tools (Figure 6-16). If you rely solely on product teams to govern their GenAI applications, you risk misaligned incentives. Product managers and developers may prioritize commercial objectives or narrow user preferences over broader societal

well-being, potentially leading them to develop systems that exacerbate inequalities, spread misinformation, or compromise user autonomy. Even with the best intentions, developers may have a limited perspective on the potential impacts of their creations, particularly at the firm or societal level. They may struggle to anticipate unintended uses, unforeseen interactions with other AI systems, or the long-term consequences of widespread AI adoption.

Governing GenAI tools and applications requires interdisciplinary collaboration, bringing together expertise from fields like computer science, human-computer interaction, psychology, sociology, law, ethics, and public policy. A multistakeholder approach facilitates this cross-disciplinary dialogue, enabling a more comprehensive understanding of potential benefits and risks.

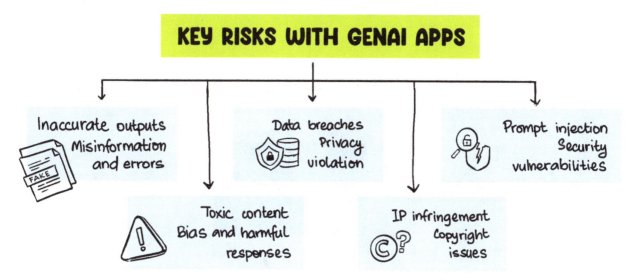

Figure 6-17. Key risks.

Establishing clear accountability mechanisms and avenues for redress is essential for building trust in AI systems. This includes mechanisms for identifying and addressing harms caused by AI, as well as processes for holding developers and deployers responsible for their actions.

Risk Mitigation

Deploying GenAI applications in enterprises carries risks such as toxic outputs, data leakage, and IP infringement that go beyond what a typical software application brings (Figure 6-17). You might need to highlight and discuss these risks specifically with your legal team when releasing a GenAI application.

When adopting or consuming a GenAI application within your organization, identify which quadrant of the IMD (impact, magnitude, duration) framework depicted in Figure 6-18 your risks will lie in, and brainstorm on the various ways that the risk could materialize.

To prevent the misuse of generative AI, you should work with your legal team to establish clear ethical guidelines and develop and enforce policies for how GenAI applications can be used. These policies should include guidelines on data access, editing, and tool use. It may be necessary to monitor the usage of GenAI technologies and implement appropriate usage policies to prevent misuse. A key aspect of your GenAI risk mitigation strategy will be to provide regular training to employees about GenAI risks and best practices. It is additionally helpful to implement access controls, update and patch systems, and track and detect unusual incidents.

To prevent the misapplication of GenAI, focus on data quality assurance by using diverse, balanced, and accurate datasets, alongside strict data validation processes and continuous updates. It is also crucial to employ comprehensive evaluation metrics to identify accuracy and performance issues. Incorporating human experts in the training and validation phases

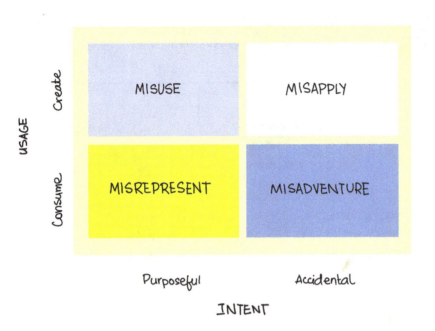

Figure 6-18. Framework to map GenAI risks. Adapted from "Mitigating Against Four Types of GenAI Risk" (*https://oreil.ly/U4VxR*), Öykü Işık, Amit M. Joshi, 2024.

can provide critical contextual insights. The line between misapplication and misuse comes down to intent, and it is important to remove temptations to cut corners by establishing clear ethical guidelines and ensuring compliance with data protection laws.

To prevent misrepresentation of GenAI, ensure that your product teams prioritize transparency and explainability in AI outputs, and couple AI outputs with fact-checking mechanisms to verify the accuracy of generated content. Create training content to promote digital literacy among users so that they can critically evaluate the information they consume. Ensure that your marketing and sales teams ground all their content in product features, and validate any GenAI-created materials before distributing to customers. As with the previous two quadrants, establishing clear ethical guidelines and regularly monitoring AI usage also

aids in preventing the spread of misleading or false information.

Finally, to prevent misadventures with GenAI, work with your IT team to focus on implementing robust security measures, including access controls and continuous monitoring, alongside ensuring data privacy through compliance with data protection laws and ethical guidelines. Prioritizing data quality with diverse, balanced, and accurate datasets, coupled with thorough validation processes and human oversight, is crucial. Regular employee training on GenAI risks and the establishment of clear usage policies can help promote the responsible and secure application of these tools.

Detecting AI-generated text

As we noted earlier in this chapter, AI detection tools do not yet work reliably, and there are concerns about their potential misuse. However,

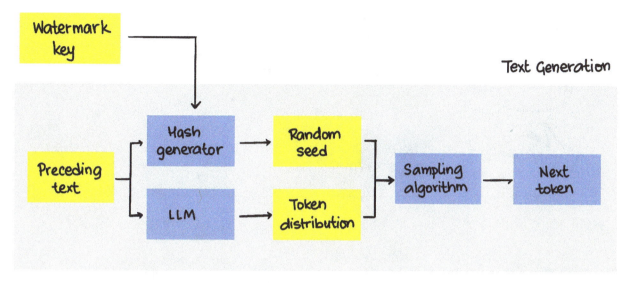

Figure 6-19. A watermark can be incorporated into AI-generated text without affecting its quality. Based on Dathathri et. al, 2024 (*https://oreil.ly/YAt8y*).

having reliable tools to identify AI-created content would help ameliorate concerns about misinformation, so developers are working to improve these tools.

An October 2024 paper in *Nature* (*https://oreil.ly/FraeD*) describes SynthID-Text, an AI watermarking technique. Recall from Chapter 1 that text generation involves sampling from a distribution of possible next tokens. One way to watermark AI-generated text is to use a watermark key as a random seed that parameterizes the sampling algorithm (see **Figure 6-19**). Because the sampling algorithm remains the same, the quality is not affected. The tool can verify how closely the given text hews to what *would* be generated if the watermark were the key.

Because this technique is based on the LLM's distribution of tokens, it works better if the distribution of tokens is high-entropy, and fails if the generated text is translated or rephrased. This implies three key limitations:

- It won't work on text generated using RAG, because factual answers powered by a limited context will be low-entropy. Most enterprise use cases involve RAG.

- It doesn't work against adversarial actors, since they can rephrase the text enough to get past the detector—but it will increase their costs, since they have to deploy their own LLM or do multiple rephrasings.

- Since it depends on the LLM provider using the watermark to generate the random seed for sampling, it won't work on text generated by open source models, where watermarking can be turned off in the code.

Situations where this technique will work include detecting AI-created novels, personalized web pages, and AI poisoning.

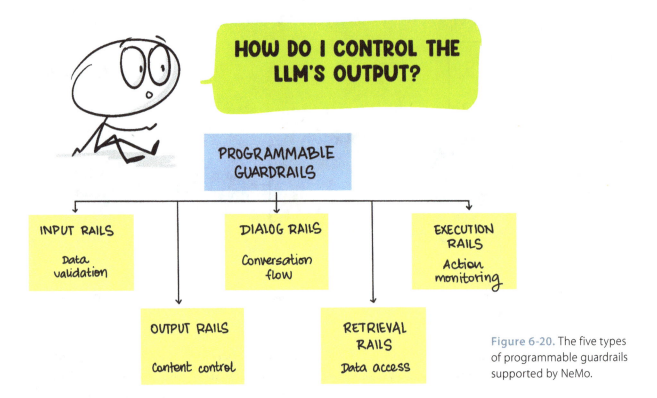

Figure 6-20. The five types of programmable guardrails supported by NeMo.

Programmable guardrails

Guardrails, often referred to as *rails*, are mechanisms to manage LLMs' output by controlling various aspects of their responses. This might include restricting discussions on certain topics (like politics), prompting the model to respond in a specific manner based on user requests, guiding the model to follow predefined conversation paths, employing particular language styles, or extracting structured data.

Nvidia's open source toolkit NeMo (*https://oreil. ly/os9r0*) allows you to add programmable guardrails to LLM-based conversational applications. It sits between the GenAI application and the LLM (**Figure 6-20**) and protects the application against common LLM vulnerabilities, such as toxicity, jailbreaks, and prompt injections.

You can set up five types of guardrails in NeMo:

- *Input rails* can reject the input being sent to the LLM and stop any additional processing (such as masking potentially sensitive data) or alter the input (by rephrasing it).

- *Dialog rails* determine if an action should be executed, if the LLM should be invoked to generate the next step or a response, or if a predefined response should be used instead. Typically, you'd use a proper LLM orchestration framework instead.

- *Retrieval rails* are used for RAG. A retrieval rail can reject a chunk, preventing it from being used to prompt the LLM, or alter chunks, such as to mask potentially sensitive data.

- *Execution rails* are applied to the input and output of tools the LLM calls.

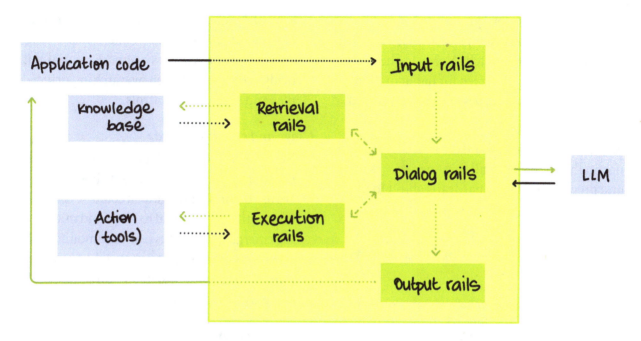

High-level flow through programmable guardrails.

Figure 6-21. High-level flow of programmable guardrails.

- *Output rails* can reject the LLM's output, preventing it from being returned to the user or altering it (such as by removing sensitive data).

Figure 6-21 shows an example of how these guardrails interact.

To use NeMo Guardrails, first set up a configuration file that lists the input and output checks you want the framework to carry out:

```
models:
  - type: main
    engine: openai
    model: gpt-3.5-turbo-instruct

rails:
  # Input rails are invoked when new
input from the user is received.
  input:
    flows:
      - check jailbreak
      - mask sensitive data on input

  # Output rails are triggered after a
bot message has been generated.
  output:
    flows:
      - self check facts
      - self check hallucination
      - activefence moderation
      - gotitai rag truthcheck

config:
  # Configure the types of entities
that should be masked on user input.
    sensitive_data_detection:
      input:
        entities:
          - PERSON
          - EMAIL_ADDRESS
```

This tells NeMo to verify inputs to the LLM, screen for jailbreak attempts, and mask any PII. The configuration also tells NeMo to check that the output is factual, screen for hallucinations, and perform specific types of moderation and truth checking.

Next, in LangChain, you'll create a chain as you normally would (let's call this one some_chain) and prepend a NeMo Guardrails object to it using the pipe (|) operator:

```
# load up the NeMo configuration file
config = RailsConfig.from_path("path/to/
config")

# Create a RunnableRails instance, and
"apply" it using the "|" operator
guardrails = RunnableRails(config)
chain_with_guardrails = guardrails |
some_chain
```

Now, when you execute chain_with_guardrails (instead of some_chain), NeMo carries out all the checks.

Governance

Setting up GenAI guardrails is not only a matter of having the technological capabilities. You also need a governance program to ensure adherence in all the applications built in your organization. The key components of a GenAI governance program (Figure 6-22) include the following:

Policy intelligence engine

The foundation of a GenAI guardrail system is a robust policy intelligence engine, such as the one from Credo AI (*https://oreil.ly/abt-bW*). This engine acts as a translator, converting high-level policies—whether legal,

ethical, business-related, or industry-specific—into practical requirements for assessing and governing AI/ML systems. Essentially, it bridges the gap between overarching principles and actionable controls.

Usage and risk dashboards

Many tools, such as GitHub Copilot, offer dashboards that provide visibility into how employees use them. This usage data could be crucial for identifying potential red flags and mitigating emerging risks. This real-time monitoring empowers governance teams to take proactive steps to ensure responsible and compliant use of GenAI across the organization.

GenAI sandbox

GenAI sandboxes can wrap commercial LLMs to provide a controlled environment for experimenting with GenAI tools.

User education

Users need to understand AI's limitations and potential biases as part of responsible GenAI adoption. User education programs also promote best practices for AI interaction and foster a culture of responsible AI usage.

Make sure that you are properly configuring or implementing these tools. This includes the following considerations:

Validate and sanitize input

Before any data is processed by a GenAI model, it should be rigorously inspected and cleaned to prevent malicious prompts or data injection attacks.

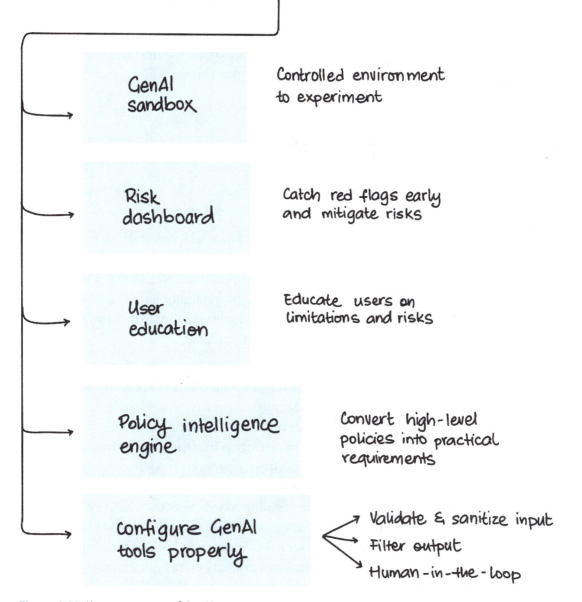

Figure 6-22. Key components of GenAI governance.

Filter output

Just as important is scanning generated content for harmful, biased, inappropriate, or inaccurate elements.

Protect data privacy and security

Protecting sensitive data entails implementing robust encryption, access controls, and data minimization practices.

Human-in-the-loop

Human oversight remains crucial for decision making and providing feedback on sensitive or potentially risky outputs.

Implementing effective GenAI guardrails is an ongoing process that requires adaptation and refinement over time.

SUMMARY AND CONCLUSION

Responsible GenAI development is not optional but essential for realizing the technology's benefits while minimizing risks to individuals and society. Technical practitioners must integrate the principles discussed in this chapter throughout the development process, from initial design through deployment and ongoing operation.

Responsible GenAI is important because of the powerful and increasingly autonomous nature of GenAI applications. The core responsible AI principles of fairness, transparency, accountability, and testing/monitoring remain valid, but there are also GenAI-specific issues like misinformation, human-AI interaction, and novel evaluation approaches that demand specialized attention.

We examined the critical role of value alignment and safety, illustrating potential pitfalls through real-world incidents and outlining best practices for ensuring that AI systems promote human interests and mitigate harm. We also discussed the ethical considerations surrounding human-AI interaction, including manipulation and anthropomorphism, and underscored the broader societal implications of GenAI on misinformation, employment, and environmental impact.

LLMOps is a crucial framework for managing the entire lifecycle of GenAI applications, ensuring responsible development and deployment through systematic experimentation, evaluation, logging, monitoring, and robust governance practices.

Congratulations! You now understand what GenAI is capable of, and the difference between snazzy demos and robust, scalable AI systems that work reliably in the real world. You've gained insights into the unique architectural challenges of generative AI, from managing its nondeterministic nature to implementing responsible AI practices that ensure your applications remain safe, ethical, and effective over time. You now know practical engineering patterns, evaluation frameworks, and how to balance creativity with reliability. We wish you great success in applying these principles to build agentic systems and deploy AI applications that deliver genuine value.

INDEX

ABOUT THE AUTHORS

Priyanka Vergadia is a senior director at Microsoft and former head of developer advocacy at Google Cloud, with more than 15 years in cloud and AI technology leadership. Author of the bestselling book *Visualizing Google Cloud*, she's known for her visual storytelling approach that makes complex cloud and AI technology accessible to millions of users worldwide. In addition, Priyanka is a keynote speaker and advises startups. She is a faculty member at University of Pennsylvania teaching cloud and AI courses and also serves on the board to define the future of online education.

Dr. Valliappa ("Lak") Lakshmanan is cofounder and CTO of Obin AI, a startup that's building deep domain AI agents for finance. He sets the technology and science direction of the company and is responsible for building the product. Prior to this, Lak was an operating executive at an investment firm, the director for data analytics and AI solutions on Google Cloud, and a research scientist at NOAA. He cofounded Google's Advanced Solutions Lab and is the author of several O'Reilly books and Coursera courses. He was elected a Fellow of the American Meteorological Society (the highest honor offered by the AMS) for his data science work.

O'REILLY®

Learn from experts.
Become one yourself.

60,000+ titles | Live events with experts | Role-based courses
Interactive learning | Certification preparation

**Try the O'Reilly learning platform
free for 10 days.**

www.ingramcontent.com/pod-product-compliance
Lightning Source LLC
Chambersburg PA
CBHW080353060326
40689CB00019B/3990